Master Addiction Counselor Exam

SECRETS

Study Guide

Your Key to Exam Success

DEAR FUTURE EXAM SUCCESS STORY

First of all, **THANK YOU** for purchasing Mometrix study materials!

Second, congratulations! You are one of the few determined test-takers who are committed to doing whatever it takes to excel on your exam. **You have come to the right place.** We developed these study materials with one goal in mind: to deliver you the information you need in a format that's concise and easy to use.

In addition to optimizing your guide for the content of the test, we've outlined our recommended steps for breaking down the preparation process into small, attainable goals so you can make sure you stay on track.

We've also analyzed the entire test-taking process, identifying the most common pitfalls and showing how you can overcome them and be ready for any curveball the test throws you.

Standardized testing is one of the biggest obstacles on your road to success, which only increases the importance of doing well in the high-pressure, high-stakes environment of test day. Your results on this test could have a significant impact on your future, and this guide provides the information and practical advice to help you achieve your full potential on test day.

Your success is our success

We would love to hear from you! If you would like to share the story of your exam success or if you have any questions or comments in regard to our products, please contact us at **800-673-8175** or **support@mometrix.com**.

Thanks again for your business and we wish you continued success!

Sincerely,
The Mometrix Test Preparation Team

Need more help? Check out our flashcards at:
http://MometrixFlashcards.com/Addiction

Written and edited by the Mometrix Exam Secrets Test Prep Team
Printed in the United States of America

TABLE OF CONTENTS

Introduction

Thank you for purchasing this resource! You have made the choice to prepare yourself for a test that could have a huge impact on your future, and this guide is designed to help you be fully ready for test day. Obviously, it's important to have a solid understanding of the test material, but you also need to be prepared for the unique environment and stressors of the test, so that you can perform to the best of your abilities.

For this purpose, the first section that appears in this guide is the **Secret Keys**. We've devoted countless hours to meticulously researching what works and what doesn't, and we've boiled down our findings to the five most impactful steps you can take to improve your performance on the test. We start at the beginning with study planning and move through the preparation process, all the way to the testing strategies that will help you get the most out of what you know when you're finally sitting in front of the test.

We recommend that you start preparing for your test as far in advance as possible. However, if you've bought this guide as a last-minute study resource and only have a few days before your test, we recommend that you skip over the first two Secret Keys since they address a long-term study plan.

If you struggle with **test anxiety**, we strongly encourage you to check out our recommendations for how you can overcome it. Test anxiety is a formidable foe, but it can be beaten, and we want to make sure you have the tools you need to defeat it.

Secret Key #1 – Plan Big, Study Small

There's a lot riding on your performance. If you want to ace this test, you're going to need to keep your skills sharp and the material fresh in your mind. You need a plan that lets you review everything you need to know while still fitting in your schedule. We'll break this strategy down into three categories.

Information Organization

Start with the information you already have: the official test outline. From this, you can make a complete list of all the concepts you need to cover before the test. Organize these concepts into groups that can be studied together, and create a list of any related vocabulary you need to learn so you can brush up on any difficult terms. You'll want to keep this vocabulary list handy once you actually start studying since you may need to add to it along the way.

Time Management

Once you have your set of study concepts, decide how to spread them out over the time you have left before the test. Break your study plan into small, clear goals so you have a manageable task for each day and know exactly what you're doing. Then just focus on one small step at a time. When you manage your time this way, you don't need to spend hours at a time studying. Studying a small block of content for a short period each day helps you retain information better and avoid stressing over how much you have left to do. You can relax knowing that you have a plan to cover everything in time. In order for this strategy to be effective though, you have to start studying early and stick to your schedule. Avoid the exhaustion and futility that comes from last-minute cramming!

Study Environment

The environment you study in has a big impact on your learning. Studying in a coffee shop, while probably more enjoyable, is not likely to be as fruitful as studying in a quiet room. It's important to keep distractions to a minimum. You're only planning to study for a short block of time, so make the most of it. Don't pause to check your phone or get up to find a snack. It's also important to **avoid multitasking**. Research has consistently shown that multitasking will make your studying dramatically less effective. Your study area should also be comfortable and well-lit so you don't have the distraction of straining your eyes or sitting on an uncomfortable chair.

The time of day you study is also important. You want to be rested and alert. Don't wait until just before bedtime. Study when you'll be most likely to comprehend and remember. Even better, if you know what time of day your test will be, set that time aside for study. That way your brain will be used to working on that subject at that specific time and you'll have a better chance of recalling information.

Finally, it can be helpful to team up with others who are studying for the same test. Your actual studying should be done in as isolated an environment as possible, but the work of organizing the information and setting up the study plan can be divided up. In between study sessions, you can discuss with your teammates the concepts that you're all studying and quiz each other on the details. Just be sure that your teammates are as serious about the test as you are. If you find that your study time is being replaced with social time, you might need to find a new team.

Secret Key #2 – Make Your Studying Count

You're devoting a lot of time and effort to preparing for this test, so you want to be absolutely certain it will pay off. This means doing more than just reading the content and hoping you can remember it on test day. It's important to make every minute of study count. There are two main areas you can focus on to make your studying count:

Retention

It doesn't matter how much time you study if you can't remember the material. You need to make sure you are retaining the concepts. To check your retention of the information you're learning, try recalling it at later times with minimal prompting. Try carrying around flashcards and glance at one or two from time to time or ask a friend who's also studying for the test to quiz you.

To enhance your retention, look for ways to put the information into practice so that you can apply it rather than simply recalling it. If you're using the information in practical ways, it will be much easier to remember. Similarly, it helps to solidify a concept in your mind if you're not only reading it to yourself but also explaining it to someone else. Ask a friend to let you teach them about a concept you're a little shaky on (or speak aloud to an imaginary audience if necessary). As you try to summarize, define, give examples, and answer your friend's questions, you'll understand the concepts better and they will stay with you longer. Finally, step back for a big picture view and ask yourself how each piece of information fits with the whole subject. When you link the different concepts together and see them working together as a whole, it's easier to remember the individual components.

Finally, practice showing your work on any multi-step problems, even if you're just studying. Writing out each step you take to solve a problem will help solidify the process in your mind, and you'll be more likely to remember it during the test.

Modality

Modality simply refers to the means or method by which you study. Choosing a study modality that fits your own individual learning style is crucial. No two people learn best in exactly the same way, so it's important to know your strengths and use them to your advantage.

For example, if you learn best by visualization, focus on visualizing a concept in your mind and draw an image or a diagram. Try color-coding your notes, illustrating them, or creating symbols that will trigger your mind to recall a learned concept. If you learn best by hearing or discussing information, find a study partner who learns the same way or read aloud to yourself. Think about how to put the information in your own words. Imagine that you are giving a lecture on the topic and record yourself so you can listen to it later.

For any learning style, flashcards can be helpful. Organize the information so you can take advantage of spare moments to review. Underline key words or phrases. Use different colors for different categories. Mnemonic devices (such as creating a short list in which every item starts with the same letter) can also help with retention. Find what works best for you and use it to store the information in your mind most effectively and easily.

Secret Key #3 – Practice the Right Way

Your success on test day depends not only on how many hours you put into preparing, but also on whether you prepared the right way. It's good to check along the way to see if your studying is paying off. One of the most effective ways to do this is by taking practice tests to evaluate your progress. Practice tests are useful because they show exactly where you need to improve. Every time you take a practice test, pay special attention to these three groups of questions:

- The questions you got wrong
- The questions you had to guess on, even if you guessed right
- The questions you found difficult or slow to work through

This will show you exactly what your weak areas are, and where you need to devote more study time. Ask yourself why each of these questions gave you trouble. Was it because you didn't understand the material? Was it because you didn't remember the vocabulary? Do you need more repetitions on this type of question to build speed and confidence? Dig into those questions and figure out how you can strengthen your weak areas as you go back to review the material.

Additionally, many practice tests have a section explaining the answer choices. It can be tempting to read the explanation and think that you now have a good understanding of the concept. However, an explanation likely only covers part of the question's broader context. Even if the explanation makes sense, **go back and investigate** every concept related to the question until you're positive you have a thorough understanding.

As you go along, keep in mind that the practice test is just that: practice. Memorizing these questions and answers will not be very helpful on the actual test because it is unlikely to have any of the same exact questions. If you only know the right answers to the sample questions, you won't be prepared for the real thing. **Study the concepts** until you understand them fully, and then you'll be able to answer any question that shows up on the test.

It's important to wait on the practice tests until you're ready. If you take a test on your first day of study, you may be overwhelmed by the amount of material covered and how much you need to learn. Work up to it gradually.

On test day, you'll need to be prepared for answering questions, managing your time, and using the test-taking strategies you've learned. It's a lot to balance, like a mental marathon that will have a big impact on your future. Like training for a marathon, you'll need to start slowly and work your way up. When test day arrives, you'll be ready.

Start with the strategies you've read in the first two Secret Keys—plan your course and study in the way that works best for you. If you have time, consider using multiple study resources to get different approaches to the same concepts. It can be helpful to see difficult concepts from more than one angle. Then find a good source for practice tests. Many times, the test website will suggest potential study resources or provide sample tests.

Practice Test Strategy

If you're able to find at least three practice tests, we recommend this strategy:

1. Take the first test with no time constraints and with your notes and study guide handy. Take your time and focus on applying the strategies you've learned.
2. Take the second practice test open-book as well, but set a timer and practice pacing yourself to finish in time.
3. Take any other practice tests as if it were test day. Set a timer and put away your study materials. Sit at a table or desk in a quiet room, imagine yourself at the testing center, and answer questions as quickly and accurately as possible.
4. Keep repeating step 3 on a regular basis until you run out of practice tests or it's time for the actual test. Your mind will be ready for the schedule and stress of test day, and you'll be able to focus on recalling the material you've learned.

Secret Key #4 – Pace Yourself

Once you're fully prepared for the material on the test, your biggest challenge on test day will be managing your time. Just knowing that the clock is ticking can make you panic even if you have plenty of time left. Work on pacing yourself so you can build confidence against the time constraints of the exam. Pacing is a difficult skill to master, especially in a high-pressure environment, so **practice is vital**.

Set time expectations for your pace based on how much time is available. For example, if a section has 60 questions and the time limit is 30 minutes, you know you have to average 30 seconds or less per question in order to answer them all. Although 30 seconds is the hard limit, set 25 seconds per question as your goal, so you reserve extra time to spend on harder questions. When you budget extra time for the harder questions, you no longer have any reason to stress when those questions take longer to answer.

Don't let this time expectation distract you from working through the test at a calm, steady pace, but keep it in mind so you don't spend too much time on any one question. Recognize that taking extra time on one question you don't understand may keep you from answering two that you do understand later in the test. If your time limit for a question is up and you're still not sure of the answer, mark it and move on, and come back to it later if the time and the test format allow. If the testing format doesn't allow you to return to earlier questions, just make an educated guess; then put it out of your mind and move on.

On the easier questions, be careful not to rush. It may seem wise to hurry through them so you have more time for the challenging ones, but it's not worth missing one if you know the concept and just didn't take the time to read the question fully. Work efficiently but make sure you understand the question and have looked at all of the answer choices, since more than one may seem right at first.

Even if you're paying attention to the time, you may find yourself a little behind at some point. You should speed up to get back on track, but do so wisely. Don't panic; just take a few seconds less on each question until you're caught up. Don't guess without thinking, but do look through the answer choices and eliminate any you know are wrong. If you can get down to two choices, it is often worthwhile to guess from those. Once you've chosen an answer, move on and don't dwell on any that you skipped or had to hurry through. If a question was taking too long, chances are it was one of the harder ones, so you weren't as likely to get it right anyway.

On the other hand, if you find yourself getting ahead of schedule, it may be beneficial to slow down a little. The more quickly you work, the more likely you are to make a careless mistake that will affect your score. You've budgeted time for each question, so don't be afraid to spend that time. Practice an efficient but careful pace to get the most out of the time you have.

Secret Key #5 – Have a Plan for Guessing

When you're taking the test, you may find yourself stuck on a question. Some of the answer choices seem better than others, but you don't see the one answer choice that is obviously correct. What do you do?

The scenario described above is very common, yet most test takers have not effectively prepared for it. Developing and practicing a plan for guessing may be one of the single most effective uses of your time as you get ready for the exam.

In developing your plan for guessing, there are three questions to address:

- When should you start the guessing process?
- How should you narrow down the choices?
- Which answer should you choose?

When to Start the Guessing Process

Unless your plan for guessing is to select C every time (which, despite its merits, is not what we recommend), you need to leave yourself enough time to apply your answer elimination strategies. Since you have a limited amount of time for each question, that means that if you're going to give yourself the best shot at guessing correctly, you have to decide quickly whether or not you will guess.

Of course, the best-case scenario is that you don't have to guess at all, so first, see if you can answer the question based on your knowledge of the subject and basic reasoning skills. Focus on the key words in the question and try to jog your memory of related topics. Give yourself a chance to bring the knowledge to mind, but once you realize that you don't have (or you can't access) the knowledge you need to answer the question, it's time to start the guessing process.

It's almost always better to start the guessing process too early than too late. It only takes a few seconds to remember something and answer the question from knowledge. Carefully eliminating wrong answer choices takes longer. Plus, going through the process of eliminating answer choices can actually help jog your memory.

Summary: Start the guessing process as soon as you decide that you can't answer the question based on your knowledge.

How to Narrow Down the Choices

The next chapter in this book (**Test-Taking Strategies**) includes a wide range of strategies for how to approach questions and how to look for answer choices to eliminate. You will definitely want to read those carefully, practice them, and figure out which ones work best for you. Here though, we're going to address a mindset rather than a particular strategy.

Your chances of guessing an answer correctly depend on how many options you are choosing from.

How many choices you have	How likely you are to guess correctly
5	20%
4	25%
3	33%
2	50%
1	100%

You can see from this chart just how valuable it is to be able to eliminate incorrect answers and make an educated guess, but there are two things that many test takers do that cause them to miss out on the benefits of guessing:

- Accidentally eliminating the correct answer
- Selecting an answer based on an impression

We'll look at the first one here, and the second one in the next section.

To avoid accidentally eliminating the correct answer, we recommend a thought exercise called **the $5 challenge**. In this challenge, you only eliminate an answer choice from contention if you are willing to bet $5 on it being wrong. Why $5? Five dollars is a small but not insignificant amount of money. It's an amount you could afford to lose but wouldn't want to throw away. And while losing $5 once might not hurt too much, doing it twenty times will set you back $100. In the same way, each small decision you make—eliminating a choice here, guessing on a question there—won't by itself impact your score very much, but when you put them all together, they can make a big difference. By holding each answer choice elimination decision to a higher standard, you can reduce the risk of accidentally eliminating the correct answer.

The $5 challenge can also be applied in a positive sense: If you are willing to bet $5 that an answer choice *is* correct, go ahead and mark it as correct.

Summary: Only eliminate an answer choice if you are willing to bet $5 that it is wrong.

Which Answer to Choose

You're taking the test. You've run into a hard question and decided you'll have to guess. You've eliminated all the answer choices you're willing to bet $5 on. Now you have to pick an answer. Why do we even need to talk about this? Why can't you just pick whichever one you feel like when the time comes?

The answer to these questions is that if you don't come into the test with a plan, you'll rely on your impression to select an answer choice, and if you do that, you risk falling into a trap. The test writers know that everyone who takes their test will be guessing on some of the questions, so they intentionally write wrong answer choices to seem plausible. You still have to pick an answer though, and if the wrong answer choices are designed to look right, how can you ever be sure that you're not falling for their trap? The best solution we've found to this dilemma is to take the decision out of your hands entirely. Here is the process we recommend:

Once you've eliminated any choices that you are confident (willing to bet $5) are wrong, select the first remaining choice as your answer.

Whether you choose to select the first remaining choice, the second, or the last, the important thing is that you use some preselected standard. Using this approach guarantees that you will not be enticed into selecting an answer choice that looks right, because you are not basing your decision on how the answer choices look.

This is not meant to make you question your knowledge. Instead, it is to help you recognize the difference between your knowledge and your impressions. There's a huge difference between thinking an answer is right because of what you know, and thinking an answer is right because it looks or sounds like it should be right.

Summary: To ensure that your selection is appropriately random, make a predetermined selection from among all answer choices you have not eliminated.

Test-Taking Strategies

This section contains a list of test-taking strategies that you may find helpful as you work through the test. By taking what you know and applying logical thought, you can maximize your chances of answering any question correctly!

It is very important to realize that every question is different and every person is different: no single strategy will work on every question, and no single strategy will work for every person. That's why we've included all of them here, so you can try them out and determine which ones work best for different types of questions and which ones work best for you.

Question Strategies

Read Carefully

Read the question and answer choices carefully. Don't miss the question because you misread the terms. You have plenty of time to read each question thoroughly and make sure you understand what is being asked. Yet a happy medium must be attained, so don't waste too much time. You must read carefully, but efficiently.

Contextual Clues

Look for contextual clues. If the question includes a word you are not familiar with, look at the immediate context for some indication of what the word might mean. Contextual clues can often give you all the information you need to decipher the meaning of an unfamiliar word. Even if you can't determine the meaning, you may be able to narrow down the possibilities enough to make a solid guess at the answer to the question.

Prefixes

If you're having trouble with a word in the question or answer choices, try dissecting it. Take advantage of every clue that the word might include. Prefixes and suffixes can be a huge help. Usually they allow you to determine a basic meaning. Pre- means before, post- means after, pro - is positive, de- is negative. From prefixes and suffixes, you can get an idea of the general meaning of the word and try to put it into context.

Hedge Words

Watch out for critical hedge words, such as *likely, may, can, sometimes, often, almost, mostly, usually, generally, rarely*, and *sometimes*. Question writers insert these hedge phrases to cover every possibility. Often an answer choice will be wrong simply because it leaves no room for exception. Be on guard for answer choices that have definitive words such as *exactly* and *always*.

Switchback Words

Stay alert for *switchbacks*. These are the words and phrases frequently used to alert you to shifts in thought. The most common switchback words are *but, although*, and *however*. Others include *nevertheless, on the other hand, even though, while, in spite of, despite, regardless of*. Switchback words are important to catch because they can change the direction of the question or an answer choice.

Face Value

When in doubt, use common sense. Accept the situation in the problem at face value. Don't read too much into it. These problems will not require you to make wild assumptions. If you have to go beyond creativity and warp time or space in order to have an answer choice fit the question, then you should move on and consider the other answer choices. These are normal problems rooted in reality. The applicable relationship or explanation may not be readily apparent, but it is there for you to figure out. Use your common sense to interpret anything that isn't clear.

Answer Choice Strategies

Answer Selection

The most thorough way to pick an answer choice is to identify and eliminate wrong answers until only one is left, then confirm it is the correct answer. Sometimes an answer choice may immediately seem right, but be careful. The test writers will usually put more than one reasonable answer choice on each question, so take a second to read all of them and make sure that the other choices are not equally obvious. As long as you have time left, it is better to read every answer choice than to pick the first one that looks right without checking the others.

Answer Choice Families

An answer choice family consists of two (in rare cases, three) answer choices that are very similar in construction and cannot all be true at the same time. If you see two answer choices that are direct opposites or parallels, one of them is usually the correct answer. For instance, if one answer choice says that quantity *x* increases and another either says that quantity *x* decreases (opposite) or says that quantity *y* increases (parallel), then those answer choices would fall into the same family. An answer choice that doesn't match the construction of the answer choice family is more likely to be incorrect. Most questions will not have answer choice families, but when they do appear, you should be prepared to recognize them.

Eliminate Answers

Eliminate answer choices as soon as you realize they are wrong, but make sure you consider all possibilities. If you are eliminating answer choices and realize that the last one you are left with is also wrong, don't panic. Start over and consider each choice again. There may be something you missed the first time that you will realize on the second pass.

Avoid Fact Traps

Don't be distracted by an answer choice that is factually true but doesn't answer the question. You are looking for the choice that answers the question. Stay focused on what the question is asking for so you don't accidentally pick an answer that is true but incorrect. Always go back to the question and make sure the answer choice you've selected actually answers the question and is not merely a true statement.

Extreme Statements

In general, you should avoid answers that put forth extreme actions as standard practice or proclaim controversial ideas as established fact. An answer choice that states the "process should be used in certain situations, if…" is much more likely to be correct than one that states the "process should be discontinued completely." The first is a calm rational statement and doesn't even make a definitive, uncompromising stance, using a hedge word *if* to provide wiggle room, whereas the second choice is a radical idea and far more extreme.

Benchmark

As you read through the answer choices and you come across one that seems to answer the question well, mentally select that answer choice. This is not your final answer, but it's the one that will help you evaluate the other answer choices. The one that you selected is your benchmark or standard for judging each of the other answer choices. Every other answer choice must be compared to your benchmark. That choice is correct until proven otherwise by another answer choice beating it. If you find a better answer, then that one becomes your new benchmark. Once you've decided that no other choice answers the question as well as your benchmark, you have your final answer.

Predict the Answer

Before you even start looking at the answer choices, it is often best to try to predict the answer. When you come up with the answer on your own, it is easier to avoid distractions and traps because you will know exactly what to look for. The right answer choice is unlikely to be word-for-word what you came up with, but it should be a close match. Even if you are confident that you have the right answer, you should still take the time to read each option before moving on.

General Strategies

Tough Questions

If you are stumped on a problem or it appears too hard or too difficult, don't waste time. Move on! Remember though, if you can quickly check for obviously incorrect answer choices, your chances of guessing correctly are greatly improved. Before you completely give up, at least try to knock out a couple of possible answers. Eliminate what you can and then guess at the remaining answer choices before moving on.

Check Your Work

Since you will probably not know every term listed and the answer to every question, it is important that you get credit for the ones that you do know. Don't miss any questions through careless mistakes. If at all possible, try to take a second to look back over your answer selection and make sure you've selected the correct answer choice and haven't made a costly careless mistake (such as marking an answer choice that you didn't mean to mark). This quick double check should more than pay for itself in caught mistakes for the time it costs.

Pace Yourself

It's easy to be overwhelmed when you're looking at a page full of questions; your mind is confused and full of random thoughts, and the clock is ticking down faster than you would like. Calm down and maintain the pace that you have set for yourself. Especially as you get down to the last few minutes of the test, don't let the small numbers on the clock make you panic. As long as you are on track by monitoring your pace, you are guaranteed to have time for each question.

Don't Rush

It is very easy to make errors when you are in a hurry. Maintaining a fast pace in answering questions is pointless if it makes you miss questions that you would have gotten right otherwise. Test writers like to include distracting information and wrong answers that seem right. Taking a little extra time to avoid careless mistakes can make all the difference in your test score. Find a pace that allows you to be confident in the answers that you select.

KEEP MOVING

Panicking will not help you pass the test, so do your best to stay calm and keep moving. Taking deep breaths and going through the answer elimination steps you practiced can help to break through a stress barrier and keep your pace.

Final Notes

The combination of a solid foundation of content knowledge and the confidence that comes from practicing your plan for applying that knowledge is the key to maximizing your performance on test day. As your foundation of content knowledge is built up and strengthened, you'll find that the strategies included in this chapter become more and more effective in helping you quickly sift through the distractions and traps of the test to isolate the correct answer.

Now it's time to move on to the test content chapters of this book, but be sure to keep your goal in mind. As you read, think about how you will be able to apply this information on the test. If you've already seen sample questions for the test and you have an idea of the question format and style, try to come up with questions of your own that you can answer based on what you're reading. This will give you valuable practice applying your knowledge in the same ways you can expect to on test day.

Good luck and good studying!

Orientation to Treatment Process

Consent

Voluntary agreement from a person able to make a meaningful choice. "Able to make a meaningful choice" indicates that the individual has the cognitive capacity to choose. "Informed consent" requires that an individual not only provide voluntary consent, but that he or she be adequately informed regarding choices, options, and outcomes to have properly understood the meaning of the consent or refusal that was given. Typically, this requires disclosure of: 1) nature and purpose of the treatment; 2) the risks and consequences; 3) the available alternatives; and 4) the risks of no treatment. "Consent for Disclosure" (or authorization for information release) refers to a consent to release information, and it falls under the guidelines of the federal Health Insurance Portability and Accountability Act (HIPAA, 1996). Mental health and substance use disorder information is considered "protected health information" (PHI) and under federal law (see 42 CFR Part 2) is afforded confidentiality standards far more stringent than HIPAA statutes, which already cover release of patient identity, diagnosis, treatment, and prognosis.

Patient Identifying Information

Any information whereby a patient can be identified, whether directly or indirectly. This also includes individually identified information transmitted in any form, whether by electronic means (except computer disk), written, oral, or any other form. Private information may not be disclosed, except as specifically authorized by a patient and as permitted by regulations. Acknowledging even the mere presence of an individual in a facility for substance use disorder treatment is only permitted if the facility is not identified as a substance use disorder treatment facility, and if the patient is not identified as a current or former substance abuser. "Incidental uses and disclosures" (being overheard talking about a patient, using sign-in sheets in waiting rooms, keeping charts at a patient's bedside, etc.) do not violate privacy standards, as long as minimum necessary safeguards limit unintended disclosures.

Code of Federal Regulations 42 Part 2

Patient information and privacy standards. The content of 42 CFR Part 2 goes beyond recognizing that patients have privacy rights, and establishes specific rights including: 1) inspection and copying of one's own records in most cases; 2) amendment of one's own record by request; 3) accounting of disclosures made (including to business associates); 4) a specific request as to restrictions on disclosure; 5) that information be communicated in a specific way; 6) receipt of a Notice of Privacy Practices; 7) the right to file a complaint with the covered entity, or with the Secretary of Health and Human Services. Identifying information may be disclosed if: 1) the client gives written consent; 2) by court order; 3) to a qualified service organization; 4) program staff; 5) for child abuse reporting; 6) to law enforcement following a crime on premises or involving personnel; 7) in medical emergencies; for research; and 8) for audit and evaluation.

Privacy of Psychotherapy Notes under the Code of Federal Regulation (42 CFR Part 2)

They are offered no protection at all. However, HIPAA (1996) does address such notes, recorded in any medium by a mental health professional during private or group sessions, as well as during any joint, couples, or family counseling. The definition of such notes, however, excludes any medication prescriptions, monitoring, start and stop times of sessions, treatment frequencies and modalities, clinical testing results, and summaries of any of the following: functional status, symptoms, diagnosis, treatment plan, prognosis, and progress. To remain protected under existing Privacy Standards, psychotherapy notes must be kept separate from any other medical record.

Code of Federal Regulations 42 Part 2.31

Minimum information required includes: 1) specific name or general designation of the program or person allowed to disclose; 2) name or title of the individual or organization to which information will be disclosed; 3) client name; 4) the disclosure purpose; 5) the kind and extent of information to be disclosed; 6) the client's signature, or that of an authorized representative; 7) the date signed; 8) a statement specifying the right to revoke at any time, except as it has already been utilized; 9) the expiration date, if not revoked earlier. In addition, Privacy Standards under 45 CFR Part 164.508(c) indicates that: 1) if an authorized representative signs for a client, the authority must be specified; 2) instructions for revocation procedure must be included; 3) a statement regarding any redisclosure must be included; 4) substance use disorder must be specified, if any such information will be released; 5) the authorization must clarify that no service, payment, or other factor was conditioned upon signing the document.

Situations Where the Therapist Is Constrained to Warn Another About a Credible Threat

The law may not protect the therapist. Federal regulations (42 CFR Part 2.20) supersede state laws, and prohibit disclosures about any patient in a covered drug or alcohol program, except by court order, or without identifying the individual. In this situation, ask: 1) Can a report be made without identifying the patient? 2) Can the report be made without identifying the client's substance/alcohol treatment? 3) If not, is there any exception in the law? 4) If an exception exists, what other limits are involved? 5) If limited, will the client sign an authorization to disclose? 6) If no, can you get a timely court order? 7) If not, does the ethical obligation still exist, given what the client has stated (e.g., imminent danger, client history of violence, capable of violence now, and has a specific plan)? If yes, consider disclosure but know that liability may result (fine up to $5,000 and potential loss of license). Report violations to US Attorney of the judicial district within 180 days.

Opiate Dependence

Opiates are central nervous system (CNS) depressants, as is alcohol (ethanol or ethyl alcohol, as opposed to "rubbing alcohol" or isopropanol or isopropyl alcohol). Opiates are able to rapidly cross the blood-brain barrier to produce a euphoric "rush," and physical dependence develops rapidly when opiates are regularly used. Withdrawal symptoms include anxiety, piloerection ("goosebumps" causing hair to stand up), insomnia, diarrhea, abdominal cramps, vomiting, muscle aches, agitation, excessive yawning, nose running, sweats, hypertension, and fever. The excessive ingestion of opiates can result in cardiac irregularities and/or respiratory depression (bradypnea, reduced breathing rate). Significant overdose, or combining opiates with other CNS depressants, such as alcohol, can ultimately lead to asystole (cessation of the heartbeat) and/or outright apnea (cessation of breathing) and death.

Screening and Client Assessment

The purpose of "screening" is to determine an appropriate initial course of action, given the client's needs, characteristics, and available resources, in conjunction with the counselor, client, and available significant others. Essential screening competencies include: 1) creating a rapport, managing any crises, and determining needs; 2) systematically collect data, including key collateral information sources and screening tools, using approaches sensitive to culture, age, gender, etc (minimum: addiction issues and history, physical and mental health, treatment history, mental status, and personal, social, environmental, and financial constraints); 3) screen for toxicity, intoxication and withdrawal, danger to self and others, and assess any comorbid mental health problems; 4) address the impact of addiction and its continuation in the client's life; 5) identify readiness for change and the related needs of significant others; 6) consider available treatment options (within clients capacity and means); 7) select treatment options in keeping with diagnostic criteria; 8) formulate an action plan with the client and involved others; and 8) pursue admission and/or referral, and ensure follow-through.

A substance "screening" is completed at the outset of the therapeutic process, while an assessment is more in depth and an ongoing activity throughout the therapeutic experience. Screening seeks to answer the question of whether or not professional help is needed, while assessment refines the nature, duration, and expected outcomes of treatment that has already been found necessary. The assessment will evaluate the client's characteristics, goals, and concerns in greater depth, and with a focus on formulation of a specific, individualized treatment plan. The goals identified and the client's progress in accordance with the treatment plan must constantly be reassessed and revised as progress continues and/or new obstacles arise. A more comprehensive assessment, supplemented with assessment instruments where helpful, can answer such questions as: 1) what is the expected outcome; 2) what therapeutic approach would be best; 3) what changes, learning, and new skills will be needed; 4) what life improvements are needed; 5) are there medical or legal problems needing to be addressed.

Levels of Care as Cited by the American Society of Addiction Medicine (ASAM)

These are: 1) Hospitalization; 2) Residential Care; 3) Intensive Outpatient Care; and 4) Outpatient Care. Some sources indicate the following levels: 1) Outpatient Treatment; 2) Intensive Outpatient and Partial Hospitalization; 3) Residential/Inpatient Treatment; and 4) Medically Managed Intensive Inpatient Treatment. Regardless, the goal is to identify the appropriate level of care a patient requires for optimal care. Numerous tools are used in the evaluation process, including the Addiction Severity Index (ASI). Because addition involves not only compulsive substance use, but other problematic behaviors, the index assesses problem severity in seven domains over the last 30 days and the last year: 1) alcohol use; 2) drug use; 3) employment; 4) family and social relationships; 5) legal; 6) psychological; and 7) medical status. The resulting "severity scores" can be used in the selection of a placement level and a treatment plan.

Substance Use Disorder Treatment Program Modalities

The modalities are: 1) detoxification (inpatient or outpatient), focused on managing withdrawal symptoms prior to entering a longer-term treatment program; 2) residential treatment (long- vs short-term), highly structured intensive settings, including "Therapeutic Community" (TC) programs using hierarchical models to enhance personal and social responsibility, restructure personality and socialization, increase skills, and integrate social norms, with stays from 12 to 24 months depending on funding; 3) outpatient drug-free (non-methadone), 6 to 12 months of drug education and counseling; 4) day treatment, 6 or fewer months of intensive day activities and home at night; 5) methadone maintenance, displacing heroin use with monitored methadone, often indefinitely. Program phases often include: 1) engagement and stabilization; 2) early recovery; 3) maintenance of recovery; and 4) transition to aftercare. Aftercare involves transitional therapy and participation in 12-step self-help groups (AA, CA, or NA) to offer social support and new lifestyle choices.

Inaccurate Expectations

Prior to treatment, clients may believe that they must up-end their lives to overcome addiction, moving away from and severing ties with all of their friends and even family. Others may believe that they must change old habits immediately, rather than recognizing the steps and stages of the change process. Still others may expect to spend numerous weeks, or even longer, in an inpatient or residential treatment setting to achieve the desired changes. Some may expect aggressive and confrontational techniques by counselors in an effort to "break" them and overcome resistance to change. There are also those who expect great laxity in a treatment setting, with counselors ignoring indiscriminate lapses and casual returns to substance use disorder. When such client expectations diverge from treatment goals and processes, the counseling and treatment experience can be significantly inhibited. Numerous studies confirm that readiness for therapy, perceived self-efficacy, expectations of positive outcome, and perceived social support can all directly correlate with more meaningful and enduring outcomes.

Educating the Client

Proper education of the client on the counseling process and the expected role of the counselor can greatly facilitate and enhance the client's growth and change. Ideally in this process, the therapeutic bond between the counselor and client will also be strengthened. Processes and expectations related to individual and group counseling should be addressed, along with treatment duration and transitions in settings and structure over time. The role of self-help programs (e.g., Alcoholics Anonymous [AA], Cocaine Anonymous [CA], Narcotics Anonymous [NA], and Al-anon) and related expectations should also be discussed. The role of the counselor is best described as that of an adviser, change facilitator, collaborator, and teacher. Although the client is encouraged to do most of the talking, a counselor must not fail to offer advice, education, and guidance as needed. Honesty, confirmation (substance testing), and accountability are keys to progress. Finally, issues of ethics, boundaries, reporting, and any special criteria imposed through employer-mandated or court-ordered processes must be reviewed and mutually understood.

Coexistence of Alcohol Use Disorder and Psychiatric Conditions

Dependent on initial presentation. Suicidality, for example, would be a particularly high treatment priority; sometimes detoxification may present the greater priority. To determine the "primary" versus "secondary" condition, consider: 1) the more enduring (preexisting) disorder is usually the primary condition; 2) secondary conditions are typically transient (e.g., depression that resolves with continued addiction treatment versus enduring bipolar disorder). A detailed alcohol, drug, and psychiatric history will be imperative. Selection of the first condition to be treated can depend on safety, resources, mode of treatment needed (inpatient vs outpatient), amenability to treatment (including honesty issues), and compliance. Secondary addictions are often easier for the client to stop, and where drug and sex addictions coexist, the sex addiction typically came first (onset at or near puberty). The least intensive level of treatment that ensures safety (e.g., suicidality, withdrawal issues) and efficacy is recommended. With both AOD and dual diagnoses, for example, the need to consider inpatient care is significant.

Crisis

The three conditions that constitute a crisis are: 1) a hazardous or stressful situation; 2) awareness of the potential for significant life disruption or emotional upset; and 3) inadequate existing coping strategies. The individual in crisis need not have done anything wrong, nor must the issue be life-threatening to precipitate a true crisis. "Critical incidents" are events that overwhelm an individual's coping skills because of the emotional intensity involved. Typical elements are experiences that are fear-inducing, grotesque, threatening, or dangerous. Once overwhelmed, the individual experiences an acute emotional response called a "crisis." Five common components of a crisis are: 1) an event that is emotionally powerful, critical, and/or threatening; 2) insufficient skills to cope; 3) mounting confusion, tension, and fear; 4) the perception of extreme discomfort; 5) a rapid-onset loss of emotional balance (disequilibrium). Crises are exacerbated by substance use disorder. "Crisis intervention" involves "strategic planning" and temporary intervention to: 1) reduce the perceptual impact; 2) facilitate normative responses; and 3) mobilize additional resources to restore adaptive functioning.

Three key features include: 1) feelings supersede thinking; 2) a sense of being out of control dominates; and 3) normal capacities become impaired. Other key concepts include: 1) an event may precipitate a crisis in one person and not in others; 2) crisis events are typically sudden and unexpected, catching individuals unprepared; 3) crisis reactions usually subside in 24 to 72 hours; 4) usual coping skills are inadequate; 5) crises may precipitate unacceptable or even dangerous behaviors in respondents; 6) those in distress tend to respond well to support from any reasonable source. Common crisis reactions are fear, helplessness, confusion/disorientation, shock, intense anxiety, denial, agitation, anger, and grief. Potential physical symptoms include heart rate changes, rapid breathing, headache, tremulousness, and nausea. Prolonged response may include apathy, social withdrawal, and decreased self-esteem.

Being very young or very old tends to heighten the intensity of a crisis response. Further, individuals who perceive themselves to be routinely in control of their lives (most commonly those in higher economic or social status) also tend to be more seriously impacted by a crisis situation. In general, 1) more powerful reactions result from more intense crisis exposure; 2) more severe reactions accrue from long duration exposure; 3) reduced reactions occur when greater family/friend support exists; 4) prior traumatic experiences may either produce greater self-confidence or intensify the trauma; 5) when concurrent stressors "pile up," personal stability is reduced on the whole and coping collapses earlier; 6) greater coping is associated with a sense of control; 7) greater resource availability leads to better coping.

Crisis Intervention

The seven principles, in order, are: 1) proximity, intervention provided in familiar surroundings; 2) immediacy, early intervention is crucial; 3) expectancy, engendering confidence that the problem(s) can be solved; 4) brevity, effective interventions need to be short and meaningful; 5) simplicity, complexity would overwhelm those in crisis; 6) creativity, innovation to accommodate circumstances is important; and, 7) practicality, impractical interventions will be seen as insensitive and draining. Other keys are: 1) know your limits and do only what you're trained to do; 2) don't open problems that can't be resolved in the time available ("unbox" only what you can "rebox" in time); 3) avoid old psychological traumas and focus on immediate concerns; 4) reasonable progress is usually sufficient, and a referral is in order if major issues persist. Primary objectives: 1) reduce the immediate trauma; 2) facilitate recovery; and 3) identify those needing follow-up support/referrals. Don't press for too much too fast.

The overarching goal of crisis intervention is to support the individual and bolster the skills needed to cope. While the other elements can be helpful, enhanced individual coping is the overarching goal. This is essential, as the short-term nature of crisis intervention underscores the fact that professional help cannot always be available. The four factors the spurred the development of crisis intervention theory are: 1) warfare; 2) natural and terrorist disasters; 3) law enforcement activities; and 4) medical events. In 1906, Edwin Stierlin utilized crisis intervention techniques following a European mining disaster. In 1944, Erich Lindemann, a Boston psychiatrist, published his findings on crisis intervention after working with the survivors of a nightclub fire in which 492 were trapped and killed. By the 1960s, medical, law enforcement, and mental health professionals were developing crisis intervention services for various events, including battered spouses and sexual assault victims. During the 1970s to 1990s hotline services and crisis centers were increasingly common.

The five main goals of crisis intervention are to: 1) control the crisis and reactions to it; 2) ameliorate distress in those involved; 3) gather necessary supportive resources to manage the trauma; 4) "depathologize" (normalize or "demedicalize") the reactions to the trauma; and 5) restore baseline (or enhance) adaptation and function. The greatest benefit is enabling people to resume reasonably normal function and avoid new long-term psychological problems. Crisis Intervention "Stage One" (of seven stages) is: Assessment is a "severity" and "situational" assessment (what has happened and what's happening now) via: a) basic information (events and complications, such as drugs or psychiatric history), witness information; b) life-threatening issues (overdose, weapons, threats); c) impact severity (mild, moderate, severe); d) symptoms (typical vs atypical with a focus on the latter); e) those needing help (e.g., children); f) special help needed (medical, police); g) timing of help (immediate vs brief delay for composure); h) the immediate resources needed.

The second Crisis Intervention Stage (of seven stages) is Establishing Rapport. Often folded into the "Assessment" stage, this involves: 1) introducing yourself; 2) demonstrating acceptance and respect; 3) providing assurance that help is available and you will assist; 4) listening well; 5) allowing time (for expressions, feelings, etc.); 6) extending warmth while remaining professional; 7) balancing (getting on the same eye level so as not to dominate); 8) using a confident, calm, controlled demeanor. The third Crisis Intervention Stage is "Exploring the Crisis Problem." This involves: 1) ask what started the crisis; 2) ask if they have ever experienced a crisis like this before; 3) ask how they coped in the past with anything of this nature; 4) address any dangerous or even possibly lethal issues in the current crisis; 5) use open-ended questioning in serial fashion; 6) prompt them to tell their story of what happened; 7) listen, using empathy; 8) reflect emotions and paraphrase what you've been told.

The fourth Crisis Intervention Stage is "Exploring Feelings and Emotions." This involves: 1) address any main emotions left unaddressed; 2) use active listening, concern, and support to open up emotional expressions; 3) Consider "what would help me or those I love" to generate further ideas for support. Stage Five is "Generating and Exploring Alternatives." This involves: 1) questioning about past crisis coping methods; 2) directly asking "what might be helpful right now?"; 3) asking if they've tried any past methods or helpful ideas yet; 4) encouraging those they've not yet tried; 5) offering suggestions where they can't think of any. Stage Six is "Developing and Implementing a Crisis Action Plan." This involves: 1) mentally brainstorming options; 2) selecting the best options; 3) implementing the option(s); 4) prompting collaboration with the plan. Stage Seven is "Checking on the Plan's Success and Following Up." This involves: 1) monitoring; 2) revising/refining; 3) continuing until resolution or hand off; 4) following up; 5) closure; 6) further assessment and referral if problems persist.

Follow-up after a crisis intervention contact is needed when: 1) medical or surgical intervention was required; 2) an individual requests it; and 3) when stress-related symptoms are severe. Like first-aid, not everyone needs more. Follow-up needs to be integrated in the crisis intervention process, and should begin immediately for those in need. Additional contacts and easily located resources should be available. The National Institute of Mental Health (2002) recommends follow-up for: 1) the bereaved; 2) those with preexisting psychiatric conditions; 3) any survivor who required medical or surgical assistance (at higher risk for stress issues; 4) any experiencing an "acute stress disorder" (early PTSD); 5) any who sustained chronic or especially intense trauma; 6) individuals who request further follow-up. Various psychotherapies can help in follow-up, including 1) Eye Movement Desensitization and Reprocessing (EMDR); 2) cognitive-behavioral therapy; and 3) trauma incident reduction.

Emotional compromise and psychological burdens can accrue readily for individuals processing the trauma of others. Emotional support for staff should be an integral part of a total crisis management program. Staff may benefit from: 1) reviewing individual interventions and related feelings with colleagues and/or supervisory staff; 2) working with fellow crisis team members to offer a team "debriefing" experience; 3) processing: a) intervention outcomes and who will offer follow-up to specific participants; b) lessons learned via an intervention; c) parts of a debriefing that generated distressing responses from participants; 4) turn to trusted friends and individual colleagues for further support; 5) attend trainings, conferences, and workshops to build knowledge, coping skills, and self-confidence through which to better cope with the tasks.

SAFER-R Crisis Intervention Model

The model is outlined as follows: "S" is stabilize the situation (protect the individual, limit interference, and reduce distraction and disruptive stimuli. "A" is acknowledge the reality of the crisis event and the understandable distress it has produced. "F" is facilitate situational understanding and develop options. "E" is encourage the development of a collaborative action plan. "R" is recovery evidence is sought out, allowing proper closure when in evidence. "R" is refer when significant impairment persists. "Critical Incident Stress Management" (CISM) programs of the 1970s were developed from group-based interventions that emerged subsequent to World War II. A variety of group models exist. The International Critical Incident Stress Foundation (ICISF) offers the most widely utilized group crisis intervention processes. The American Red Cross and the National Organization for Victim Assistance use other models. The ICISF models called "Demobilization" and "Crisis Management Briefings" work well for disaster-generated large groups, while "Defusing" and "Critical Incident Stress Debriefing" work better in small group situations.

Demobilization

"Demobilization" is designed as an information-only, very brief, large group (20+) intervention for operations personnel (ie, "first responders" such as ambulance staff, police, and firefighters). It involves a 10-minute session of useful information addressing typical symptoms, coping options, and resources for further help. It may be followed by a 20-minute rest and food break before release from work to return home. The information is provided, but no interaction is solicited. "Crisis Management Briefing" differs from Demobilization in the following ways: 1) it is designed for nonprofessionals (e.g., community members in a disaster area); 2) it is minimally interactive (questions are taken and factually answered regarding what occurred and what is being done, with a goal to inform and calm the community); 3) information is provided by a "team" of respondents (e.g., from various responder services); 4) information provided (e.g., handout materials) is primarily for health and safety, rather than being focused on emotions management; 5) the time allotted is typically 45 to 60 minutes.

Critical Incident Stress Debriefing

Critical Incident Stress Debriefing (CISD) is seven phases of "structured storytelling" to help normal people cope with abnormal events. In brief, it consists of: 1) an introduction with summary of the purpose and format; 2) incident descriptions with each individual sharing what they experienced; 3) personal thoughts of each participant telling their thoughts about the event as they experienced it; 4) the worst is each participant describing the worst part for them personally; 5) distress signals is the entire group contributes signs and symptoms of distress they are experiencing; 6) normalization is practical information offered about common signs and symptoms, and optimal ways to cope; and 7) a summary segment is offered by which to conclude the CISD intervention. Further evaluation and referrals may be needed if any participants are experiencing complicated grief, emotional trauma, or loss of coping capacity. A CISD is typically conducted by a team (a counselor and paraprofessionals) with a small group (under 20), within the first several days, and last 2 to 3 hours.

Crisis Management "Defusing" Model

Designed for use with small groups (less than 20), it is an abbreviated version of Critical Incident Stress Debriefing. Participants should be as homogenous in their experiences as possible (ie, having witnessed the same traumatic event at a similar level and degree of exposure). Participants who are familiar with each other on some level, and who share similar roles in the event, are ideal (ie, firefighters, or hotel personnel survivors of a facility fire). Using this approach with mixed groups should be entirely avoided. The primary goal is discussion of the shared experience, and the provision of practical information oriented toward recovery. Active interaction between the crisis response team and the participants is encouraged, allowing brief experiential stories to be drawn forth for crisis leaders to respond. In this way, the experiences can be "processed" and "normalized," and suggestions regarding stress, self-care, interactions with loved ones, eating, sleeping, and activity levels can also be offered. Finally, in this way those needing further help can also be identified.

Therapeutic Relationships That Are Respectful Versus Confrontational and Aggressive

Past views suggested that aggression and confrontation were necessary to "break through denial." Current theory recognizes aggression engenders defensiveness, and that therapeutic success depends on respectful treatment that empowers the client. Other facilitative qualities include: 1) cultural sensitivity is appreciating differences, and understanding the cultural context and cultural factors that relate to problem development and treatment success; 2) empathy is vicariously receiving the attitudes, feelings, and thoughts of the client; 3) genuineness is avoiding a contrived or false presentation of oneself or role; 4) immediacy is remaining focused on immediate issues in the "here and now'; 5) respect is responding to clients as competent adults able to take responsibility for their own lives; 6) warmth is remaining accepting, open, and responsive to all clients. "Motivational interviewing" can help, as it aids clients to explore and resolve ambivalence, elicits motivation rather than imposing it, acknowledges that denial is a function of therapeutic interaction rather than part of the client's character, and thus helps to build a full partnership.

Assessment

Competent Assessment

Competent assessment requires a process sensitive to client demography, disability, and personality with specific inclusion of: 1) current substance abuse status; 2) past alcohol and drug use history; 3) addiction treatment history; 4) physical and mental health (past and present); 5) family, work, and career issues; 6) legal/criminal history; 7) psychological, emotional, and worldview issues; 8) exploration of spirituality; 9) current legal standing, lifestyle choices, and socioeconomic characteristics; 10) current use of community resources. Various assessment tools may also be helpful. Assessment data must be analyzed and interpreted in order to derive treatment recommendations. Consultation may be required, and findings and recommendations must be recorded.

Physiological and Psychoactive Effects of Alcohol Ingestion

Alcohol (EtOH) rapidly enters the bloodstream via the stomach and small intestines (slower if ingested with food). Its sedative properties affect the central nervous system and spinal cord and then progress to the brain, penetrating its outer and finally inner layers. Outer layer penetration produces intoxication, and "social drinkers" moderate drinking to minimize this effect. Toxic to all cells in the body, prolonged high EtOH levels can produce permanent brain damage called "organic brain syndrome." Weakening the heart, it is primary cause of hypertension in the United States. Inflammation of the pancreas is a serious problem because this organ produces insulin. Liver cirrhosis (hardening) can back blood up into the veins of the esophagus. If they rupture, death can result. Rates of esophageal cancer are higher in drinkers as well (likely due to the carcinogenic urethane contamination found in most alcohol beverages). Stomach inflammation can lead to hyperacidity and ulcers, and the resulting bleeding/hemorrhaging can also be fatal. Depressed genital reflexes can lead to transient or even permanent impotency.

Role of Behavior in the Development of Chemical Dependency

Current behavioral perspectives focus on behavioral stimulus events, reinforcement, and punishment. While acknowledging the disease model of addiction, they recognize that behavior and learning may play an important role. The basic behavioral tenets of addiction acquisition include the following: 1) discriminating stimuli exist for all persons all the time; 2) a range of drinking responses exists, mediated in part by learning and environment; 3) some behavioral consequences will enhance the probability of a behavior being repeated; and 4) punishment will decrease the likelihood of a behavior being continued. Bandura (1969) borrowed from Social Learning Theory to develop a framework of learning, cognition, and reinforcement that helped to explain many psychosocial and cultural predispositions for alcohol use and abuse. Mello (1972) and Sobell and Sobell (1978) offered the best-known applications of learning theory to alcoholism, as they largely succeeded in using operant theory to help some (but not all) abusive drinkers to recover and establish appropriate social drinking patterns.

Alcohol Use Inventory (AUI)

Horn, Wanberg, and Foster developed the 147-item self-administered AUI in 1974 as a screening scale for the evaluation of drinking behaviors. The instrument offers 17 primary scales that directly measure the use and misuse of alcohol, and 6 second-order factors used to broadly evaluate the following: a) drinking to enhance functioning (e.g., social, emotional); b) the degree of obsession with alcohol; c) the degree of life disruption resulting from alcohol use; d) anxiety about the problems resulting from alcohol use; e) the level of awareness that alcohol is a problem; and f) the breadth of alcohol consumption and impairment. The results of the test then offer an aggregate score that reflects the level of alcohol use and misuse. As a longer, more intense screening tool, it is useful not only in assessing the degree of alcohol use disorder but also in evaluating the degree of impairment in numerous life domains.

Comprehensive Drinker Profile (CDP)

Incorporating information much like that found in the MAST (Michigan Alcoholism Screening Test), the Comprehensive Drinker Profile (developed in 1971) expands to cover a much wider array of information about an individual's drinking patterns. Administered as a structured intake interview, the CDP produces numerous quantitative indices in multiple dimensions such as family drinking history, duration of the problem and quantities consumed, range of beverages used and in what situations, the emotional features driving the drinking, life problems, and substances other than alcohol concurrently or episodically used. Because of the complexity of the 88 areas covered, the intake interview must be conducted by an evaluator familiar with the information it contains and well-rehearsed in administering it. In spite of these demands, however, the instrument is the most comprehensive and empirically validated instrument of this nature, and it offers substantial sensitivity in an assessment of the issues addressed.

MacAndrew Alcoholism Scale

The MacAndrew Alcoholism Scale was designed for administration to psychiatric patients to separate alcoholics from nonalcoholics. Based on 49 items from the Minnesota Multiphasic Personality Inventory (MMPI), the scale assesses both general features of alcoholism and specific alcoholic drinking behaviors. Researchers have found the scale to have both reliability and validity in a much more rapid administration format as compared with the extensive MMPI instrument. As with other screening instruments, the MacAndrew Alcoholism Scale can be helpful in diagnosing an alcohol problem and in developing a treatment plan for chemically dependent individuals. By identifying behavior patterns, appropriate goals and interventions can be more meaningfully and effectively designed and implemented.

Minnesota Multiphasic Personality Inventory (MMPI)

The Minnesota Multiphasic Personality Inventory (MMPI) is a self-administered 566-item personality test that is constructed in a true-false response format. Researchers have found the MMPI to be useful in the assessment of alcoholism, as a limited number of personality profiles have been consistently associated with alcoholism. Specifically, the 4, 3-4 or 4-3, and 4-9 configurations are frequently associated with substance abuse, as these profiles indicate issues with inadequate personality, passive-aggressive behaviors, immaturity, irresponsibility, and impulse control problems. However, the 2-7-4 profile is the most consistent indicator of an addictive personality, with issues of depression, obsessive-compulsive traits, anxiety, phobias, irresponsibility, poor impulse control, acting out, and immaturity as prominent features. One drawback to using the MMPI is that scoring and interpretation can only be completed by a properly trained psychometrician, limiting its use in many settings.

Cocaine Assessment Instruments

The 1984 Gold cocaine addiction instrument was developed to provide a self-administered tool by which to determine if an individual suffers from an addiction to cocaine. While all self-administered tools are impaired by issues of denial and dishonesty, this 50-question tool has an educational component that can be of particular value to the respondent even while important information about use and abuse patterns is being gathered. In 1980, McLellan, Luborsky, and O'Brien produced the Addiction Severity Index. It evaluates seven areas that are typically impaired by any substance addiction. The test is arranged in a series of questions about the preceding 30 days as well as over the course of the person's lifetime, so the responses can reveal the significance of the identified problems as well as their severity. Again, minimization, poor memory, and dishonesty can influence the quality of the findings.

Questions About Substance Use Disorders That Must Be Asked

The client's pattern of substance use disorder should be ascertained at intake, including 1) drugs used (combinations used, primary drug of choice); 2) overall usage patterns (lifetime usage for all drugs, age at first use, changes in usage over time, general usage in the past 30 days, detailed daily usage in the last 7 days); 3) current and preferred mode of administration (may reveal much about drug depth and malignancy); 4) amount and frequency of use (quantified in dollars per day, if necessary); 5) setting and circumstances of use (gives clues to use triggers: where, when, with whom, what emotional precursors, what goals of use). A trial period of abstinence may reveal much about the impact of drugs in the client's life.

Units of Measure for Common Substances of Abuse

Alcohol is usually measured in ounces. One can of beer, an 8-ounce glass of wine, and one shot of distilled alcohol will each contain roughly equivalent amounts of alcohol. Heroin is often sold in "dime bags" ($10 bags), with an IV addict using 3 to 10 bags during a day. Crack cocaine is often sold in plastic vials containing 1 to 3 pea-size "rocks" at $5 to $30 per vial. Cocaine is sold by the gram: 1 oz (28 grams), a "quarter" ounce (7 grams), or an "eighth" ounce (3.5 grams), at $40 to $50 per gram. Marijuana is sold by the ounce, in dime bags of loose material from which 2 to 3 joints can be rolled, or per cigarette ("joint" or "reefer") for a few dollars each. Binge use complicates the addiction picture. Crack cocaine offers a very brief high followed by a dysphoric crash that propels further use. Crack binges often last 2 to 3 days, until funds run out or extreme exhaustion results. Binge drinking ("benders") often extend several days.

Dopamine

The neurotransmitter dopamine plays a key role in initiating and maintaining the brain's biochemical "reward system." Other neurotransmitters largely only interact with the dopamine reward system. Any activity that stimulates the brain's powerful reward system (e.g., sexual expression) can lead to addictive behaviors. The areas of the brain involved in the neurochemical reward system include the "ventral tegmental area" (VTA), found in the anterior ventral midbrain, along with the "nucleus accumbens" (NA), situated in the ventral forebrain. The brain regulates dopamine via the "mesolimbic dopamine system." The cell bodies of the brain's dopaminergic neurons are found in the VTA, and the terminals of the neurons are found in the NA. Neuroimaging studies reveal that the brain's reward system can be boosted by cocaine, opiates, and alcohol. Further, however, anticipation of other external nondrug stimuli (e.g., sex, money, status) can also activate a similar neurobiological pathway in the brain. Thus, biochemical reward-boosting thoughts and behaviors can produce similarly addictive results.

Adaptive Consequences

"Adaptive consequences" are behavioral enhancements that preserve family dysfunction. Researchers have noted that couples were often more relaxed and communicative when the alcoholic partner was drinking, as opposed to abstaining. Thus, the behavioral patterns associated with substance abuse can sometimes offer positive reinforcements (ie, adaptive consequences) that sustain and perpetuate the problematic behavior regardless of other causative factors. Bowen (1974) has noted that problematic nuclear family symptoms are often expressed in three areas: 1) marital conflict; 2) spousal dysfunction (e.g., substance abuse); and 3) projection onto one or more children (ie, the "family projection process"). The children who receive projections become "symptom bearers" and are referred to as "identified patients" who serve to express the entire family's pain. Individual differentiation is often low in substance abusing families, where personal needs are sacrificed to protect the family system. Both projection and low differentiation patterns lead to intergenerational transmission of problems, such as addictions.

Principal Behavioral Feature(s) of Addiction

These include: 1) obsession/preoccupation with the behavior or drug; 2) continued use/conduct despite serious negative consequences; 3) compulsive/out-of-control behavior. Obsession involves constant preoccupation or fantasy with the addictive issue. Serious consequences include gambling into poverty or drinking with life-threatening liver disease. Compulsive loss of control can be grossly overeating, pornography viewing, drinking, etc. When all three categories exist, an addiction is present. Behavioral addictions often involve a physiological component (e.g., gambler's "rush" of adrenaline), and commonly coexist with substance/alcohol use disorder, and often run in families. Legitimate behavioral addictions (e.g., work, cleaning) also exist. Sexual addictions may meet the same criteria. However, sex addicts have, on average, three out-of-control behaviors; some are "normal" (masturbation, promiscuity) and others are disordered "paraphilias" (e.g., exhibitionism, sadomasochism, pedophilia, voyeurism). One-third of all sex addicts are women, who tend more toward exhibitionism (in dress) and fantasy sex, while men tend more toward voyeurism, patronizing prostitutes, and anonymous sex. A careful history is important.

Personal Areas/Domains Directly Impacted by Substance Use Disorder

The six artificial divisions of substance use disorder that are directly impacted are as follows: 1) physical (e.g., altered health, including using to affect sleep and/or relieve stress, as well as problems with internal organs, nutrition, immunological compromise, blackouts, impaired sexual function); 2) behavioral (e.g., preoccupation with the substance, avoidance of boasting of use as abuse grows, episodic abstinence to gain control, shifting preferred drinks, rushing drinks/sneak hits, lying about use, missing social and employment commitments, increased aggression and unpredictability; WART: "With Alcohol, Repeated Troubles"); 3) emotional (remorse and guilt at loss of control and related problems, mood swings, irrationality, and grandiosity); 4) social (withdrawal and isolation, and marked discomfort at events lacking substance abuse); 5) spiritual/moral (gradual breakdown in values and ethics; progressing to routinely broken promises, lying, stealing, etc., as the chemical dependency worsens); 6) volitional (impaired capacity for making choices; eg, when, how much, and where to drink).

Gender Issues

Males (compared with females) are younger with their first drink, encounter physical dependency earlier, drink more and earlier in the day, binge more, encounter delirium tremens and blackouts more, and have more social, legal (arrests), work, and academic problems due to alcohol. Women, however, drink alone more, are more aware of alcohol problems, and have more suicide attempts. Chemical dependency among women tends to be more stigmatizing than with men, and they are less likely to seek help. Thus, while substance use disorder rates may appear to be lower for women than men, research suggests rates are much closer and may even be equal. Families report women's substance use disorder less; prescription drug abuse is more common among women and also easier to dismiss. Because men drive more (and women are more likely to be simply warned), DUI rates are somewhat biased as well. Entry into the workplace, however, has heightened awareness.

Physiological factors: Research suggests that the weight-adjusted metabolic rate of women introduces alcohol into their systems more readily than men's. Hormonal fluctuations due to menstruation and other endocrinological factors may also influence addiction. Finally, health complications such as cirrhosis may emerge more readily in women than men.

Social factors: Role stressors: a) stay-at-home family pressures; b) achieving career goals in a male-dominated working world; c) dual home and work roles; d) "empty nest" influences (potentially filled via drug use); e) single-life loneliness; f) postpartum- and menopausal-induced emotional crises. Many women point to loneliness and isolation as key precipitants motivating substance abuse. A tendency toward self-blame and over-assumptions of responsibility can also contribute to addictive tendencies.

The average woman seeking help is 44 years of age, married with children, and employed. Kirkpatrick (1977) notes that women do better in all-female groups where sex-typed nurturing roles do not as readily constrain the counseling process. Lemay (1980) noted that women have unique needs in the treatment process: 1) understanding male-female sex-typed roles; 2) identifying women's conflicts with sex-typed roles; 3) teaching women to assume responsibility for defining the roles they assume; 4) identifying sexual relationships and inherent sexual conflicts; 5) learning assertiveness training and the insights necessary to avoid seeking unrealistic approval from others; 6) understanding that a "perfect" relationship is not the key to personal happiness; 7) becoming informed of basic personal rights (e.g., financial, legal) and tools for self-efficacy.

Culture

Swidler (1986) incorporated beliefs, values, and worldview into the meaning of "culture." An individual's "racial identity" may also shape each of these cultural features, as can patterns and practices of substance use disorder. Thus, culture is best understood through open discussion. Sue and Sue (1990) suggest raising cultural awareness in counseling via: 1) addressing and resolving cultural differences as they arise; 2) openly exploring how a client may feel about working with a counselor of another race or ethnic background; 3) evaluating the possibility that cultural norms may limit a client's disclosure of personal information; 4) identifying the extent to which family is a source of support (ie, "familism" or its absence); and 5) examine any culturally driven expectations and perceptions a client may have about counseling.

Review Video: Multicultural Counseling
Visit mometrix.com/academy and enter code: 965442

Cultural Humility

The approach that Tervalon and Murray-Garcia (1998) recommend is called "cultural humility." Research reveals that client and staff ethnic/racial matching (including language and culture) has not enhanced treatment service utilization. Rather, staff should practice cultural humility to optimize the interaction and treatment process. Cultural humility requires that the staff person incorporate five relational keys: 1) recognize that the client is the "expert" in his or her culture; 2) utilize self-critique and self-reflection when interacting with culturally diverse clients; 3) offer mutual respect; 4) commit to continuous cultural learning; and 5) humbly accept that he or she cannot know all that is culturally relevant. To maximize cross-cultural treatment effectiveness, Finn (1996) encourages: 1) an individualized treatment approach; 2) the avoidance of assumptions; 3) the establishment and nurturance of trust; and 4) identify and address substance use disorder issues rooted in aspects of culture.

Acculturation

The term "acculturation" can be defined as "adoption of a host society's culture." The process of accommodation and integration of the host culture is a transitional period during which individuals are at greater risk of substance use disorder and HIV exposure, especially if the host culture is more permissive and/or the stresses accompanying the process are high. In such situations, substance use disorder can emerge as a coping mechanism. A consistent research finding is that the influence of acculturation on alcohol and illicit drug use and abuse is stronger for women than for men. The stresses of acculturation are heightened by the social and familial disruption caused by migration, resulting in reduced social support and mobility. Migration and acculturation often also lead to increased poverty and racial discrimination.

Asians

Numerous individuals of Asian descent (50%) have one or more inactive copies of the liver enzyme acetaldehyde dehydrogenase, which is necessary to metabolize acetaldehyde. As a result, they tend to require longer periods of time to metabolize alcohol out of the body. The genetic variant is evident by marked facial flushing and nausea in those carrying the inactive gene copies. For many, these negative associations cause them to self-limit their drinking. Consequently, rates of alcoholism are lower among Asians than among other groups. It is important to note, however, that affected individuals do not become intoxicated faster or experience a higher blood alcohol proportionate to the alcohol consumed. Further, not all Asian groups have similar alcohol use disorder patterns. For example, Koreans and Korean Americans have higher alcoholism rates than Chinese and Chinese Americans. While alcoholism rates are particularly high among Native Americans and Native Alaskans, there are no known genetic causative factors.

Asians have the lowest use of alcohol of any major racial/ethnic group in the United States. In a 2005 to 2006 survey by SAMHSA's Office of Applied Studies, when asked about any alcohol use in the past month, 35.4% of Asians, 36.7% of Hawaiian/Pacific Islanders, 37.2% of Native Americans (American Indians/Alaskan Natives), 40.0% of African Americans, 41.8% of Hispanics, and 55.8% of Caucasians responded affirmatively. Males use alcohol more than females (57% vs 45.2%). By age, 16.6% of those 12 to 17, 61.9% of those 18 to 25, and 53.7% of those age 26 and older responded affirmatively. According to the National Comorbidity Study (1996), mental illness is accompanied by substance abuse about 29% of the time, though actual alcohol dependency among that group is only 7.2%. However, although 3.3% of Hispanics, 3.1% of African Americans, and 2.6% of Caucasians were in need of substance abuse treatment, only 15.9%, 28.7%, and 15%, respectively, of those in need received treatment.

Genetics and Metabolic Factors

Four types of study suggest genetics plays a role in substance use disorder: 1) alcoholism tends to run in families (although postnatal environmental factors may also play a role); 2) animal studies have identified inherited factors that influence the tendency to drink and the amount ingested; 3) twin studies reveal a two times greater risk of alcoholism in identical twins compared with fraternal twins; and 4) adoption studies reveal a greater than four-fold risk of alcoholism in birth-adopted children of alcoholics (without background knowledge of or contact with the natural parents) as compared with nonalcoholic birth-adoptees. Neurochemicals such as serotonin, dopamine, THP, and other biochemicals also appear to mediate alcohol use and abuse. For example, blood acetaldehyde levels reach much higher levels with the same amount of alcohol (and breakdown much slower), when compared with nonalcoholics, and react with brain amines to produce morphine-like compounds that trigger the need to drink.

Psychosocial Assessment

It is essential for a clinician to have a broader understanding of a client for the counseling process to be optimally effective. A complete psychosocial assessment should include the following: 1) client identification and demographic factors, 2) presenting problem/complaint, 3) referral source, 4) past substance use and abuse history (current and past drugs of choice, use and abuse patterns, and treatment), 5) psychiatric history and treatment provider(s), 6) legal history, 7) relevant medical history, 8) educational history, 9) employment history, 10) family history, 11) available support systems, 12) religious views and practices, 13) sociocultural factors that might influence treatment, 14) language and cultural barriers, and 15) client strengths and weaknesses. Tools that can help to elicit this information include the New York State Office of Alcoholism and Substance Abuse Services (OASAS) Comprehensive Psychosocial Evaluation and the Addiction Severity Index (ASI), which covers seven areas: medical status, employment and support, drug use, alcohol use, legal status, family/social status, and psychiatric status.

Family System

Families are integrated as a "system" of interrelated members. Distortions in relationships produced by compensating efforts (e.g., avoidance, covering) lead to situations of "codependency," preoccupation with the user and the circumstances he/she creates to the point that various mutual support and maintenance behaviors develop. Children growing up in a codependent environment often lag in emotional maturation and normal role development, and may later be angrier with their enabling parent (who should have "saved" them) than their using parent (who "couldn't help him/herself"). For example, a chemically dependent family member produces an enabling response from the others as they seek to cover for and assume the roles and responsibilities of the faltering family member. "Functional" users (e.g., still able to maintain employment, home activities) still impact others with their dysfunctional emotions and behaviors. Achieving change can be difficult because of the influence of "homeostasis," the need to maintain the status quo because it feels familiar in the face of a stressful, threatening, anxiety-producing circumstance.

Family Responses to Alcoholism

Kinney and Leaton's (1987) six stages of family responses to alcoholism are as follows: 1) denial: there either is no problem, or the problem can easily and logically be explained away; 2) bargaining: attempts to extinguish the problem via pleading, threats, and throwing the substance(s) away are often concurrently attempted; 3) disorganization and chaos: family balance is lost, finances become compromised via the substance abuse, children often begin acting out, and a spouse may seek outside help; 4) reorganizing around the problem: efforts to reform the user cease, and family members divide and accept assignments for the roles the substance abuser is no longer able to carry out; 5) efforts to escape: family members emotionally or even physically distance themselves from the home (e.g., children strive to leave, divorce may occur); 6) family reorganization: the user is eventually excluded, and must reenter the family as a "different" (ie, sober) person, which may cause considerable distress as roles and assignments are again reorganized.

Chemically Dependent Family

Chemically dependent family boundaries may be diffuse or rigid, but the most common presentation is rigid. For this style, the common rules of a chemically dependent family are as follows: 1) well-maintained homeostasis is paramount (sub-rules: don't talk/share, don't trust, and don't feel); 2) chemically driven roles must be retained; and 3) something outside or someone else creates any observed problem, not the chemical dependency. The chemically driven family dynamic may be many generations old, as a user and a spouse may have actually found one another to transmit and continue familiar (homeostatic) roles and responsibilities from their prior upbringing.

Codependency

Key features of codependency include the following: 1) "denial": refusing to accept the magnitude of the user's problem; 2) "bargaining": offers of reciprocal favors (or threats) to control the user's abuse (pushing into counseling is popular, but either the counselor misses the problem if not told of it directly, or the user accuses the sober member of "telling lies" and exaggerating, etc.); 3) "disorganization/dysfunction": as crises arise ever more frequently and intensely, the family can lose themselves in "putting out fires" that arise from the user's abuse; key home problems are finances, legal problems, unemployment, children's failures in school, etc.; 4) "reorganization": the development of new family roles and responsibilities to again achieve "homeostasis."

Chemically dependent families desperately want homeostasis (balance), given all the chaos introduced by the user. When all coping options fail, families will reorganize as rapidly as possible, producing new roles for each other. Common roles are as follows: 1) "chief enabler": typically a spouse or parent, with characteristics of excessive concern, fear, guilt, and need for control/power, this person overcompensates and leads covering and denial; 2) "hero": typically an oldest child, often enmeshed with the "chief enabler," their job is to overachieve and keep things "looking good" to others (often at the expense of their childhood); 3) "scapegoat": usually a male middle-child, the acting-out child who shifts focus away from the substance abuser (potentially by using drugs, too); 4) "lost child": characterized by seriousness, low self-esteem, isolation, withdrawal, and avoidance (with commensurately poor social skills) to prevent "gumming up" the complex family dynamics; 5) "mascot/placater": youngest child, uses shallow levity and "showy" immature behavior to distract or cover their pain (hypochondriasis, drugs, and promiscuity may also become a problem).

The predominant codependency treatment approach is the "disease model." Used in AA and Al-Anon settings and other treatment centers, this model was co-opted from the treatment chemical dependency itself, in spite of the fact that codependency treatment focuses on mental, emotional, and spiritual healing, as opposed to physical recovery. In treatment, family members are assisted in seeing their distorted roles and in modifying these roles to allow for a wholesome, chemical-free lifestyle. The alternate treatment approach is the "developmental-symbiotic model." This approach avoids references to disease, illness, and sickness, and instead addresses the arrested developmental growth. Codependent behaviors are construed as "normal," given the abnormal circumstances, and "symbiotic" in their unhealthy family relationship constructs. The focus is on proper family development by identifying arrested developmental points (stages) and learning how to get "unstuck" and move forward. Physical and emotional techniques are used to aid clients in feeling and entering earlier developmental stages, by which to reengage the natural maturational process.

Regardless of the therapeutic approach used, all codependents must: 1) identify abuses from their past, as personally perceived (as opposed to factual reality), as beliefs and related feelings are more important that technical accuracy; 2) put words to their pain, as open and honest discussion is essential to resolve related anger, grief, and shame–there is no timeline for this step, and it is often benefited by broad participation in and support from additional groups such as AA, Al-Anon, Alateen, and/or ACA (Adult Children of Alcoholics) as therapy allows personal expression and larger groups offer mutuality in the painful experiences; and 3) abandoning the victim lifestyle through understanding and forgiveness, where forgiveness does not refer to a return to abusive vulnerability, but rather an awareness of circumstances that drove the abuser and actual reconciliation only where appropriate and safe.

Review Video: Addictions
Visit mometrix.com/academy and enter code: 460412

ADULT CHILDREN AND GRANDCHILDREN OF CHEMICAL DEPENDENTS

Common characteristics of adult children of chemical dependents include the following: 1) people pleasing (due to an inability to trust one's own feelings secondary to an inconsistent upbringing); 2) abandonment fears (resulting in either attachment rejecting or overly dependent behaviors that intensify over time); 3) dysfunctional relationships (due to attraction to other chemical dependents and/or codependents); 4) fear of failure (fought off by overachieving or living below one's talents); 5) untoward guilt (over wishing parents dead, and worse if they do die prematurely leaving no hope for resolution); 6) resentment (toward the sober parent who did not flee the situation); 7) rigidity (lack of spontaneity to fend off fears of a return to past chaos); 8) fear of confrontation (particularly "hero children" avoid conflicts at all costs); 9) immaturity (particularly "scapegoats," "lost children," and "mascots") avoid responsibilities and have truncated developmental experiences; 10) compulsive substance abuse tendencies (due to their need to "numb" the distress in their lives–85% of those with one user parent will abuse substances, and 90% if both parents used substances).

Key ACA common personality characteristics include the following: 1) hyper-responsibility or total irresponsibility; 2) anger or fear over authority, producing an avoidance or inability to hold others accountable; 3) low self-esteem/self-efficacy resulting in hyperachieving or achievement avoidance; 4) hypersensitivity to others' feelings and actions (to avoid their own feelings); 5) lack of spontaneity and over-seriousness, or taking nothing seriously; 6) exaggerated fears of abandonment (causing clinging dependence or commitment avoidance); 7) reluctance to forgive (if ever) and intense judgments of self and others; 8) addiction to excitement (seen in compulsive behaviors, workaholism, and/or deadline procrastination); 9) commitment avoidance in everyday or long-term circumstances (e.g., chronic tardiness); 10) hyperdependency or extreme independence in interpersonal relationships; 11) chronic feelings of "oddness" yet uncertain what "normal" looks like; 12) high need for external affirmation of self, potentially evidenced in compulsive fabrications; 13) over-intellectualization or outright obliviousness to feelings; 14) strict regimentation or overly casual approach to situations, people, and activities; and 15) poor self-care (emotional and physical).

Whether chemically dependent or not, adult children of chemical users transmit codependent and victimization patterns to their children. A distorted family image results in recreated roles like those in the family of origin. Over-parented, they lack adequate coping skills. Family secretiveness is perpetuated by tradition. If they escape chemical abuse, they may well seek out other compulsions (e.g., work, many superficial relationships, food). Anxiety and depression are common, producing feelings of confusion and guilt in the absence of any apparent emotional triggers. Family approval is paramount, entrenching a "don't talk, don't trust, don't feel" collaboration (Black, 1981). Other key elements are a closed family style to avoid outside criticism; rejection of help because of trust issues; a strong sense of negative fate; and a defensive reaction in life, rather than proactive action. Treatment is similar—with permission, family rules are broken and secrets revealed to promote openness and understanding. ACA groups can be very helpful in breaking the codependency cycle.

As adults, most "heroes" tend to be successful. However, many have such a high need for achievement and control that they are unable to enjoy life, and many are unable to express feelings or manage intimate relationships because of a lack of trust. Adult "scapegoats" persist in inappropriate social relationships and remain rebellious and act out. The result is chemical dependence and encounters with the legal system. Others become victims of abuse because they invite abuse through their servile and acquiescent natures, leading to high-stress lives and illnesses. Adult "lost children" are often accommodators who are largely adrift and seek out troubled others to continue their roles. Adult "mascots" (placaters) remain unable to identify and meet their own needs, and either refuse to take life seriously or become enmeshed in real or supposed illnesses. Many do not live out their adult lives differently from the "special child" status.

Addiction Severity Index (ASI) Is Appropriate

The Addiction Severity Index (ASI) is used primarily to explore the nature and severity of issues common to substance use disorder. It has numerous strengths: 1) considerable research has shown it is a reliable instrument, 2) it requires only one hour to administer, 3) it is comprehensive, 4) it can be helpful in identifying dually diagnosed patients, 5) readministration at different points in treatment can help track progress, 6) its wide acceptance by national organizations allows for comparative use, and 7) it can accommodate multiple counseling and interviewing styles. Limitations include poor outcomes with severe and persistent mental illness; it is not appropriate for use with adolescents; because it focuses on the 30 days prior to assessment, it is less effective for clients who are hospitalized/institutionalized for long periods; and although it addresses some lifetime problems, it cannot derive a baseline needed to measure change over time. It does not provide quantity estimates of ethyl alcohol (ETOH) (the focus is on patterns), it doesn't address human immunodeficiency virus (HIV), and some feel that it doesn't adequately incorporate women's issues.

Adult Substance Use Survey (ASUS)

The Adult Substance Use Survey (ASUS) is a 64-item self-report survey. The administration time is 8 to 10 minutes. It takes less than 5 minutes to score, and it requires no training to administer. The Alcohol Use Disorders Identification Test (AUDIT) is a 10-item instrument with three subscales. It is self-administered or given via interview; the administration time is 2 minutes. It must be given by a trained health professional or paraprofessional. The CAGE questionnaire is a very brief alcohol screen of four items, which is self-administered or given via interview. The administration time is less than 1 minute, and no training is required.

The CRAFFT is a six-item screen for alcohol and drug use among adolescents; it is self-administered in less than 1 minute. The Drug Abuse Screening Test (DAST) has 10 items, is self-administered or given via interview in 2 minutes, and no training is required. The Michigan Alcohol Screening Test (MAST) is a 25-item instrument, which is self-administered or given by interview in 10 minutes, with no training required. The UNCOPE is a six-item screen designed to identify alcohol and/or drug abuse or dependence, it is self-administered or given by interview in less than 2 minutes, and no training is required.

Assessing a Family History of Addiction

Obtaining a family substance use disorder and psychiatric history can greatly illuminate the depth of a client's challenges and the unique issues within the larger family support system. Issues of depression, suicide, and major mental disorders can be particularly important when treating clients with dual diagnoses (substance use disorder and psychiatric conditions). The University of New Mexico, Center on Alcoholism, Substance Abuse and Addictions (CASAA) offers a Family History Questionnaire that explores 27 extended full and partial family relationships as relevant to substance use disorder history. The Addiction Severity Index (ASI), through its multidimensional risk profile, offers less detail in the familial history, but it expands the relational evaluation into peer and extended social relationships. The National Institute on Drug Abuse, in "NGC Domain #11: Family history information," recommends drawing a "family pedigree chart" and including substance use disorder (even tobacco) and psychiatric history information for all familial relationships. Finally, Weissman et al. (2000) offer the Family History Screen, covering family information on 15 lifetime psychiatric disorders and/or suicide attempts.

Self-Esteem

Poor self-image and low self-esteem are major risk factors for drug experimentation, and drug use damages self-image and self-esteem. Adolescence is a particularly risky developmental period. Self-esteem is increased in three ways: 1) Acceptance and respect from significant others (shifting from primary family to peers around age 11). Acceptance is defined as an investment of care, warmth, and interest without substantial "strings" of secondary gain for the family member or peer. 2) A positive history of success and achievement defined in terms of social approval. 3) Adequate skills to cope with failure. Children who are either over- or underindulged typically lack these skills, as they were either overly protected from failure, or were labeled a failure to the point of perpetual hopelessness. Positioning children for success, praising their successes, as well as allowing some failures, can be protective from future drug experimentation.

Identifying Why a Client Has Come to Seek Treatment

Clients may come in for treatment for many reasons: 1) a desire to stop using; 2) pressure from family; 3) a requirement for continued employment; 4) due to court order. Substance-abusing clients typically present in crisis or under pressure, and crisis intervention may be required. Where the visit was externally coerced: 1) acknowledge and sympathize with appropriate negative feelings; 2) accept without critique the client's primary desire to relieve pressure from the external source; 3) compliment the client on keeping the appointment; 4) point out that keeping the appointment was a positive choice; 5) emphasize that you do not want to continue the coercion, but instead simply want to help. If reports must be submitted (e.g., to a court), note this upfront, emphasizing that the goal is to help, not coerce.

Circumstances, Motivation, Readiness, and Suitability (CMRS) Questionnaire

The four primary scales in the CMRS are: 1) Circumstances; 2) Motivation; 3) Readiness; and 4) Suitability. "Circumstances" refers to external motivation; "Motivation" refers to internal motivation; "Readiness" refers to openness to treatment; and "Suitability" refers to a perception of the client's appropriateness for the proposed treatment modality. Rating the client's level of motivation and readiness is important both for the client's ability to benefit from a given program, and in terms of the impact the client will have upon others in the program. Currently, up to 70% of clients referred for treatment don't even show up for evaluation, and 40% to 60% will drop out during the course of treatment (usually during the beginning phases of treatment). To maximize the potential for success, all barriers (child care needs, transportation, accessibility, etc.), should be minimized or eliminated, and a trusting and positive therapeutic relationship with involved counselors should be carefully established.

Recidivism (Reoffense) Rate Following a Drunk Driving Arrest

About one-third (33%) of individuals arrested for drinking and driving will reoffend. Most states set the blood alcohol concentration (BAC) at either 0.08 or 0.10, though driving skills may be compromised at as little as 0.02 percent. One hour after two standard drinks on an empty stomach, a 160 lb man will have a 0.04 BAC. Other problems associated with alcohol use include: 1) crime and violence (half of arrestees had used alcohol recently and 21% were intoxicated); 2) sexual assault (one-half of perpetrators had been drinking at the time of the crime, and were more likely to target strangers); 3) child abuse (research suggests increased risks of both physical and sexual abuse, which often leads the child to future alcohol problems).

IV Drug Paraphernalia Prone to HIV Transmission

Recent research suggests that all elements of IV drug paraphernalia can harbor and transmit the HIV virus, and potentially other infectious diseases, such as hepatitis C. IV drug users require needles, syringes, "cookers," cotton swabs, and rinse water to carry out their habit. First the drug (typically a powder or crystal) is placed in a small container called a "cooker," often a bottle cap, spoon, or other metal receptacle. Water is then added, and the solution is mixed and heated from below if necessary (e.g., cocaine HCl needs no heat, but heat is needed for some forms of heroin and for time-released pharmaceutical drugs to remove the waxy filler; amphetamines may lose potency when heated). Water-insoluble heroin (ie, European heroin) is made soluble by the addition of an acid (citric acid, ascorbic acid, or even lemon juice or vinegar). Vinegar and lemon juice are also used with crack cocaine. Once dissolved, the solution is drawn through a filter (e.g., a cigarette filter or cotton swab).

Effect of Amprenavir (*Agenerase*) and Ritonavir (*Norvir*) on Methadone Treatment

Amprenavir (*Agenerase*) and ritonavir (*Norvir*) can both decrease methadone levels, and patients can even experience methadone withdrawal unless the methadone doses are increased to compensate. However, because these reactions are extremely idiosyncratic, it is essential to tailor all dose patterns to each individual's unique response. In like manner, both ritonavir and delavirdine can reduce the body's ability to metabolize both ecstasy (MDMA) and amphetamines. In consequence, these substances can reach toxic, potentially lethal blood levels (deaths have been reported). Protease inhibitors tend to increase THC levels in marijuana users, as can delavirdine, and clinicians must be alert to the potential consequences. In contrast, efavirenz and nevirapine are capable of decreasing THC effects. Clearly, it is important to understand the potential interactions between drugs of abuse and HIV treatment medications in order to respond properly.

Length of Time It May Take for a Hepatitis C–Infected Individual to Experience Symptoms

Most individuals don't develop symptoms until years after exposure. Hepatitis C virus (HCV) is bloodborne, so most infections are acquired through IV drug abuse (30% to 40% of all cases; 50% of all new cases). About 1% to 2% acquire the infection via sexual intercourse, 2% via occupational hazards, less than 1% via blood transfusion (none in the last decade), and 4% of babies born to infected mothers will acquire the disease. About 75% show no initial symptoms, and the other 25% develop only mild to moderate flu-like symptoms. About 15% to 25% of all infected will recover completely. However, most (75% to 85%) will harbor a chronic infection for 10 to 20 years or more. Of these, 20% will develop liver cirrhosis or liver cancer. Treatment involves ribavirin and the antiretroviral medication interferon. These medicines cause many side effects, including flu-like symptoms (e.g., fever, fatigue, nausea, muscle and joint pains), and not all will benefit from or even need these treatments. HIV and HCV are commonly shared infections, and those at risk for either one should be tested for the other.

Percentage of the General US Population with a Mental and/or Addictive Disorder

Approximately 28% to 30%. The 2001 report of the office of the US Surgeon General ("Mental Health: Culture and Ethnicity") notes that approximately 20% of the population has a diagnosable mental disorder during any given year (the "1-year prevalence rate"); some 3% have combined mental and addictive disorders; and approximately 6% will struggle with an addictive disorder only. Thus, 28% to 30% are affected. In children, the prevalence of mental disorders is also about 20%, and 5% to 9% have serious emotional disturbances. Ethnic variation and burdens of assimilation are factors in poverty, and poverty is related to substance use disorder. Thus, it is helpful to note the rates of the following various ethnic groups encountering poverty: black (22.7%); Hispanic (21.4%); non-Hispanic white (9.9%). Men consistently have higher levels of drug use compared with women (8.7% vs 5.5% in the 2001 National Household Survey on Drug Abuse [NHSDA] survey). This disparity persists even when comparing lifetime psychotherapeutic drug use with lifetime illicit drug use rates (19.4 vs. 14.8 for illicit drugs, and 11.1 vs 7.6 for psychotherapeutic drug use).

Composite International Diagnostic Interview (CIDI)

Designed and used by the World Health Organization (WHO), the Composite International Diagnostic Interview (CIDI), version 3, is composed of a total of 42 interview sections. It is recommended that every participant complete Section 1 because it explores general health and screens for primary disorders addressed elsewhere in the survey. In this way, a clinician is less likely to miss other relevant issues and conditions that may not yet have been a focus of treatment. Following the screening, however, a clinician may use any section that seems most relevant to the respondent's situation. This can be particularly important in situations in which a respondent might not cope well with the administration of a more extensive instrument. Examples include the following: Section 11, alcohol use; Section 12, illicit drug use; Section 14, tobacco; Section 26, functioning over the past 30 days; Section 27, symptoms in the last 30 days; and, Section 28, assessing for personality disorders.

Personality Characteristics and the Cognitive Health of Chemically Dependent Individuals

Research suggests that many chemically dependent individuals share common personality characteristics, including poor frustration tolerance, impulsivity, manipulative traits, and/or excessive dependency needs. Recognition of these assumptions has led to treatment approaches focused largely on confrontation, accountability, boundary setting, and teaching coping skills needed to remain sober. Other issues of mental health also appear to be relevant. Alcohol use and affective disorders (primarily depression) are closely correlated. Depressed alcoholics are usually one of the following four subtypes: 1) drinkers depressed because of alcohol's effects, which resolves after detoxification; 2) drinkers with a reactive depression due to other life problems; 3) drinkers using alcohol to treat an endogenous (biochemical) depression; 4) drinkers in the midst of an affective disorder, using alcohol to cope. Schizophrenia and Borderline Personality Disorder tend to predispose to substance use disorder, as well. However, psychiatric evaluations should be conducted only after detoxification.

Cognitive Deficits That Arise with Long-Term Alcohol Use Disorder

Long-term heavy drinking can produce cognitive impairment evident in both recent and remote memory. Cognitive problems are particularly common with high blood alcohol concentrations. Wernicke syndrome occurs from an alcohol-related thiamine deficiency. The encephalopathy is also significant for sixth nerve palsy and ataxia; all can be reversed with thiamine deficiency correction. Korsakoff syndrome arises from the alcohol toxicity and is less reversible. Symptoms include profound recent memory amnesia, inability to learn, confabulation, hallucinations, deficits in abstract and conceptual reasoning, and visuospatial impairment. Wernicke encephalopathy and Korsakoff psychosis are now referred to as "Alcohol Amnestic Syndrome." Peripheral neuropathy (with numbness, tingling, and paresthesias) occurs in 5% to 10% of alcoholics. Alcoholism can be brought on by a number of potential factors. Genetics play a well-known role. Alcoholism is particularly likely among those who began drinking as teens and progressed quickly to alcohol use disorder. By contrast, those who did not begin drinking until young adulthood were more likely to self-medicate for anxiety, and progressed into alcoholism more slowly.

Assessing Homeless and Comorbid Patient Populations

The Seattle, Washington, Downtown Emergency Service Center (DESC) recommends the Vulnerability Assessment Tool (VAT) with homeless men and women. The VAT addresses ten domains: 1) survival skills, 2) basic needs, 3) indicated mortality risks, 4) medical risks, 5) organization/orientation, 6) mental health, 7) substance use, 8) communication, 9) social behaviors, and 10) homelessness status.

The New South Wales (NSW) Clinical Guidelines for comorbidity screening recommend the following: 1) the Mental Status Exam (MSE), which is more extensive than the Mini-Mental State Examination (MMSE); 2) the Alcohol, Smoking and Substance Involvement Screening Test (ASSIST); 3) the Alcohol Use Disorders Identification Test (AUDIT); and 4) skillful clinical questioning.

Key questions for mental health problems include the following: 1) past mental health care, 2) past psychiatric medications, 3) whether the client is currently seeing a mental health provider, 4) problems sleeping, 5) changes in appetite, and 6) difficulties concentrating.

Substance use disorder screening problems include the following: 1) drug history, 2) time of last drug use, 3) drug of choice, 4) use frequency, 5) quantity, and 6) increases/decreases in use. Screening for suicidality is also indicated. Finally, collateral contacts (health-care providers and/or family) can be crucial, within the bounds of confidentiality and permission.

About 30% of those diagnosed with psychiatric disorders also engage in substance use disorder. Conversely, 36.6% with alcohol use disorders and 53.1% percent with other substance use disorders are mentally ill. Those with bipolar disorder are five times more likely and schizophrenics are four times more likely to have a substance use disorder or alcohol problem. Given these rates, it is essential to appropriately evaluate substance use disorder clients for a potential dual diagnosis and to meaningfully assess both conditions over time. Co-occurring disorders can often exacerbate each other, making diagnoses far more difficult. Detoxification may facilitate diagnosis. A commonly used interview tool for assessment is the Psychiatric Research Interview for Substance and Mental Disorders, version IV (PRISM-IV). The Young Mania Rating Scale (YMRS) and the Angst Hypomania Check List (HCL) may be used to assess hyperactivity, hypomania, manic, and bipolar evaluation). The Inventory of Depressive Symptoms (IDS) and the Montgomery-Åsberg Depression Rating Scale (MADRS) are helpful in cases of chronic depression. A careful mental status exam can better guide the clinician to the proper assessment tool.

ADDICTION

The term addiction is used to describe "an intense attachment to or dependence on any substance, idea, thing, or person that avoids reality and is pursued in spite of the consequences." The term first appeared in a seventeenth century reference to Roman law (1625), referring to formal surrender to a court sentence. By 1641 the term had broadened to refer to devotion to specific pursuits or habits in daily life. A connection with a compulsion or craving as related to the ingestion of a drug did not emerge until the eighteenth century. Today, the term remains primarily associated with physiological dependence on a drug. However, research increasingly suggests the root of many compulsions may arise with the brain's "reward systems" in ways similar to the neurological rewards of substance abuse. Thus, use of the term addiction is trending toward including compulsive behaviors that exhibit addictive features (ie, gambling, shopping, pornography viewing).

Review Video: Addictions
Visit mometrix.com/academy and enter code: 460412

PROCESS ADDICTION

Process addictions, also known as "behavioral addictions," fall into the category of nondrug addictions that exhibit similar addictive qualities. Certain human activities are particularly likely to stimulate the release of natural psychoactive neurotransmitters in the brain, just as certain chemical substances stimulate the release of those same psychoactive substances. Whether the "high" is chemically stimulated by an ingested substance, or induced by fiercely competitive computer games or experienced through the intense experience of high-stakes gambling, there may a similar biological substrate for both. Thus, engaging in any activity that profoundly and dependably produces intense emotionally charged experiences produces the possibility for an addiction to emerge (e.g., running, eating, gambling, computer gaming, debating/arguing, pornography, shopping). Many researchers agree that even intense and continuously ongoing negatively stimulated emotions (e.g., abusive or drama-driven relationships) can produce process additions.

Alcohol's Influence on the GABA (Gamma-Aminobutyric Acid) System

GABA (gamma-aminobutyric acid) is a key inhibitory neurotransmitter that is affected by alcohol. Normally, when GABA binds to its target receptor, neuronal cell activity is inhibited. In the presence of alcohol, that process of inhibition is further facilitated, which accounts for the behavioral changes. All psychoactive substances interact with one neurotransmitter system or another (e.g., opiates via the endogenous opioid system), and all ultimately interface with the brain's reward system in one way or another. Propensities to addiction as well as certain compulsive and impulsive behaviors appear to be a function of various genetic phenotypes, indicating that addictive tendencies may be related to an individual's genetic makeup.

Obsessive-Compulsive Disorders

Obsessive-compulsive disorders can be distinguished from addictions by the presence of ego-dystonic qualities. Addictions tend to result in ego-syntonic feelings, a sense of well-being and relief of psychological stress, at least until after the fact (ie, until after the "high" of gambling, shopping, or taking drugs has waned). Thus, most addictions arise from what are perceived as positive experiences, and many people are unaware that they are developing an addiction until the addiction is well entrenched. By contrast, obsessive-compulsive behaviors (and other psychiatric illnesses) tend to be accompanied by marked ego-dystonic (ego-alien) thoughts and distress. There is a desire to be rid of or free of something that is continuously troubling, distressing, or concerning in one way or another. Consequently, there is no "high" involved, but only the transient relief of distress when obsessions or compulsions are indulged.

Drug-Abusing Smokers and Nondrug-Abusing Smokers

Six key differences: 1) they tend to have started smoking at younger ages; 2) they tend to be more addicted (averaging 10 cigarettes more per day) and report more withdrawal symptoms, with 72% smoking two or more packs per day versus 9% of nondrug-abusing smokers; those smokers with a severe drug problem smoke two to four packs per day; 3) they have more cognitive deficits (perhaps due to the drug use); 4) they have more psychological problems (depression, anxiety, and personality disorders); 5) they have more medical problems (e.g., heart disease, cirrhosis, pancreatitis, and upper digestive and respiratory cancers); and 6) they have less self-efficacy in smoking cessation. Though most want to stop smoking, those desiring cessation are fewer than nondrug-abusing smokers (50% to 75% vs 80% to 90%). However, if they remain in recovery, 45% to 65% eventually stop smoking (about equal to or even somewhat higher than nondrug-using smokers at 45% on average). Thus, the goal of ceasing all substances of abuse is certainly achievable.

Smoking Cessation for Substance Abusers Already in Treatment

Polydrug users may turn to drug substitution. Smoking cessation is not easy, as tobacco use is as addictive has heroin. Thus, individuals in recovery for another drug are 30% to 65% less likely to succeed in smoking cessation in the same number of attempts as individuals attempting to quit nicotine alone. Even so, tobacco is the number one behavioral killer, and therefore is not relatively harmless. Further, about one-half of all house and forest fires are caused by smokers; half of all smokers will die from smoking-induced health problems; smoking is directly linked to sudden infant death syndrome (SIDS); and some 53,000 people die each year from "secondhand" smoke. Twelve-step programs can work well with all addictions, including smoking, and should be used to preserve the life of the user. AA founders Bill Wilson and Dr. Bob Smith did both stop drinking, but both also died prematurely from tobacco-related illnesses (emphysema and pharyngeal cancer, respectively). Stopping all dangerous addictive substances simultaneously is increasingly found to be successful, and advisable.

Percentage of Inpatient Drug Users Who Attempt to Stop Smoking Via an Initial Cessation Program and Remain Smoking-Free 6 Months Later

Around 12% or less. Therapists need to recognize if an individual is still both smoking and using drugs and wants to cease all (initial cessation), has only recently quit (early recovery and stabilization), or is well into recovery (middle or later recovery). In "initial cessation," individuals may experience added symptoms (e.g., 2 weeks of withdrawal symptoms for tobacco; overlapping 1 week for alcohol). However, stopping only one substance may be problematic, as one may "cue" the use of the other. The first 3 months have the highest rates of relapse for most substances. Maximal success requires social support and avoidance of places where tobacco (or any addictive substance) is used. Successful smoking cessation prior to 3 months is about 25%, and rises to 60% beyond that mark. After 3 to 6 months, smoking cessation success rates for drug users approach those of nondrug users. Delaying smoking cessation may be helpful when many sources of stress and strong urges to use remain unaddressed.

"Five As" of Tobacco Treatment

Ask, advise, assess, assist, and arrange. The "Smoking Cessation Practice Guidelines" recommend: 1) *ask* regarding tobacco use (as a rule, a pack or more a day indicates a strong addiction); 2) *advise* smoking cessation in a "strong and personalized manner," describing the risks and health benefits involved, and clarifying that tobacco in any form is not safe; 3) *assess* a client's willingness to stop in the next 30 days, and provide resource materials; motivation may include keeping a log, writing down pros and cons, encouraging tapering back, etc.; 4) *assist* with nonconfrontational counsel, mobilization of social support, and pharmacotherapy referral if appropriate; and 5) *arrange* to assess the individual's use in subsequent follow-up. Effective support includes multiple therapeutic sessions, offering training in problem solving and coping, bolstering social support including a smoking cessation support group, reminders that many attempts are often required, pointing out excusive defenses (e.g., rationalization, denial), and identification of fears in quitting.

Drug Abuse Treatment Providers Who Also Smoke

Approximately 30% to 40%, and 50% to 60% of recovering providers. Staff who quit smoking will be better equipped to aid clients to stop as well. Any drug user preparing to stop smoking should obtain a medical clearance, as there may be hidden medical issues. Once cleared, research demonstrates that providing clients with a smoke-free environment considerably enhances their ability to stop smoking. This can be particularly difficult when staff smoke, and other clients are also permitted to smoke. The individual's home environment also needs to be addressed, as there may well be smokers in the home (40% of the time for nondrug users, and 53% of the time for drug users). A family agreement to move all smoking outside, or to limit smoking to only one room, or to aid the individual in leaving areas when smoking is to occur, can be very helpful.

Mood-Elevating Effects of Nicotine

Many drug users have a history of depressive symptoms, and smoke to cope with those negative effects. Nicotine offers certain stimulant effects that can assist with mood elevation. Smoking does not, however, reduce insomnia, enhance smell or taste, or increase stamina. Alternative mood management strategies may be needed for the individual to avoid relapse. Cognitive-behavioral strategies include relaxation training, increasing enjoyable activities and social interactions, and assertiveness training. Antidepressant pharmacotherapy may also be indicated. Belief system strategies include incorporating nicotine as just another substance of addiction, rather than as a special entity of its own, and focusing on the 12-step philosophy of recovery (powerlessness, need for a higher power, seeking to make amends, etc.). Language strategies involve using affirmative statements (e.g., "one moment/day at a time") and replacing negative self-talk with positive self-talk.

Antidepressant Medication Compatible with the Anti-Smoking Medication Bupropion

Bupropion (also known as *Wellbutrin*, *Zyban*, *Budeprion*, or *Aplenzin*; formerly known as amfebutamone) can be used with both serotonin reuptake inhibitors (SSRIs) and tricyclic antidepressants. Thus, where an SSRI is being used, it may be preferred to add bupropion rather than discontinue the SSRI. Best practice smoking treatment guidelines emphasize five first-line nicotine replacement therapy (NRT) options: nicotine gum, lozenges, patches, vapor inhaler, nasal spray, and bupropion. Second-line medications include clonidine, nortriptyline, etc. Use of nicotine patches lead to consistent compliance and high rates of smoking cessation, but high rates of subsequent relapse. If the individual smokes more than one pack per day, medical supervision in the use of multiple patches for NRT and tapering may be advisable. It is important to emphasize, however, that many smoking cessation treatments may be contraindicated in certain medical situations. Thus, a proper medical assessment is essential before undertaking any smoking cessation medication regimen.

Eating Disorders

Eating disorders and substance disorders commonly coexist. Studies have revealed higher than expected rates of eating disorders (15% with anorexia or bulimia) among women undergoing alcohol and other drug (AOD) treatment. Anorexia nervosa involves severe caloric restriction due to issues of control, body image, etc. Bulimia nervosa involves "binge eating" and "purging" (vomiting or misuse of laxatives). A new category of binge eating disorder (without purging) has also been proposed. Eating disorders involve a continuum of behaviors, from rigid over-control to profound loss of self-control. A dual diagnosis involving an eating disorder can be particularly difficult to treat, as treatment of one tends to worsen the other.

Multiple Addictions

Multiple addictions tend to interact and reinforce each other. A substantial intertwining can occur with multiple addictions (e.g., food, sex, and cigarettes are often interrelated). The nicotine's neurochemical effect reinforces the addiction in the brain, while advertisements "sell" slimness and sexiness through smoking. Behavioral addictions are "ritualistically reinforcing" (e.g., setting up the sexual "score," or the "big" gambling win), which can release endogenous chemicals in the brain that offer collateral pleasure. Compulsive sexual behavior is present in 70% of all cocaine users (of both genders); in one urban area 70.5% of crack cocaine users sold sex, versus 4.3% of abstainers; 37% of women had more than 100 male partners, versus 3% of non-crack smokers. Alcohol and cybersex often track closely; drinking alone often includes solo-sex behaviors that should be discussed. Cigarette smoking and gambling are highly correlated, with about two-thirds of pathologic gamblers being daily cigarette smokers. Alcohol and cigarettes are also closely intertwined, with 28% of smokers having a lifetime alcoholism history (14% are currently alcoholics).

Neuroadaptation

Neuroadaptation is the body's tolerance and withdrawal reactions to chemical substances. With persistent use of a drug or other substance, the body attempts to create an accommodation for the continuous presence of the drug or substance. This may include the increased production and release of various hormones, neurotransmitters, and other mediating responses. The goal of the body is to maintain functional equilibrium. When successful, the frequent result is tolerance, the need for increasing amounts of the drug or substance to achieve disequilibrium (the "high"). In some cases, the body's mechanisms of accommodation result in severe feelings of illness if the drug or substance is withdrawn. This response is known as withdrawal. The term neuroadaptation encompasses both of these physiological phenomena.

Dual Diagnosis

The term "dual diagnosis" refers to coexisting addiction and psychiatric problems. The 1990 Epidemiological Catchment Area (ECA) study revealed that 37% with alcohol abuse or dependency had one or more diagnosable psychiatric disorders: 53% for non-alcohol abusers and 76% for cocaine abusers. Inversely, 81% of individuals with mental disorders have a substance use disorder (referred to as mentally ill chemical abusers [MICAs]). In addition, the ECA study revealed that 18% of those with an alcohol abuse or dependency disorders also had a second drug dependency ("alcohol and other drugs" [AOD]). Identification of individuals with dual diagnoses is crucial because: 1) cognitive issues may limit the addiction treatment process; 2) the mental disorder may need treatment first; 3) treatment interventions may need modification (e.g., confrontation may increase psychosis); and 4) AOD clients relapse at a greater rate, often because of underlying mental disorders or behavioral addictions. AOD may initiate, exacerbate, mask, or mimic psychiatric disorders, and vice versa.

Psychiatric Disorders

The rate of psychiatric disorders among substance-abusing clients is over 50%. Because co-occurring mental health problems are so prevalent, substance use disorder counselors need to make screening for psychiatric problems a routine part of assessment, along with seeking consultation and treatment coordination with mental health specialists. In like manner, mental health specialists need to screen for substance use disorder issues, and seek consultation and treatment coordination with addiction counselors as well. Data gathering also must explore each client's readiness for change. Change stages include precontemplation, contemplation, preparation, action, and maintenance. Failing to recognize that a client is still in the precontemplation stage, for example, will result in an action plan that misses key motivational issues. Therefore, mapping the client's progress through these stages can be crucial to effective interventions and planning.

Assessing Psychiatric Status

Psychiatric assessment tools fall into two broad categories: 1) screening tools (helping to rule-out major disorders or suggest their possible presence) and 2) evaluation tools (helping to identify and refine a diagnosis). The most common general psychiatric screening tool is the Folstein Mini-Mental State Examination (MMSE). The MMSE evaluates seven cognitive domains, with a score range from 0 to 30 points and a dementia/impairment cutoff at about 24 points. Other common condition-specific evaluative tools include 1) depression, commonly assessed using the Patient Health Questionnaire (PHQ-9); 2) anxiety, assessed via the Generalized Anxiety Disorder 7 (GAD-7), a seven-question screening tool that identifies whether a complete assessment for anxiety is indicated; 3) bipolar disorder, often via the Mood Disorder Questionnaire (MDQ), with 13 bipolar symptom questions; 4) posttraumatic stress disorder (PTSD), via the Life Events Checklist (LEC), a

17-item screen for 16 events known to predispose PTSD; and 5) suicidality, via the Columbia-Suicide Severity Rating Scale (C-SSRS).

Spirituality

Alcoholics Anonymous emphasizes that their reference to a "higher power" need not be limited to a Judeo-Christian conception, but can encompass any commitment to principles higher than one's own selfish desires. Consequently, a higher power may refer to God for some, but it can also be a morally centered organization or moral code. Spirituality is an external life force that generates the energy necessary for commitment to rules, goals, and causes greater than ourselves. Spirituality is crucial, because addicted individuals tend to lose sight of the truly important things in their lives. It also cultivates a sense of gratitude and humility that is essential to the recovery process.

Heroin

While oral ingestion of heroin will produce a psychoactive effect, the bioavailability is only about 35% and the protracted period of effects will not produce the intense "rush" valued by abusers. Until recently, injecting heroin into a vein ("mainlining") was the most common method of abuse, with subcutaneous injections ("skin-popping") and intramuscular injections used if veins collapsed. Now, with increased drug purity, the drug is more commonly smoked (as "black tar" heroin) and snorted (in crystalline powdered form). Irregular, recreational drug use (called "chipping") typically occurs via "snorting" when heroin is used.

Percentage of College Students That Drive under the Influence of Alcohol

Approximately 25%. As many as 40% binge drink, and the rates are highest at campuses with a focus on sports and a fraternity/sorority system that fosters drinking. The result is 500,000 injuries, 1,400 fatalities, and 70,000 sexual assault incidents annually. Prevention efforts include enforcing age-related drinking laws, establishing drug and alcohol prevention centers, screening and treatment referrals through student health centers, and greater education efforts. Prevention in the workplace tends to be secondary, via Employee Assistance Programs (EAPs) and employment-related drug testing programs. The most effective prevention for Fetal Alcohol Syndrome (FAS) and Fetal Drug Syndromes (FDS), particularly among Native Americans, is preventing substance use disorder altogether. Education is also important, as many women are unaware that FAS/FDS does not require severe abuse, but rather simply the occurrence of abuse at key developmental junctures. Illicit drug use in the elderly is very low, but 16% are heavy drinkers. The Michigan Alcohol Screening Test-Geriatric Version (MAST-G), Short MAST-G, or CAGE can help identify problems.

Most Dangerous Way to Take a Drug

The most dangerous way to take a drug is via injection. Generally, ingestion (eating) is the safest route of administration, but all routes can be made safer. Some guidelines include: 1) Smoking: short-acting drugs (nicotine, cocaine, etc.) start fast, but are over too soon, typically leading to greater usage; pace/time these drugs. 2) Snorting: Cocaine and "speed" are corrosive, so mix with water and spray, or line the inside of the nose with Vitamin E oil; crushed pills don't "snort" well, so just swallow (whole or in water). 3) Drinking/eating: use on a full stomach for a slower but safer and longer "high;" start small (e.g., one-quarter of a small brownie) and wait an hour to experiment with oral doses safely. 4) Pills: know the difference between manufactured and homemade; research online for efficacy and safety guideline. If an untoward effect occurs, don't go off alone and do call 911 or poison control. Never leave someone intoxicated alone, as they may die if not watched.

Sex Addiction

The overarching goal of sex addiction treatment is healthy sexual expression. Combination therapy typically works best (e.g., group and individual counseling, 12-step programs, education, shame reduction, coping skills, cognitive-behavioral relapse prevention strategies). Family involvement and couples therapy are highly recommended/needed. Sexual addictive patterns include: 1) obsessive fantasies; 2) seduction for conquest; 3) voyeuristic sex (e.g., peeping); 4) exhibitionistic sex (to arouse shock or interest); 5) anonymous sex (one-night stands); 6) prostitution services; 7) sex for power (trading, selling, using sex to control of others); 8) intrusive sex (e.g., frotteurism–uninvited touching); 9) sadomasochism (sex coupled with pain); 10) exploitative sex (e.g., via power or via partner vulnerability, such as child molestation, incest, rape). Sex addiction may present via: 1) client evaluation; 2) client disclosure; 3) unexpected STDs; 4) arrest for sexual issues; 5) loss of job due to sex issues (harassment, etc.); 6) financial problems due to sex costs.

Assessing Sexual History and Sexual Preferences

Individuals struggling with substance use disorder often have complicated sexual lives. Issues of indiscriminate sex, sex for money, and unprotected sex can greatly complicate their health and relationships. It is therefore essential for substance use disorder counseling to address these important concerns. Special attention should be given to issues of human immunodeficiency virus (HIV) and other particularly problematic sexually transmitted infections (STIs). Partner preferences (heterosexual, homosexual, or bisexual) should also be elicited to allow for more specific discussions about safety, protection, and risks. Counselors should establish routine systems for collecting client sexual histories and practices. One abbreviated method for routine assessment is to discuss the "five Ps" with all clients: partners (number, gender[s], and needle-sharing risks and patterns); sexual practices (vaginal, anal, oral, and with or without condoms); past STIs (kinds contracted, treatments obtained, and continuing); pregnancy (history and plans); and protection from STIs (methods, competency, and familiarity in use).

Sexual Orientation and Its Relationship to Substance Use Disorder Issues

Heterosexism is a belief system that favors heterosexuality and rejects homosexuality. Inversely, "homosexism" rejects heterosexuality. "Discrimination" is to act based upon one's biases or prejudices. Homophobia is a bias against the LGBT community; heterophobia is the reverse. Issues of sexual orientation and HIV may affect whether individuals seek treatment for their HIV and/or IV drug use. According to 2008 CDC data, 77% of all white males contracted HIV via homosexual contacts alone. This number rises to 86% when homosexual IV drug users are included (route of transmission uncertain). However, fully 26% of blacks and 25% of Hispanics acquire HIV via IV drug use alone (compared with only 8.8% of whites diagnosed with HIV). Both black and Hispanic cultures are comparatively more homo-aversive. Given that only 2.8% of men and 1.4% of women identify themselves as homosexual/bisexual, there is a reluctance by these heterosexual drug-use-only individuals to seek treatment for HIV and/or IV drug use if the diagnosis may categorize them unfavorably.

Substance Use Disorder Among the Lesbian, Gay, Bisexual, and Transgender (LGBT) Community

The rates are generally higher than the non-LGBT population. There are few statistics for substance use disorder among the LGBT community, in part because of wide variation in definitions of LGBT (ie, any same gender experience after puberty at about 9.8% for men and 5% for women; same gender sexual interest at about 8% for both genders vs adult self-declared LGBT orientation at 2.8% of men and 1.4% of women). Other issues preventing clear data are the inability to determine exact figures for LGBT numbers regardless of definitions used, and the typical denial and secrecy that surrounds issues of alcoholism and substance use disorder among every population. In 2010, Healthy People 2020 was released, and included LGBT as a new category for data collection. Goals are reflected in the most current Healthy People 2030 to target health concerns in the LGBT population, including drug use and abuse. For instance, one Healthy People 2030 goal is to decrease the percentage of LGBT adolescents, grade 9-12, who reported using illicit drugs from 23.1 % (in 2017) to 16.1% in 2030.

Addressing Whether an Alcoholic in AA Who Has Significant Pain, Depression, and/or Other Issues That Would Typically Benefit from Mind/Mood-Altering Medications

Research indicates that individuals with sobriety, actively in AA, with family support, generally do well with any medical treatment needed. AA's official position supports treatment (it is "wrong to deprive any alcoholic of medication which can alleviate or control other disabling physical and/or emotional problems"). Individuals with a history of opioid dependency have more complex relapse issues. Using a family/friend "dispenser" to distribute and monitor medications (with an agreement never to pressure them) can make a difference. Individuals actively abusing alcohol/drugs may need to start with sobriety first. Benzodiazepines often need to be avoided altogether, as abuse potential is high, relief is transient, and legitimate need is typically low.

Assessing Socioeconomic Status and Social Support System

Substance use disorder invariably has negative influences on social and financial resources. When client stability in either of these areas is compromised, relapses and treatment failure become far more likely. Exploration of a client's finances should include all available resources: income (current and potential), family financial support, significant assets, and other resources that can aid the client in establishing and maintaining financial stability. Eligibility for financial and in-kind support (food stamps, etc.) via local and state programs should also be explored. Social support systems play a pivotal role in successful recovery. Therefore, a client's social network and the level of support from all available individuals should be carefully evaluated (e.g., extended family, friends, and religious and social organizations). Collateral contacts can greatly expand insights into a client's social network. It is also important for the client have a positive perception of available social supports because he or she may otherwise be inordinately pessimistic and therefore more prone to relapse and failure. The 12-item Multidimensional Scale of Perceived Social Support (MSPSS) evaluation tool can assist in measuring and enhancing the client's understanding.

Ongoing Treatment Planning and Implementation

Laboratory Screening

Laboratory screening has an important role in the diagnosis and screening of substance use disorder. Blood alcohol testing is the most widely used test, and it yields a level of intoxication measure that can be interpreted for quantity ingested and how recently the ingestion occurred. Routine urine testing can be used to detect a variety of other substances of abuse. It can reveal trace residues of barbiturates, cocaine, nicotine, opiates, and Quaaludes, as well as various tranquilizers. The presence or absence of marijuana use can be detected via urine testing, but not the level of intoxication or the time of ingestion. Even so, a cannabis urine test is reliable and sensitive (even after extended periods of storage), and requires a very minimal sample quantity.

Overlooking Substance Use Disorder

Substance abusing clients may well present for counseling with a chief complaint that is actually rooted in substance use disorder, but which the client does not recognize as such. Examples include marital discord, medical problems, or work issues. Regular substance use disorder can result in symptoms of nearly every psychiatric disorder, and can lie at the heart of many other mood, interpersonal, and health problems. Clinicians may be reluctant to inquire about substance use, particularly illicit use, and especially if the client seems insightful, educated, and articulate. Consequently, it is essential that intake assessments include questions about substance use and abuse. While it is assumed that clients will avoid disclosure, practice reveals that many clients may be surprisingly forthright, especially if they don't view their use as a clinical problem requiring a treatment focus.

20 Questions List

The Johns Hopkins University 20 Questions List is perhaps the most widely used screening instrument for alcoholism. Self-administered, the tool addresses the impact of alcohol in various areas of an individual's life, ranging from family and social associations, to work, emotions, health, cravings, and self-confidence. A positive answer to any single question raises a warning, two affirmative responses suggests a probability, and the identification of three positive answers is considered determinative for alcoholism. A primary drawback of the screening instrument is that self-reports can be significantly skewed by the presence of active denial, rationalization, and minimization. Nevertheless, it is a valuable preliminary screening tool.

Michigan Alcoholism Screening Test (MAST)

The Michigan Alcoholism Screening Test is a 25-question tool for the identification of alcoholism. Introduced in 1971, it can be administered in as little as 10 to 15 minutes. Each question offers

a 0 to 5 weighting that can be summed into a total score. Three or fewer points rule out the likelihood of alcoholism. Five or more points are suggestive of alcoholism. Ten points are the usual threshold for the identification of alcoholism, with higher scores further validating the presumed designation. Some criticism of the tool has been noted, however, as research suggests a relatively high rate of false-positive alcoholism identification. Even so, it remains a valuable screening tool when used in conjunction with other data and information

Adolescent Alcohol Involvement Scale

Traditional scales for the screening of alcoholism are difficult to apply because adolescents have much shorter drinking histories. An effort to address this shortcoming was made in 1979 with the formulation of the Adolescent Alcohol Involvement Scale. An important aspect of the scale is its awareness that alcohol use among teens involves a greater measure of clandestine activity. This was addressed by the addition of questions addressing how the adolescent obtains alcohol, as well as where and with whom drinking occurs. A 14-question scale, the highest possible score is 79. Scores from 42 to 57 suggest "alcohol misuse" and scores from 58 to 79 identify "alcoholic-like" drinking.

Problem Drinking Scale (PDS)

George E. Vaillant developed the Problem Drinking Scale (PDS) in 1983 in an effort to capture the number of life problems arising from drug or alcohol use by participants in a longitudinal study. Therefore, it can also be used to roughly quantify the seriousness of an individual's substance use disorder. Consisting of 14 items, the Problem Drinking Scale (or Problem [Drug] Scale, by substitution) weighs each issue equally, covering complaints by employers (e.g., tardiness, sick leave), a spouse, family members, and friends, as well as job losses, medical problems (including blackouts and tremors), a physician-determined diagnosis, and substance-related arrests, and are each scored. Finally, getting "on the wagon" and admission of a problem are accounted for. A score of four or more on the scale suggests a likely substance abuser. If an individual is able to remain entirely problem free for a full year, the designation can be considered resolved.

Simpson's Four-Part Model of a Drug Treatment Delivery System

The model specifies: 1) referral; 2) induction; 3) intervention; and 4) transition. Referrals may be received from individuals, families, employee assistance programs, social services and public health/community agencies, HIV/AIDS outreach programs, centralized intake units, and the criminal justice system. Induction refers to entrance into a treatment program. Intervention and treatment strategies typically involve detoxification and stabilization, motivation and commitment, and rehabilitation. Finally, clients are transitioned out to "aftercare" programs (e.g., AA, CA, NA). Comprehensive care requires many programs and services to meet diverse needs and widely ranging recovery stages. Optimal programs include: 1) pharmacotherapy to reduce distressing withdrawal symptoms and minimize relapse; 2) cognitive and/or behavioral therapy to address the underlying psychosocial roots of the problem; 3) supportive services for collateral concerns (e.g., medical care, employment, transportation, child care). Further, aftercare is needed to aid individuals in resisting urges to relapse, of which drug testing is a crucial part.

Referral Process

The referral process has eight elements and is used to determine if other community resources and support systems are needed in the treatment of a client.

The elements are as follows:

- A relationship should be established with other agencies, community groups, and professionals
- Continual re-evaluation and assessment of sources to find out how appropriate they are
- Be able to determine the difference between a situation where the client can refer himself and when the counselor should refer
- Meet the client's needs by referring him to other agencies, programs or professionals
- Be able to make a clear explanation to the client about why he or she needs the referral
- Exchange information which is important to the treatment with the referral agency

- Be aware of the importance of confidentiality
- Determine the effectiveness of the referral

Diagnostic Formulation Summary

An effective treatment plan requires proper assessment and diagnosis of the primary and collateral problems involved. Key to effective assessment is the clinical interview. It will ideally be comprehensive, and it can be enhanced with collateral contact information (from family, prior treatment providers, records, and other testing results). For substance use disorder, it is essential to identify the substances being used, frequency, duration, and amounts along with the symptoms produced (agitation, hallucinations, and/or depressive intoxication) and the related degree of tolerance, dependence, and withdrawal symptoms. Psychiatrically, mood, behavior, and cognitive symptoms must be organized using a reliable classification framework such as the International Classification of Diseases (ICD) or the Diagnostic and Statistical Manual (DSM) of the American Psychiatric Association, in their current versions. Although the final diagnosis is intended to be clear and distinct, the process of formulation is more subjective, starting with the presenting problems and key symptoms and concluding with an explanatory summary that justifies the diagnosis(es) given and foreshadows the treatment and/or recovery plan.

Formal Treatment Plan

Where time and resources allow, a formal treatment plan generally consists of: 1) client demographics; 2) a *DSM* diagnosis; 3) brief history; 4) case formulation; and 5) short- and long-term goals (including interventions, anticipated time frames, and measurement criteria). However, where limits exist, the plan may simply incorporate a client's goals as follows: Desired Outcome #1: Abstinence. Steps: a) monitor cravings and use; b) identify trigger situations; c) determine avoidance and coping strategies in trigger situations; d) attend training on new coping skills; e) reorganize thinking and environment; f) use relaxation techniques to cope with trigger stimuli and life stressors. #2: Enhance social opportunities. Steps: a) join AA/NA and find a sponsor; b) participate in at least one new weekly social activity beyond AA/NA; c) attend social skills training. #3: Initiate career planning. Steps: a) bolster current work habits; b) attend a career assessment at a local employment agency; c) consider career change options; d) narrow long-term career goals; e) avoid rapid changes.

Marijuana Ingestion

Marijuana is primarily ingested via smoking but may also be eaten. Selective cultivation has produced plants with levels of THC (the primary psychoactive ingredient) much higher than in the past (increasing from 1% to 6% to 8%). These levels are much closer to that of hashish (a concentrated marijuana preparation with THC levels from 3% to 14%). Recent studies reveal mild physical dependencies with long-term use, though psychological dependency may be the primary motivator of abuse. With higher tar levels than cigarettes, as few as three "joints" per day can cause serious pulmonary damage over time (the equivalent of three entire cigarette packs per day). Cancer risks also follow. Other problems include impaired sexual function, impotence, and reduced sperm count and motility. Women may experience disrupted menstruation, ovulation, and greater rates of miscarriage. Marijuana produces impaired perceptions related to time, speed, and distance, a consequence that predisposes to accidents. Long-term users may develop permanent impairment in emotions, behavior, and the capacity to carry out complex tasks requiring memory and information analysis.

Tranquilizer Ingestion

There are two broad categories of tranquilizers. Anxiolytic (antianxiety) medications such as *Valium*, *Miltown*, *Librium*, *Equanil* (so-called "minor" tranquilizers) used in the treatment of stress, anxiety, insomnia, and behavioral agitation. Other uses include treatment of lower-back pain, convulsions, panic attacks, and alcohol or barbiturate withdrawal. Neuroleptics or antipsychotic agents (previously called "major" tranquilizers), such as *Haldol*, *Mellaril*, and *Navane*, are used primarily in the treatment of major mental disorders, such as schizophrenia and psychosis. Both can be taken orally or intravenously, and low-dose anxiolytics offer much the same calming and disinhibiting effects of alcohol. Increasing doses move from sedation to confusion and unsteadiness. Combined with alcohol, respiratory depression and death become profound risks. Physical dependence and withdrawal symptoms can occur, including anxiety, insomnia, anorexia, vomiting, and fever, when stopping an extensive habit. Although abuse is down as physicians have become more aware of the problems, some inappropriate usage continues.

Cocaine Ingestion

Cocaine can be inhaled, smoked, or injected intravenously. Typically called "coke," street names include flake, snow, blow, liquid lady (cocaine and alcohol), speedball (cocaine and heroin), and (in freebase form for smoking) crack, rock, and base. In 1914 the Harrison Narcotic Act misclassified cocaine as a "narcotic" (grouping it with opiates), though psychoactively it is a stimulant. Ingestion produces 15 to 30 minutes of euphoria (with a more addictive but shorter high following IV use). This is followed by depression, agitation, and irritability, prompting users to serial doses to avoid these effects. A mix of cocaine and marijuana may help reduce the negative effects. Small doses slow the heart, while high doses accelerate it and induce shallow breathing, anxiety, confusion, and fever, and may result in convulsions and respiratory arrest (especially if the purity of the cocaine is misjudged). Due to vascular constriction, cocaine can also induce heart attacks. Dependence is characterized by a compulsion to use the drug and withdrawal symptoms, including cravings, lethargy, depression, sleeplessness, and irritability.

Review Video: Addictions
Visit mometrix.com/academy and enter code: 460412

Noncocaine Stimulant Ingestion

Amphetamines may be used to treat obesity, sleep disorders, depression, and some forms of ADHD. Methamphetamine ("speed" or "meth") is derived from amphetamine (methylated phenylethylamine) when it is methylated twice. Double methylation produces a stronger, quicker effect on the body. Breaking down into amphetamine, urine tests for "meth" often indicate only amphetamines. Abuse is due to its profound euphoria and its ease of illicit production; simply mixing cold medicine with hydriodic acid. Amphetamines are typically capsules or tablets, while methamphetamine is a crystal or powder. Street names include bennies, uppers, and crystal. Stimulant effects produce increased blood pressure, pupil dilation, rapid respiration, appetite suppression, and decreased fatigue. Modest doses in some, however, can result in agitation, confusion, anxiety, heart irregularities, and even amphetamine psychosis. Death (uncommon) usually involves vascular rupture in the brain (hemorrhagic stroke), high fever, or heart failure. A long half-life (10 to 30 hours) means some of its effects may persist long after ingestion. Withdrawal symptoms include profound fatigue, hunger, cramps, and depression.

Sedative-Hypnotic Drug Ingestion

Beyond alcohol (the leading sedative), other sedative-hypnotics include the barbiturates (e.g., amobarbital, butabarbital, pentobarbital, secobarbital). Slang names include reds, blue devils, yellow jacks, and downers. Usually bitter-tasting white powders, they are marketed as capsules, tablets, and liquids to be taken orally. After ingestion, the onset of effect can occur in about 20 minutes, with symptoms similar to those of alcohol, such as relaxation, sleepiness, poor coordination, and decreased inhibitions. At higher doses, feelings range from euphoria to hostility and aggression, and finally reaching confusion, slurred speech, stupor, and sleep. Amphetamines may be used to "bring the user down." Concurrent alcohol and/or amphetamine use has a multiplying effect, enhancing the drug's impact on the body. Once dependence and tolerance develop, overdose is a great risk, with problems, such as respiratory depression, grand mal seizures (up to 2 weeks after stopping), coma, and/or possibly death. The risk of seizures, along with severe withdrawal symptoms, such as anxiety, dizziness, nausea, and vomiting, warrants withdrawal under medical supervision.

Narcotic Drug Ingestion

Narcotics are primarily drugs derived from the Oriental poppy plant (e.g., opium, heroin, morphine). Other narcotics are synthetic (laboratory) chemicals that mimic natural narcotics (e.g., hydrocodone, oxycodone, meperidine, methadone). All are highly addictive. Heroin (ie, "smack," "junk," "horse") remains the most commonly abused narcotic. A typical dose produces 2 to 6 hours of effects: a rush followed by a sense of detached contentment. Intermediate doses suppress breathing and heart rate, and may produce nausea and vomiting. High doses result in confusion, loss of consciousness, coma, and ultimately death. Low-dose irregular use produces only flu-like withdrawal symptoms. Heavy regular use produces painful, severe withdrawal symptoms like those of alcohol or barbiturate withdrawal. Symptoms present in 6 to 12 hours after the last dose, peak between 26 to 72 hours, and may persist for up to a week. Complete resolution may require 6 or more months. IV abuse of impure drugs can produce hepatitis, skin scarring and infections, and collapsed veins. Needle sharing exposes users to numerous infections, including AIDS.

Hallucinogenic Drug Ingestion

Hallucinogens produce distortions primarily in auditory, visual, tactile, and time perception. Sensations of anxiety, paranoia, and isolation, along with bizarre delusions and "flashbacks" (primarily from LSD, even weeks to months after the last ingestion) make hallucinogen abuse very problematic. Popular hallucinogens are LSD (acid) and PCP (angel dust, super weed, THC, dust). A white, water-soluble powder, PCP is often smoked. At lower doses it produces a sense of euphoria for 3 to 5 hours, or 5 to 8 hours if swallowed. Effects include lost sensation in the limbs that may result in significant injuries without awareness, drowning from poor airway protection, heart failure, hemorrhagic strokes, jumping from windows in attempts to fly, etc. PCP impairs hormonal development and results in poor cognitive and social functioning. Crystalline LSD is usually diluted in liquid and taken orally, but is sometimes injected. Total tolerance develops in days, but passes in around a week between uses. Intoxication "trips" are highly variable, with exaggerated and "mixed" senses (synesthesia). Purity issues are common and dangerous.

Solvent and Inhalant Ingestion

The use of solvents and inhalants has generally decreased since the peak epidemic of glue-sniffing in the 1960s. Even so, the abuse if substances such as gasoline, aerosol sprays, model glue, and nail-polish remover, continues. A common method of inhalation is to put the substance on a rag and then draw in the fumes. The resultant intoxication produces feelings of elevated mood, a sense of well-being, and reduced inhibitions. At higher levels, the fumes may cause a sense of floating, and laughter and giddiness for 5 to 60 minutes, along with delusional thoughts and disinhibition. Negative effects include neuromuscular impairments, nausea, vomiting, with anesthetic-like effects, sleepiness, and depression at higher doses. Deaths are not common, and usually involve suffocation due to fainting. However, brain damage and injury to the lungs and other body organs, such as the liver and kidneys, are more frequently encountered.

Determining a Client's Readiness for Treatment

Clients that present for treatment may not be ready to make changes — as many as 70%. If interventions are not properly matched with the client's readiness for change, this can produce high levels of resistance or premature treatment termination. The transtheoretical model of behavior change identifies the stages of readiness: 1) precontemplation (not ready), 2) contemplation (getting ready), 3) preparation (ready), 4) action, and 5) maintenance. Its 10 requisite change processes are as follows: consciousness raising (awareness), seeking dramatic relief, self-reevaluation, environmental reevaluation (how behaviors affect others), social liberation (positive social awareness), self-liberation, establishing helping relationships, counterconditioning (substituting healthy for unhealthy behaviors), reinforcement management (finding rewards), and stimulus control (reminders and cues for healthy behavior). The clinical interview is key to determining readiness for change, and several instruments can assist in evaluation. The Readiness Ruler is a self-administered screening tool that uses a scale of 1 to 10, with 1 being "not prepared" and 10 being "already changing." The Stages of Change Readiness and Treatment Eagerness Scale (SOCRATES) can be used to evaluate change readiness for alcohol and drug addiction.

Reward Deficiency Syndrome

Reward Deficiency Syndrome occurs when the dopamine system is hypoactive/hypofunctional. The result is a low level of pleasure, which may induce greater activity in behaviors designed to stimulate the dopamine reward system. During drug use, the dopamine reward system may be chemically stimulated to a greater or lesser degree based upon the kind of psychoactive substance used and the route of administration. Thus, orally ingested cocaine stimulates the reward system to a lesser degree (though typically over a longer period) than injected cocaine, due to its slower entry into the blood stream. By contrast, injected or "snorted" (inhaled) cocaine will enter the bloodstream quickly and profoundly stimulate the dopamine reward system (but over a much shorter period of time). The quality and persistence of an addiction may therefore vary according to the substance utilized and the route of administration used.

Self-Help Groups

The use of self-help groups in treating chemical dependency dates back to at least 1935 with the introduction of Alcoholics Anonymous. A simple definition of group counseling is "group interaction to facilitate self-understanding as well as individual behavior change" (George and Dustin, 1988). Through the sharing of common experiences, attitudes, and experiences, group members establish roles and norms that guide the change process. Weiner (1984) has noted that any group experience can positively impact all who are involved. However, leadership by a trained and experienced moderator can ensure an optimally effective process. Collective sharing reduces self-disclosure inhibitions and boosts feelings of cohesion and belonging. Chemically dependent individuals are often in need of positive group experiences, as other relationship experiences are frequently poor. Social influence, conformity needs, and peer pressure can further aid in self-assessment and behavioral change. More experienced group members can further benefit others, offering comparisons regarding effective versus ineffective change efforts.

Therapeutic Elements That Produce Positive Change

Key therapeutic elements that benefit participants in group settings include the following: 1) a sense of hope (past serial failures to change often produce a sense of hopelessness in the chemically dependent person, and testimonials and the lived evidence of change in others helps overcome this); 2) feelings of security and support (requires evidence of unconditional acceptance, trust, and understanding); 3) cohesive belonging (where altruism, empathy, and intimacy facilitates listening, acceptance, tension relief, self-disclosure, and efforts to influence and be influenced by others); 4) universality (discovering that they are not so unique in their problems; sometimes facilitated by the anonymous exchange of "fearful secrets" collected and redistributed as written notes); 5) vicarious learning (insights gained from observation and imitation); and 6) interpersonal learning (e.g., enhanced understanding, insights including corrections and challenges, self-esteem, security) via sharing and feedback.

Addiction Recovery Peer Group Support Systems

The first peer group support system for addiction was Alcoholics Anonymous (AA), with its 12 steps, 12 traditions, and its slogans. Other similar programs that are constructed in the AA model include Narcotics Anonymous (NA) and Cocaine Anonymous (CA). While it is possible to maintain sobriety without the use of a support program, it is far more difficult. Thus, involvement in a 12-step program is basic advice for all individuals struggling with addiction. Bill Wilson, with assistance from another alcoholic, Dr. Bob Smith, formally established AA on June 10, 1935 to combat his feelings of isolation in overcoming alcoholism. The first edition of Alcoholics Anonymous (the "Big Book" as it has come to be known) was published in 1939. Using its principles, researchers have learned that nearly 60% who regularly attend AA will remain sober for more than a year. AA uses no threat, guilt, intimidation, or judgment. The initial admission that the person needs help is the central feature.

AA's Twelve Steps and Traditions

Individuals engage in the steps in chronological order, but may frequently return to earlier steps to remain sober. A genuine commitment to the entire program is required for optimum benefits. "Working the program" requires Honesty, Openness, Patience, and Effort (acronym: HOPE). Key features include the following: 1) acknowledging that powerlessness over alcohol and the unmanageability of an addicted life cause one to seek help; 2 and 3) believing in and turning life over to a "higher power" produces flexibility and acceptance of outside resources; 4) a "moral inventory" reveals both flaws and strengths; 5) admitting wrongs improves both honesty and self-acceptance; 6 and 7) preparation and a request for freedom from "defects of character" enable the process of change; 8 and 9) listing "harm" done and "making amends" engages personal humility, responsibility, and correction; 10) ongoing "inventory" and admissions of wrongs reinforces continuous recovery work; 11 and 12) commitment to a new way of life and helping others is established.

The Twelve Traditions guide the 12-step process, the AA organization, and its members. Key features of each tradition include: 1) Establishing the necessity to see the needs of others. 2) No single individual holds authority over anyone else. 3) Enshrines "desire" (not status, success, finances, etc.) as the single eligibility criterion. 4) Group autonomy is paramount, barring harm to others. 5) Finding and helping others in need is a key purpose of each group. 6) Ensures that AA never becomes a commercial enterprise. 7) Self-reliance as a group is fundamental (never look outside the group to meet needs). 8) The focus remains on alcoholic-to-alcoholic support, not on professionals. 9) Any necessary leadership is focused on service, not on control. 10) As an entity, AA avoids all public controversies outside its recovery focus. 11 and 12) Anonymity prevents self-promotion.

AA Slogans

AA slogans are intended to provide alcoholics with ready reminders for the maintenance of sobriety. Perhaps the most famous slogan is, "One day at a time." It is intended to help reduce the sense that remaining sober for a lifetime is an overwhelming task. By focusing on only the present day, the task can seem far more manageable. Other slogans include "easy does it" (aimed at curbing stress and agitation), "let go and let God" (a reminder of the Higher Power involved), "live and let live" (prompting tolerance and forgiveness), and "walk the talk." Each slogan can be empowering if conscientiously and regularly referenced and applied.

Advantages and Limitations of Group Therapy

Key advantages of group therapy include: 1) reduced sense of isolation due to recognition of a common problem; 2) firsthand observations of those making progress, thus fostering hope; 3) learning by watching; 4) moderates self-concept distortions; 5) the reparative "family" context models improve family functioning; 6) conflicts typically managed more productively and positively; 7) hearing of others' substance use challenges heightens the need to remain relapse-free; 8) the higher accountability of a therapy group (as opposed to a self-help group) bolsters retention, as early warning signs tend to be more readily noticed. Key limitations: 1) group members must be carefully matched (e.g., demographically, drug type and mode of use, level of severity) for optimum functioning; 2) comorbidity may preclude participation; 3) groups for family members (e.g., ACOA) may well overlook other family members' drug use issues.

Review Video: Group Work and its Benefits
Visit mometrix.com/academy and enter code: 375134

DSM-5

The DSM-5 is a manual which provides a common language and standard criteria for the classification of mental disorders. It is also a classification system with periodic revisions. It includes comprehensive descriptions of the symptoms and manifestations of mental disorders and associated information such as prevalence. It does not discuss causation (etiology). The DSM offers specific criteria for clinicians to diagnose disorders. The DSM also takes cultural context, cultural belief systems, and cultural differences between client/worker into account and includes Culture-Bound Syndromes. The DSM also presents a Defensive Functioning Scale, which assesses the client's defenses or coping patterns at time of the evaluation and just preceding it.

DSM-5 Categories:

- Neurodevelopmental disorders
- Schizophrenia spectrum and other psychotic disorders
- Bipolar and related disorders
- Depressive disorders
- Anxiety disorders
- Obsessive-compulsive and related disorders
- Trauma- and stressor-related disorders
- Dissociative disorders
- Somatic symptom and related disorders
- Feeding and eating Disorders
- Elimination disorders
- Sleep-wake disorders
- Sexual dysfunctions
- Gender dysphoria
- Disruptive, impulse-control, and conduct disorders
- Substance-related and addictive disorders
- Neurocognitive disorders
- Personality disorders
- Paraphilic disorders

- Other mental disorders
- Medication-induced movement disorders
- Other conditions that may be a focus of clinical attention

Substance Related Disorders and Their Treatment

Substance related disorders may be caused by abusing a drug, by medication side-effects, or by exposure to a toxin.

Substance intoxication or withdrawal—the behavioral, psychological, and physiological symptoms due to effects of the substance. It will vary depending on type of substance.

Substance related disorders includes the following classes: caffeine; hallucinogens; alcohol; cannabis; stimulants; tobacco; inhalants; opioids; other; and sedatives, hypnotics and anxiolytics. The severity of the particular substance use disorder can be determined by the presence of the number of symptoms.

Also present may be substance induced delirium, dementia, psychosis, mood disorders, anxiety disorder, sexual dysfunction, or sleep dysfunction.

Treatment should focus first on the substance. Treatment options include outpatient or inpatient; residential or day care; group, individual, and/or family counseling; methadone maintenance (for opiates); detoxification; self-help groups; or a combination of therapies and medication.

Substance-related and addictive disorders now include gambling disorder, as evidence shows that the behaviors of gambling trigger similar reward systems as drugs.

Comorbidity

Comorbidity refers coexisting disorders (29% of all mental disorders involve concurrent substance use disorder). Common comorbidity includes 1) anxiety disorders (panic disorder, post-traumatic stress disorder, 20% to 59%), and social phobia (precedes alcohol abuse 66% to 85% of the time; overall, 50% more likely to abuse alcohol); 2) disruptive behavioral disorders (oppositional defiant disorder [ODD], conduct disorder, and attention-deficit hyperactivity disorder; in adolescents, ODD rates ranged from 30% to 68%, and ADHD ranged from 30% to 50%); 3) eating disorders (bulimia nervosa and anorexia nervosa, 35% to 75%); 4) impulse control disorders (especially pathological gambling, 30% to 50%, and intermittent explosive disorder; for children and adolescents: ODD and conduct disorder); 5) mood disorders (bipolar disorder and major depressive disorder; 40% to 50% of cocaine users meet mood disorder criteria; 25% to 30% of bipolar patients misuse substances; for adolescents, 8% to 11% for bipolar, 5% to 34% dysthymic, and 18% to 35% for major depression); 6) personality disorders (34% to 38% of abusive drinkers and 90% of multi-substance users [especially antisocial (95%) and borderline disorders (28% to 34%]); 7) psychotic disorders (lifetime rate of substance abuse for someone with schizophrenia is about 50%).

DSM Diagnosis

A formal *DSM* diagnosis cannot fully encapsulate all features of a client's condition. Early impressions are tentative, time may be required for full diagnostic clarity, and a diagnosis can also evolve over time. Diagnosis of a substance use "disorder" requires lack of control in the face of behavioral, cognitive, and/or physiological symptoms that have persisted at least 1 month.

Classification of being in remission from substance abuse according to the DSM-5:

- The type of remission is based on whether any of the criteria for abuse/dependence have been met and over what time frame:
- Early Remission: After the criteria for a substance use disorder have been met, none of those criteria are fulfilled (except for the criteria for craving) for at least three months but not more than 1 year.
- Sustained Remission: After the criteria for a substance use disorder have been met, none of those criteria are fulfilled (except for the criteria for craving) for 1 year or longer.
- If the client is in remission in a controlled environment, this should be specified.
- Maintenance Therapy- a replacement medication that can be taken to avoid withdrawal symptoms. The client could still be considered in remission from a substance use disorder if while using maintenance therapy, they do not meet any criteria for that substance use disorder except for craving. For tobacco use disorder this would include using nicotine replacement systems. For opioid use disorder this could include medications such as methadone.

Key Psychodynamic Feature Recurring in Chemically Dependent Clients

The key psychodynamic feature recurring in chemically dependent clients is "denial." Not only do these clients typically deny their problems initially and attempt to cover up their abuse at the outset of treatment, but they also very often cycle back into denial. This can recur even after they initially admit a problem, and at times even after they are well along in the treatment process. Usually this is seen in renewed expressions of doubt that they actually had a significant substance use disorder problem. Consequently, chemical dependency counselors must utilize confrontation techniques more often compared with other therapeutic areas. Clients must be regularly reminded of their need to continue in a recovery program to ensure they do not relapse. Otherwise, the basic array of counseling techniques and strategies are fundamentally similar to those used within any selected theoretical orientation (e.g., Adlerian, behavioral, client-centered, cognitive, Gestalt).

Treatment Medications Compliance

Compliance is often poor when there are numerous medications, poor communication between patients and providers, the medication regimen is complex, there are special storage requirements, if the medication interferes with lifestyle, or the side effects are severe. Medication compliance is enhanced with: 1) regular follow-up with ample discussion; 2) care that is readily obtained; 3) extra support for weekends and holidays; 4) changes are planned ahead of time; 5) a set time and place for taking medications; 6) an individualized plan meeting client needs; 7) a medications diary; 8) all questions are clarified in advance. Adjunctive medications may be needed in situations of pain, which afflicts 75% of individuals with AIDS (e.g., due to cancer, neuropathy). While nonsteroidal medications (e.g., aspirin, ibuprofen) are helpful, opioids (e.g., hydrocodone, oxycodone, codeine) may be needed. Adjuvant symptom moderators (e.g., anticonvulsants, corticosteroids, antidepressants) may also be needed, especially with neuropathy. Counseling patients and providers around addictive issues in pain medications is important, as undertreatment of pain is common in this population.

Client's Need to Understand the Treatment Process

The client's understanding of the treatment process is essential, as a lack of complete commitment and buy-in can confound the treatment process. The Addiction Technology Transfer Center (ATTC) National Curriculum Committee (1998) affirms this, adding that assessment understanding is a client's right, and requiring that addiction counselors be: 1) willing to negotiate and communicate interactively with clients; 2) respect client and others' input, values, and goals; 3) remain sensitive to client needs and perceptions, as well as gender and cultural issues; 4) recognize the importance of client input regarding the specific processes, outcomes, and goals involved; and 5) remain open to considering a variety of approaches and methods by which to achieve change. Potential high-priority client goals include: 1) becoming financially stable and/or pursuing new educational and/or career goals; 2) clearing up legal issues; 3) enhancing and maintaining quality family relationships; 4) bolstering social skills and social support systems; 5) improving life management skills (e.g., stress management, decision making and problem solving, emotional/mood control, relaxation); and 6) improving health and fitness.

Substance-Induced Disorders

Substance-induced disorders refer primarily to psychiatric symptoms brought on by substance use disorder. There are eleven substance-induced disorders: 1) intoxication; 2) withdrawal; 3) delirium; 4) persisting dementia; 5) persisting amnesia; 6) psychosis; 7) mood disorders; 8) anxiety disorders; 9) sexual dysfunction; 10) sleep disorders; and 11) hallucination disorder. Some substances (such as alcohol) can result in or induce all eleven, while caffeine will lead to only three. Determine if the presenting disorder was induced or preexisting, as this will likely affect treatment. Useful guidelines for a differential determination include: 1) secure a complete history (including collateral contacts, such as family and friends); 2) delay any determination for a month following the client's cessation of the substance; 3) evaluate the potential that the substance was used to self-medicate (ameliorate symptoms). Where reports indicate preexisting symptoms, and symptoms persist longer than a month after cessation, and where short-term symptom amelioration was realized via the substance, the likelihood is that the symptoms represent a preexisting condition.

Reviewing Assessment Data with the Client

A crucial aspect of substance use disorder counseling is client participation in creation of the treatment plan in order to ensure buy-in, motivation, and compliance. It is not possible for clients to meaningfully participate in treatment planning and decision making unless they are well informed about their testing results. Research in clinical practices reveals that 71.3% of counselors "usually, almost always, or always" provide direct in-person assessment feedback to their clients and/or their involved families. As many as 46.6% also provide assessment feedback to their clients in writing. Fully 72% of clients indicated that this information (especially direct discussion) was helpful and positive. Direct feedback was typically provided through open dialog, often lasting around one hour. In some situations, assessment findings and reports needed to be rewritten more simply to ensure clarity for the client. Written feedback also allowed the client to review, follow, and compare progress and evolving issues over time. Clients report feeling greater motivation and commitment to goals and progress when feedback is provided. Thus, neglecting client feedback is a profound clinical oversight that should not continue.

Counselor-Client Treatment Plan Formulation

Counselors should actively collaborate with clients in the identification of goals and treatment strategies. Key treatment planning competencies include: 1) gathering and interpreting essential assessment information; 2) explaining assessment findings to all involved; 3) offering clarification and added information as needed; 4) considering the treatment implications in collaboration with all involved; 5) determining the readiness of the client and others for treatment; 6) prioritizing issues requiring treatment; 7) designing treatment goals and outcomes that are mutually agreed upon and measurable; 8) creating workable strategies to achieve each goal and outcome; 9) organizing and coordinating resources and activities to meet the client's prioritized needs, diagnosis, and placement criteria; 10) designing an action plan and monitoring process that is effective and mutually acceptable; 11) maintaining client confidentiality and ensuring informed consent and understanding regarding applicable policy and outside regulations; 12) determining criteria for regular reassessment of the treatment plan, both at appropriate intervals and in response to changing circumstances.

Addiction Counseling Practices and Prevention

Identification and Fulfillment of Needs

An addict's need to get drugs has been the uppermost thing in his life. Very often other needs are not met or even recognized during addiction. He may feel that he does not have the right to have his needs met. The counselor should help the patient to identify the needs that need to be met and to introduce the various behaviors in which needs can be met. He should be encouraged to practice assertive behavior to meet needs. Frequent practice of this skill can lead to better ways to meet needs.

Assertion means to stand up for one's personal rights in direct, honest, and appropriate ways. Nonassertion has to do with letting others violate one's rights. Characteristic behaviors include not being honest with others or not being assertive about expressing one's thoughts and feelings.

Aggression is standing up for one's rights by dishonesty and inappropriate behavior. The goal is domination.

Maintaining Abstinence

The stage known as "maintaining abstinence" occurs when the addict has achieved abstinence.

- He or she now can recognize the triggers (environmental, emotional, and psychosocial) that cause the drug use.
- The addict is also developing healthy coping skills for the stresses of life.

The most important thing to address during this stage is the danger of relapse. Being honest about feelings and attending self-help groups are both good things for the addict to do. The role of the counselor during this stage is to help the patient to maintain abstinence. Encouragement,

teaching, assisting, and helping are ways that the counselor can help to achieve the goals. During this stage the patient is practicing the "drug-free" lifestyle. He or she must keep a humble attitude toward their addiction and not take the abstinence for granted.

Skills That Prevent Relapse

Being able to recognize when one is headed for a relapse is a valuable preventive skill. Those danger signals are negative changes in attitudes, feelings and behaviors. The addict must develop the skill to deal with these feelings without using drugs. The counselor can teach the addict how to recognize these signals. Then the addict needs to be taught how to intervene and change these feelings and behaviors. A plan should be developed that includes concrete behavioral changes that will need to be made in order for the patient to be successful.

More frequent attendance at meetings of AA or similar groups, avoiding environmental triggers, putting more structure into their lives, and spending more time with people who are supportive of their recovery are behavioral changes which will be helpful in preventing relapse.

SAMI

SAMI is an acronym for Substance Abuse and Mental Illness. SAMI programs provide assessment, consultation, and treatment for individuals with concurrent diagnoses of substance use disorder and serious mental illness. Individuals coping with substance use disorder and mental illness or other co-occurring issues (e.g., criminality, HIV/AIDS, pregnancy) typically need more than counseling and clinically monitored activities to achieve recovery. "Case Management" may be needed to assist the recovering individual in areas of education, housing, employment, transportation, child care, etc. The goal of Case Management is the provision of a continuum of services to reestablish relationships, enhance self-image, and engage prosocial activities, and to further attenuate drug use via both therapeutic and rehabilitative services. Other case management–oriented programs such as Treatment Accountability for Safer Communities (TASC) emerged to offer, for example, mandatory treatment and multimodal support in lieu of incarceration.

Social Service Case Management Models

Four. 1) Broker/Generalist identifies client needs and links them to resources or services; ideal where treatment and social services are integrated, advocacy/monitoring needs are minimal, and clients are motivated, psychologically intact, and financially stable. 2) Strengths-Based Perspective uses client strengths and assets, prompts goal-making, and then motivates clients to search out needed resources and support networks. It aids clients in finding needed resources/services, counters the common "dysfunction stigma" that hinders treatment, and focuses on client skills and capacity instead of pathology. 3) Clinical/Rehabilitation combines resource linking and clinical support in one provider for greater effectiveness. One variation is "multisystemic therapy" (e.g., therapists that coordinate directly with community resource providers. 4) Assertive Community Treatment is intensive case management for highly compromised clients (e.g., severe mentally ill, heavy substance users, HIV-infected with multiple daily medicines). It includes: 1) home/community visits; 2) frequent (potentially daily) contact; 3) medications monitoring; 4) problem solving; 5) advocacy; 6) small caseloads; 7) a team approach; and 8) long-term enrollment.

Case Managers

Case management requires a working familiarity with a great variety of issues, interventions, and resources. Consequently, case managers function best within a "generalist" practice framework. Within a substance use disorder treatment framework, case management consists of seven core social service functions: 1) engagement (establishing a positive relationship, and demonstrating prompt and effective service [eg, form completion assistance]); 2) assessment (typically focused on immediate goals and needs); 3) planning (usually involving sequential, escalating progress); 4) linkage (agency/program referrals); 5) monitoring (tracking progress); 6) advocacy (assertive client representation); and 7) disengagement (appropriately timed case closure). The principal focus of case management, however, is typically on its hallmark functions of linkage and advocacy. The parameters of case management are frequently mandated by the interdisciplinary team and institution through which the case manager works.

Case management practice activities do not include the direct provision of treatment/counseling, but include: 1) Assessment and planning via a "holistic" evaluation well beyond substance use disorder issues, often best accomplished by organizing information into "life domains" (e.g., health, occupation, family, legal) from which to identify resources that will sustain recovery and barriers that might impede it. The case management plan incorporates the overall recovery plan, psychosocial planning, and sequencing and coordinating necessary services. 2) Referrals that identify properly tailored resources and services, educating the client, providing specific contact persons, and then following-up to ensure client follow-through. 3) Service Coordination and Documentation includes ongoing advocacy, continuing client education, social support development (family, friends) within the bounds of confidentiality, resource sequencing, and careful record-keeping of progress and ongoing issues and concerns and how they are being addressed and resolved.

Support Groups for Family Members of Alcoholics

The impact of substance use disorder is felt by family members and even friends, and over time will shape their own thinking and living patterns. The alcoholic's cessation of drinking did not necessarily bring these patterns back to normal. The wives of early AA members recognized this and a support group for intimate others was eventually formed. Known as Al-Anon and patterned after AA's 12-step model, this group assisted its members in developing an appropriate lifestyle that was independent from the actions of the alcoholic. In like manner, Alateen was developed to aid teenaged children of alcoholics cope with their uniquely related issues. Both are peer-driven, and are built upon the powerlessness of loved ones over the alcoholic's drinking. Each helps its members cope with the stigma and stressors that accompany living with an alcoholic, whether recovering or sober. Both offer very valuable support.

Heroin Abuse

Common health problems associated with intravenous heroin abuse include the following: vascular collapse, tissue abscesses, respiratory and cardiac depression, HIV/AIDS (with needle sharing), heart and heart valve infections, and liver disease. Further, illicitly obtained heroin is often "cut" (diluted) with other substances. When the "cutting" (diluting) agent is insoluble, vascular clots and occlusions may result. Withdrawal symptoms may set in within hours, peak in 48 to 72 hours, and last about a week. Symptoms include muscle and bone pain, restlessness, cravings, and vomiting. Overdose is characterized by respiratory and/or cardiac depression, convulsions, coma, and death).

Prolonged Marijuana Use

There are many potential health pitfalls with prolonged marijuana use. The THC in marijuana can interfere with the function of the hippocampus in the brain, and prolonged disruption can result in lasting memory impairment. Marijuana smoke contains more tar and more harmful substances than cigarette smoke, is held in the lungs longer, and is inhaled more deeply than cigarette smoke. This can greatly increase the odds of developing lung cancer for frequent marijuana smokers. Other potential problems include cognitive impairment, cardiovascular disease, a compromised immune system, and respiratory illness. Certainly, the intoxicating effects of use can lead to a greater likelihood of accidents and injuries. Psychologically, persistent use can lead to depression, panic attacks and anxiety, irritability, personality problems, and decreased activity and motivation.

Ketamine

Ketamine is known for its "dissociative" "out-of-body" psychedelic properties, as well as its anesthetic qualities. The drug has increasingly been associated with the "dance culture," where its effects (including the near-death experience) are particularly desired. Street names include K, special K, and vitamin K. When injected, ketamine can induce profound analgesia, amnesia, respiratory depression, and cardiovascular stimulation. Even low doses can produce memory impairment, poor attention, and a reduced ability to learn. Extended abuse been associated with considerable psychological addiction. Further, individuals who frequently use ketamine develop tolerance to the drug, requiring higher doses for the same desired effect. Since 1999, ketamine has been a Schedule III drug under the Controlled Substances Act.

Intergenerational Transmission of Addictions

The capacity to develop personal differentiation (ie, a high sense of self in the face of competing demands) is protective against intergenerational transmission of problems such as addictions. Other protective factors include "selective disengagement" (moving 200 or more miles away and limiting family contact to two times per year) and "deliberateness" (taking control of one's life and carefully selecting a healthy mate). Further protection can be generated through sustained positive "family rituals" (e.g., family holiday activities, vacations, visits, meals). Through positive family rituals, enhanced transmission of values, roles, expectations, and boundaries are cemented, which can then overshadow the addictive problems of an individual family participant with substance use disorder issues. When positive family rituals are disrupted (e.g., by heavy drinking), the intergenerational transmission of problems is increased.

Risk Factors for an Addictive Disorder

It is known that addictive disorders tend to run in families and appear to have genetic components. Those most at physiological risk of alcoholism may have: 1) an alcoholic parent or grandparent; 2) a higher threshold for intoxication effects (more alcohol resulting in fewer effects); and 3) a tendency to drink heavily at the outset of life drinking. The biological tendency tends to be blurred between addiction and compulsion for behavioral problems (e.g., gambling, sex, shopping). Personal psychological factors can also play a role. Poor attachment development to a primary caregiver during infancy and childhood, particularly poor attachment to a father, is highly predictive of drug use among adolescents, as is a poor self-image. However, a sense of clear parentally defined conduct norms (referred to as "control") is protective against drug abuse, most likely because it reduces childhood and adolescent anxiety levels and confusion.

Parenting Styles and the Risk of Developing an Addictive Disorder

There are four styles of parenting that can increase addictive risk. First is the "teetotaler" parent. Although substance use disorder (including alcohol) is lower among children from such families, those children who do breach the family standard are more likely than other children to develop drug or alcohol use problems, likely due to a suppressed need to rebel. Second is the "overly demanding" parent (including over-achieving parents that seem to set exceptionally high standards for children to follow), resulting in self-worth issues. Third is the "overly protective" parent who does not allow a child to experience natural negative consequence or inhibits the child's development of self-sufficiency, resulting in a poor sense of self and innate uncertainty. Fourth is the "addicted/alcoholic" parent who models addiction, produces an unpredictable and chaotic home life, and induces anxiety and poor self-worth.

Psychological Risk Factors for Addiction

Key psychological risk factors for addiction include: a) poor intra- and interpersonal skills; b) inadequate decision making/judgment skills; c) high faith in problems solved via "miracles." Other psychological risk factors include low identification with the primary reference group (typically their family); low identification with available role models (inducing a distorted self-concept); and inadequate systemic skills (ie, adaptability, flexibility, and responsibility skills needed to cope with family, social, legal, and other societal systems). Eight sociocultural factors that reduce the risk of alcoholism are: 1) early childhood exposure to alcohol in family and/or religious circumstances; 2) parents that drink moderately only; 3) alcoholic beverages typically well diluted with nonalcoholic liquids; 4) a lack of moral significance attached to alcohol; 5) alcohol use not related to status or rites of passage (e.g., adulthood, personal virility); 6) alcohol seen as "food" served with meals; 7) excessive alcohol consumption and intoxication seen as unacceptable, and abstinence as an acceptable option; 8) a virtually fully unified family standard regarding proper drinking behavior.

Two Categories and Three Types of Children of Alcoholics

The first category contains the obviously troubled children in an alcoholic family. They act out, misbehave, and otherwise cause turmoil in the family. The second category includes preternaturally mature children who overachieve and behave. She divided these children into specific types: 1) the "adjusters" who are perpetually flexible to family needs, but feel they are powerless over their own lives; 2) the "placaters," who are emotionally sensitive, see to others needs first, and soothe feelings, but neglect themselves and feel they have little self-worth; and 3) the "responsible" child (often the oldest) who becomes adult-like and self-reliant, takes little time for fun or play, and is often lonely. Black also noted that family roles operate through family rules, which may be both "overt" and "covert" in alcoholic families (e.g., keep secrets). Black's three rules for alcoholic children are: 1) don't talk; 2) don't trust; and 3) don't feel." Ignoring intoxication is safest, promises are not kept, and denying feelings is functional.

Children's Risk Factors If an Alcoholic Parent Obtains Treatment

An alcoholic parent obtaining treatment is never truly protective, regardless of child age or in-home status. Common factors placing children at the highest risk for alcoholism include 1) being raised in a low socioeconomic home; 2) being younger than 7 years during the time of parental alcohol abuse; 3) experiencing or witnessing violence; and 4) living in a non-supportive family. Children in alcoholic homes report their primary concerns were parental arguments and fighting, and the consequent lack of interest in them by both such highly addiction-preoccupied parents. Among the factors most damaging are 1) the lack of structure (highly variable/changeable and/or contradictory family rules during "wet" [drinking] and "dry" [sober] cycles), and 2) inconsistent parenting. The four most commonly observed problems include 1) neglect or outright abuse; 2) acting out/destructive behaviors (e.g., aggression, substance abuse); 3) interpersonal/social deficits (poor trust, adjustment, development, and feeling unloved, abnormal, overly responsible); and 4) emotional reactions (depression, suicidality, poor self-confidence, fears of rejection/abandonment, high needs for perfection).

Percentage of Children of Alcoholics Who Will Become Alcoholic

Approximately 25% to 30% (70% to 75% do not). Researchers now warn against pathologizing all Adult Children of Alcoholics (ACOAs). Numerous factors may intervene, including child age at onset of parental drinking; whether both parents were alcoholic; duration and severity of the alcoholism; the extent of family history; recovery status; parental mental illness history; violence or sexual abuse; economic stability; the availability of compensating external support systems; and the personality of the child. "Resilient" children (who go on to do well) typically demonstrate: 1) insight (sensing problems, leading to knowing a problem exists, and finally obtaining an understanding); 2) independence ("straying" in search of distance from problems as an adolescent); 3) rationally separating (as an adult); 3) relationship compensation ("connecting," "bonding," and "interacting"); 4) taking initiative (survivor pride, appreciating challenges, self-trusting, and exploring, working, and generating success); 5) exercising creativity (including active imagination); 6) using humor (finding laughter); and 7) exercising morality (judging, valuing, and serving others with an informed conscience).

Substance-Induced Illnesses Likely to Cause the Demise of Individuals Treated for Alcoholism

Illnesses involving tobacco use. Smoking is common in combination with both alcohol (60%), heroin (nearly 100%), and other substances. Tobacco smoke creates a negative "synergistic effect" on the body, making the deleterious health effects of both substances much greater together. Substance abusers typically smoke more cigarettes, more often, and more effectively (obtaining more carcinogens, tars, etc.). Thus, more alcoholics die from tobacco-induced diseases than from alcohol-induced problems. Aiding substance users to also abandon cigarettes is deemed important for at least four reasons: 1) the high incidence of substance abusers using tobacco increases the likelihood of an continuing smoker making contact with other substance users; 2) a substance user's social circle typically has both substance users and smokers, enhancing the likelihood of relapse; 3) the problematic synergistic effects of tobacco combined with other substances (including marijuana) is highly deleterious to health; and 4) overcoming all substances of abuse can be an empowering and effective way to enhance recovery.

Addiction Treatment

Basic principles include: a) education about general and specific addiction theory; b) individual and group therapy, and an introduction to 12-step programs; c) life skills training; and d) family involvement where possible. Inpatient versus outpatient treatment decisions are easier using the American Society of Addiction Medicine (ASAM) *Patient Placement Criteria for the Treatment of Psychoactive Substance Use Disorders* (1996). Many sex addicts are also addicted to alcohol and other drugs (AOD). In such situations, treatment of the AOD addictions must be primary. "Sequential treatment" involves targeting the addiction most problematic for the client. "Concurrent treatment" involves separate but simultaneous treatment of each addiction present, focusing on their unique features. "Combined treatment" posits that all addictions are similar, and thus can be treated in a group setting with a primary chemical dependency focus, behavioral addiction augmentation, and tailored individual counseling and 12-step involvement. Ideally, an integrated approach using all three can be drawn up where sufficient counselor/facility expertise exists.

Special Needs Populations in Drug Addiction Treatment

Special needs populations include: 1) criminal substance abusers: individuals involved in criminal behavior (often related to sustaining their addiction) are at high risk for ongoing problems, and appear to do best when community treatment programs are combined with criminal justice orders and supervision; 2) dual diagnosed: those with coexisting addictive and psychiatric disorders that complicate the treatment process, especially as related to mood disorders, medications management, and the cognitive and emotional capacity to generate and sustain change; 3) women: issues of pregnancy and childrearing make this population particularly problematic, as do histories of physical and/or sexual abuse that may contribute to ongoing issues; 4) adolescents: issues of maturity, peer environments, self-esteem, and ongoing physical, emotional, and psychological development make this population particularly vulnerable to ongoing substance abuse.

Cognitive Restructuring

Cognitive restructuring centers around the concept that belief systems produce thought patterns that in turn produce feelings and behaviors. Consequently, revising the way an individual thinks about a situation can produce needed feeling and behavioral changes. Ellis (1962) proposed the ABCDE Principle of Emotional Disturbance to assert cognitive control over emotions. A is the external event; B references beliefs, attitudes, or interpretations of "A." C is the consequence or emotional reaction. D refers to "disputing/intervening" for change. E represents the "effects" or results of D. Ellis postulated that B (belief about A) causes C. Three common irrational ideas driving B include: 1) I must have the approval of others; 2) how you treat me must be proper or necessary; and 3) I should always receive what I want. Successful restructuring requires the client to: 1) recognize the irrational idea; 2) believe that thinking patterns can be changed; and 3) establish more rational thinking, ideas, and philosophies in order to avoid irrationality.

Behavior Contracts

Behavior contracts are used to help clients determine in advance the kind of conduct they desire, and specific steps they will take should they find themselves at risk of undesirable behavior. Behavior contracts are valuable in many ways. First, they help clients meaningfully clarify the behaviors they are seeking to ensure. Second, they allow public revelation of goals, which can be an important aid in keeping commitments. Third, they include a specific relapse-prevention plan–what to do if circumstances or thinking again predispose a return to old behavioral patterns. Successful behavioral contracts, whether oral or written, require reality, specificity, an absence of coercion, and flexibility. Full mutual agreement, clear response time frames, and adequate counselor support (not just after relapse) are other key features. Milestone mementos, positive feedback, and learning reviews are all additionally useful interventions.

Social Learning and Assertion Training

Social learning refers to the process of change achieved by observing and adopting the conduct of others. This can be accomplished by behavioral modeling—demonstrating a desired behavior or response either directly (requesting the client's observation) or indirectly (displaying desirable conduct that the client eventually adopts naturally). Role playing (producing scenarios that are then enacted together), role taking (assuming another's role to gain greater insights), and observational learning (watching the enactments of others) are all additional ways to facilitate social learning.

Assertion training aids individuals to more successfully extend themselves in particular situations by showing affection, expressing feelings, saying "no," defending oneself, etc. Learning to be properly assertive (e.g., without self-abnegation or being over critical of others) can be facilitated through the numerous social learning techniques described above.

Relaxation Training and Aversion Training

Significant relaxation and marked anxiety cannot coexist. Therefore, learning techniques to facilitate relaxation are key to coping with stress and anxiety. Given the typical poor coping skills of chemically dependent clients, this can be an important relapse prevention tool. Jacobson's (1938) progressive muscle relaxation approach, as well as transcendental meditation, guided imagery, music therapy, and other tools for relaxation training can all be very helpful.

Aversion training seeks to pair an unpleasant stimulus with a behavior or scenario that one seeks to avoid. This can be accomplished by use of aversive imagery (e.g., nausea and vomiting, medications that react negatively to the consumption of substances of abuse). Although used much less commonly today, aversion training (particularly in regard to imagination-generated negative mental associations) can be particularly useful in certain situations or at key points in client interventions.

Relapse

While 70% of recovering addicts will relapse at some future time, fully 37% of these will relapse within the first 12 months (1 year). Denzin (1987) proposes four relapse phases: 1) lax or permissive thinking about recovery commitments; 2) actual ingestion of a mood-altering substance; 3) the experience of intoxication; and 4) seeking help again. Post-relapse counseling involves: 1) the search for triggers (internal and external pressures, etc.) in a search for identifiable patterns that can be avoided in the future; 2) discovering what needs were being met by using; 3) revealing excuses (without generating crushing guilt). The optimum approach may be prevention by identifying triggers or danger signs (especially those accompanied by feelings of anger, fear, guilt, inadequacy, covered by arrogance and self-centeredness) and retrenching into strict honesty with themselves and others. Danger signs fit in four categories: attitudes/thoughts, feelings, behaviors, and delusions of control.

Cognitive-Behavioral View of Addiction and Relapse Prevention

In contrast to a disease model of addiction, cognitive-behavioral theorists view addiction as a maladaptive coping pattern arising out of stress. Cognitive-behavioral relapse prevention models typically utilize self-management approaches, sometimes with and sometimes without 12-step programs. Some proponents of 12-step programs are often averse to cognitive-behavioral models, as the idea of self-help is incongruent with admitting powerlessness. Others may be supportive. Self-management approaches focus on lifestyle changes, behavioral skills training, and cognitive interventions, largely based on the idea that although addiction may have occurred outside one's awareness, recovery is a matter of personal control.

Alcohol Relapse Symptoms

Common relapse symptoms include 1) abstinence is all that's needed; 2) overconfidence regarding recovery; 3) compulsive behaviors; 4) self-isolation; 5) depression; 6) painful life failures; 7) overreacting to stress; 8) excessive daydreaming; 9) feeling hopeless about problems; 10) haphazard or unrealistic planning; 11) avoiding fun; 12) blaming others; 13) doubting the disease (addiction); 14) fatigue and/or poor sleep; 15) loss of daily routine; 16) sporadic attendance at aftercare meetings (e.g., AA); 17) a "don't care" attitude; 18) rejecting help; 19) hoarding things; 20) dishonesty; 21) rationalizing drinking; 22) drinking fantasies; 23) self-pity; 24) feeling overwhelming emotions; 25) visiting places or people around which drinking will occur; 26) encountering a major life change; 27) substance substitution; 28) being easily irritated with family and friends; 29) living in the past; 30) doubting the ability to stay sober.

Remaining Drug Free

The duration of time retained in treatment is among the most significant of all factors in terms of relapse prevention. Studies indicate that 50% of all patients in both outpatient and residential program dropped out of treatment in 3 months or less, yet retention in treatment is positively correlated with benefits in abstinence and functioning. Retention strategies include: 1) enriched treatment with more treatment options, frequency, and intensity (improving retention by up to 15%); 2) client satisfaction (also correlated with the previously stated enriched treatment options); 3) treatment stability (low counselor turnover rates, contingency management strategies, reduced fees, etc.); 4) careful patient-treatment modality matching. Effective treatment requires: 1) comprehensive assessment and diagnosis; 2) individualized treatment plans; 3) essential services; 4) regular treatment plan reassessment and revision; 5) aftercare enrollment and adequate support systems.

Categories of Prevention Cited by Public Health Service

The three categories are primary, secondary, and tertiary: 1) Primary prevention addresses nonuser education; 2) secondary prevention targets the initiates or drug users; and 3) tertiary prevention involves relapse prevention among drug users. Primary prevention can be subdivided into three types: 1) Universal addresses all demographic populations; 2) selective focuses on at-risk subgroups (e.g., offspring of those incarcerated, Native American children); and 3) indicated singles out those with known predisposing precursors (thrill-seekers, delinquent, conduct disordered, and the aggressive). Effective approaches for demographic groups include: 1) child-only, informational education ("DARE" programs), social skills, and competency, and mentors range in "effect" outcomes in the very small .05 to 1.0 range; 2) family-focused approaches (parenting, skills training, family therapy, in-home support, etc.) demonstrated an average effect size nine times that of child-only models; 3) community coalitions such as Communities That Care (CTC) models are also helpful.

Easiest Ways to Manage Drug or Alcohol Use

One of the easiest ways to manage drug or alcohol use is by controlling where you use. The setting will often determine what drugs you use (e.g., in a bar = alcohol; in a club = club drugs). Make sure you have the drugs you want to avoid trying something on the spur of a moment's choice. Use in safe places (e.g., well-lit, clean, running water, private so not rushed) to increase safety. Plan your use in advance. Consider: 1) a designated driver; 2) clean equipment prepared in advance; 3) whom you're with and where (especially when using hallucinogenics); 4) have sufficient water and food; 5) limit eating with psychedelics, as they may induce emesis; 6) consider alternating alcohol with other beverages, and include a glass of water between each in order to minimize the "hangover" response so common following a night of drinking. Harm reduction is an important part of safety for those who are not yet ready to abstain from all substance usage.

Tension-Reduction Model

The tension reduction model views substance use disorder as a method of reducing environmentally conditioned anxiety. The relief of anxiety provided by the substance reinforces its repeated use. Cappell and Greeley (1987) conducted a careful evaluation of literature on this model and rejected it as a single-factor explanation, in part because substances of abuse do much more than alleviate tension. This led to the stress-response-dampening model (Sher, 1987), which sees substance use disorder as providing an expectation of stress relief, derived in part via peer and family modeling and direct and indirect substance use experiences. Expectations include mood alterations, enhanced social comfort, an increased sense of control and power, and (eventually) an expectation of cravings compelling one to continue the substance use disorder. This led Marlatt and Gordon (1985) to develop a successful social-learning relapse prevention model that viewed addictive behaviors as habits that can be analyzed and changed, as with any habit. Chemical-aversion therapy has largely been abandoned in favor of these behavioral approaches.

Attribution of Responsibility

Brickman, et al described four models that vary in determining who is held responsible for creating problems and problem-solving: 1) the Moral Model, the individual creates and must solve all personal problems; 2) the Medical Model, individuals are held blameless for their problems and are not responsible for finding solutions; 3) the Enlightenment Model, individuals create their own problems, but should not be held responsible for resolving them; and 4) the Compensatory Model, individuals are not seen as responsible for personal problem creation, but must be held responsible for solving them. Alcoholics Anonymous follows number 3; a Higher Power is sought to resolve the problem (though taking steps to this end fits number 4). A common modern treatment model is number 4; addiction is an unexpected lapse into a disease, but the individual must work to master and resolve the problem.

Action Counseling Model

The Action Counseling Model was designed to aid those treating the chemically dependent (CD) to more effectively structure the counseling process. The model offers the following three stages: Stage 1) Establishing therapeutic rapport, information gathering, and problem assessment. This stage focuses on self-exploration, gaining insights, finding relationships between identified concerns, and determining the major issues requiring address. Stage 2) Client determination of changes desired, goal setting, and establishing commitment (requires overcoming insight and judgment limits). Stage 3) specific action steps, interventions, and strategies to achieve change (e.g., requires agreements, contracting). Other common Stage 3 strategies: assertion training, behavioral contracts, cognitive techniques, and relaxation therapy. In counseling CD clients, careful attention to nonverbal cues, empathy, confrontation, and immediacy skills are important. However, genuineness and acceptance ("positive regard") are primary keys, as CD clients typically come from poor trust/acceptance environments.

Review Video: Basic Skills of a Counselor
Visit mometrix.com/academy and enter code: 965456

Attending

Attending refers to nonverbal behaviors that demonstrate attention. Attending behaviors are essential in the counseling process, without which clients can readily feel devalued and unheard. Egan (1986) proposed the acronym of SOLER to identify key attending behaviors: S = squarely facing the client (degrees of turning lessen the sense of contact and invite the inclusion of other external stimuli); O = open posture (e.g., uncrossed arms, open relaxed hands); L = leaning slightly forward (showing invested concern; too far forward can be intimidating); E = good eye contact (unless culture limits this); and R = relaxed posture (e.g., normalizing the experience and easing stressful communications).

Empathy

To hone empathic skills, Egan (1975) suggests the following: 1) see empathy as a "way of being," not a role to be played; 2) listen carefully for client views and feelings; 3) suspend biases and judgments long enough to step into the client's perspective; 4) seek "core" client messages; 5) ensure a grasp of context as much as expressions; 6) briefly but frequently acknowledge core client messages; 7) ensure flexible and tentative responses to avoid circumventing client views; 8) gently ensure a focus on major issues; 9) address core messages without emphasizing one over another without specific cause; 10) engage sensitive feelings and topics gradually; 11) carefully look for cues that support or obviate the accuracy of your responses; 12) ensure your empathic responses clarify/develop key issues and keep the client focused; 13) determine if client resistance or stress emerge because of your inaccurate versus overly accurate responses; and 14) remember that empathy is a tool to clarify and manage problems more effectively and not an end in itself.

Confrontation

Confrontation is used to increase a client's awareness of themselves, their environment, or the way they interact with their environment. Further, confrontation can be used to help clients see reality as opposed to wished for preference. Finally, confrontation can be used when a client ignores, avoids, or denies issues or feedback. If managed properly, confrontation can markedly improve client behaviors and enhance their relationships. However, it can also polarize and alienate individuals. To avoid this, confrontation should only be used in a relationship of clear caring and trust. It must never be used as a punitive tool or as a means for releasing frustrations and anger. Sensitivity, careful timing, and a keen awareness of the client's capacity to cope with the information offered are absolutely essential for confrontational success.

Self-Disclosure

Self-disclosure refers to personal revelations by a counselor to a client, and it can take many forms, such as: 1) disclosing past personal experiences and problems, along with related feelings and concerns, and/or processes that led to overcoming past issues; 2) reactions and feelings arising about the client and/or his or her circumstances; and 3) feelings about the counseling experience itself. Self-disclosure can be problematic. First, it can shift the focus from the client to the counselor. Second, it can suggest equivalence between the client and the counselor's experiences and leave the client feeling defensive and marginalized. Third, where the counselor overcame issues, it can leave the client feeling substandard and inferior. Fourth, it can diminish the counselor in the client's eyes. Self-disclosure of feelings is more likely to be helpful, even powerful, if it models appropriate expression, is kept brief and genuine, and if it occurs in a trusting/accepting atmosphere.

Self-disclosure as a leader does not refer to revelations of personal demographics or history, but the revelation of feelings and reactions to group experiences and events. This promotes openness and personalizes the leader (as someone authentic, trustworthy, and human enough to be emulated). Authenticity is crucial to help members avoid the trap of social pretending to avoid perceptions of undue self-exposure of inadequacies, etc. Occasional direct personal questions of a leader can be answered (e.g., age, years in practice), but the continuous use of such questions suggests the members need to deflect attention away from themselves because of anxiety and fears. This should be noted, kindly but directly: "Perhaps you're feeling attacked, as you seem to be asking questions in an effort to try and shift the focus off yourself and onto me. Can we talk about that?"

Immediacy and Role Playing

Immediacy refers to an undistorted (or minimally distorted) awareness of emotion in the immediate present. It is the ability to identify and express feelings of anxiety, boredom, frustration or discouragement. In a group setting, immediacy can be revealed by turning members' attention inward, by identifying patterns in eye contact, seating, sharing, etc., but without the leader's interpretation when possible (ie, the group should interpret, unless an interpretation example is needed to grasp the concept: "Does your bouncing foot suggest you are agitated right now?"). Leader self-disclosure of feelings may help.

Role playing refers to group members acting out situations and relationships of significance to them. In this way, rehearsal for improved interactions can be secured, and insights from group feedback can be gained. Alternative behaviors can also be more fully explored for greater self-efficacy and learning.

Confrontation and Cognitive Restructuring

Confrontation in a group setting can help group members to recognize and overcome issues of which they may be effectively unaware, such as addiction severity and overall denial. As long as confrontation is used to produce insight and growth, it is therapeutic and positive. Where it is used punitively or in hurtful ways, the outcome is invariably negative and counterproductive. To ensure positive processes, confrontation should always be delivered from a position of caring concern, not domination or control.

Cognitive restructuring is useful when group members express irrational and illogical ideas, which can be challenged by the use of reason (logic), exaggeration (for perspective), and/or humor (e.g., to reduce thought-impairing tension).

Group Leadership Styles

White and Lippitt (1961) identified three key group leadership styles: 1) Authoritarian: makes all policy, activity, and technique decisions and dictates to the group, makes comments (praise, confrontation, etc.) directly to involved persons, and remains relatively aloof; the style fosters group dependence on the leader. .2) Democratic: policy, activity, and technique decisions derived via discussion, becomes warmly involved, and makes objective (rather than personal) comments; results in friendly and cohesive groups. 3) Laissez Faire: supplies materials and only gives information when asked; results in less organized (and less satisfied) groups. Barlow, et al (1982) note two additional styles: 4) Speculative: speaking more for him/herself and a focus on others' behaviors; and 5) Confrontive: focused on the group's impact on him/herself, documentation of statements, and leans on personal charisma (runs risk of members idealizing him/her and seeing accomplishments as not their own). Each style may be helpful (new group: authoritarian for a time; democratic as they grow; laissez faire when seasoned).

Group Process

Considerable overlap occurs. Stage 1) Orientation and Exploration: meeting, structuring, setting goals (an "agenda go-round" approach may be helpful), establishing trust, etc. Key: Anxiety reduction is crucial to early learning. Stage 2) Transition: mixed feelings and attitudes emerge, along with conflicts, confrontations, resistance, and domination issues; individual roles and group norms solidify; pressures to conform emerge and shape participants. Leaders model openness and conflict resolution. Stage 3) Action: change begins as intimacy, closeness, and acceptance grow, and as conflicts and competition decrease. Difficult issues can be revealed, and shared understanding encourages further self-disclosure. Key issue: retrenchment to conflict-avoidance may prevent further learning; the leader must continue to model challenging each other to promote growth. Stage 4) Completion: reviewing insights and learning, looking to future goals, and providing concluding group experience summaries. Key issues: coping with anxiety at group termination, ensuring a positive focus during closure sharing sessions, and emphasizing continuing work to maintain progress and continue forward.

Motivational Interviewing

Unlike a the typical confrontation-of-denial technique, motivational interviewing involves the following: 1) avoids the acceptance of labels as being necessary for change (e.g., "addict," "alcoholic"); 2) focuses on personal choice and responsibility as the key to recovery; 3) sees client resistance as an outgrowth of the clinician's interactions with the client; 4) views goal negotiation as superior to unconditional acceptance of unilaterally recommended treatment; 5) views ambivalence as the central issue, as opposed to denial. This technique is seen as a leap forward in overcoming clients' resistance to giving up their drug use. It also proposes that the therapist's behavior is the greatest predictor of the interaction outcome (as opposed to blaming the substance user alone, as has been common in the past).

Self-Medication Hypothesis Model

The "self-medication hypothesis" is a psychodynamic model of substance use disorder that frames substance use/abuse as an effort to self-regulate where deficits in interpersonal relationships, affective functioning, and self-care/self-esteem exist. Individuals with self-regulation deficits (especially when also combined with a genetic predisposition) are much more likely to develop a substance use disorder than those without such features. Therefore, an individual with bipolar disorder may use substances to modulate manic episodes; an individual with a social phobia may use substances to cope with social fears; and an individual with attention-deficit hyperactivity disorder may use substances to self-medicate feelings of agitation and distraction.

General Systems Theory

Ludwig Von Bertalanffy. "Systems thinking" allows one to move beyond "linear" cause-and-effect thinking. The system is "more than the sum of its parts," by which it produces "wholeness" (ie, a watch has individual parts, but assembled it also displays time). Drawing from cybernetics, the mathematician Weiner postulated the "feedback loop" enabled self-correction; "positive" amplifies deviation, and "negative" reduces a deviation (e.g., high temperatures trigger a thermostat to cool to an original temperature). Bateson used the feedback concept to postulate "circular causality," psychopathologies maintained by circular feedback loops. Thus, families are studied for: a) behavioral rules; b) sequences of events and patterns around a problem; and c) negative feedback loops that do not solve a problem, and/or positive ones that do not press for solutions. For example, an alcoholic family develops entrenched feedback loops: secrecy, problem avoidance, accommodation, and stasis, which sustain continued alcoholism. Bowen examined "differentiation" ("separated" vs "fused" family members). The "undifferentiated family ego mass" leads to high emotional reactivity and the "multigenerational transmission" of problems (e.g., substance abuse).

Homeostasis

Family balance through equilibrium. Don Jackson coined the term, and described families like an artistic mobile, where movement in one causes movement in others and tends to return to an original configuration. Ewing and Fox (1968) applied the concept to alcoholism, where change is resisted by rigid family roles. Should the alcoholic stop drinking, the disequilibrium can easily induce relapse or tear the family apart (e.g., divorce). In the presence of addictions, family member roles are typically highly scripted and rigid. Children quickly blame themselves for pain and problems, and rigidly play out their roles in the family paradigm. The early family therapist/researcher Virginia Satir identified family roles when under stress, and labeled them: the "blamer," the "placater," the "irrelevant," and the "super-reasonable." Wegscheider (1981) added the "family hero" (usually the oldest), the "scapegoat," (acts out to divert from the family problem), the "lost child" who is withdrawn, and the "mascot" (often the youngest) who distracts with humor and fun, but is often insecure, fearful, and lonely.

Family Systems Therapy

During the 1950s, substance use disorder treatment moved from being seen as an individual problem to one of family dysfunction with multigenerational processes. Among the earliest paradigms published was a paper describing four types of spouses of alcoholics: 1) the "sufferer" who punishes herself by staying with the alcoholic; 2) the "controller" who attempts to change the alcoholic; 3) the "waverer" who is insecure and fearful, functionally competent, but unable to induce change; and 4) the "punisher" who operates as superior and dominating and drives the spouse to drink. Over time, the literature uncovered four key areas for research: 1) biological/genetic influences; 2) environmental influences; 3) children's risk factors; and 4) treatment outcome evaluation. Today, behavioral couples therapy, family therapy, and community reinforcement and family training are seen as far more effective than individual treatment alone.

Review Video: Bowen Family Systems
Visit mometrix.com/academy and enter code: 591496

Structural Family Therapy

Structural Family Therapy was developed by the Argentinian psychiatrist Salvador Minuchin. He recognized that many family problems were a result of dysfunctional relationships with problematic roles, rules, alignments, coalitions, and boundaries. His approach was to "join" the family and then destabilize and reorganize family interactions, leading to change and enhanced function. The approach did not require that the family focus on insights into problems, but simply trust and collaborate with the therapist to achieve change. Strategic Family Therapy was developed by Jay Haley. The approach is based on a similar view of family problems, but the focus is on insight, understanding, and the completion of behavioral tasks that enable change to occur. Further, the interaction moves past dyadic interactions, and expands to include "triangulations" or "perverse triangles" in family relations that prevent change. In 1962 Minuchin and Haley formed a partnership and considerable blending of the approaches has since occurred.

Family Boundaries

Enmeshed boundaries are diffuse in nature. They arise in families where "sameness" and "belonging" are stressed over individuality in an effort to produce a sense of cohesion and closeness at the expense of personal realization. Disengaged boundaries are common in alcoholic families. The boundaries are rigid and serve to isolate family members through family rules, secrets, and avoidance. Healthy boundaries are at mid-continuum, and are called "clear" boundaries. At polar boundary ends, individual survival requires the development of coalitions and alliances. An alliance involves two people, but a "coalition" of two people against a third person is usually required to form a stable, interactive triangulation (e.g., a mother and son generate a cross-generational alliance against an alcoholic father for their safety). Problematic family symptoms arise when a family system stagnates, leaving the family unable to move forward through the family life cycle (e.g., separation and individuation).

Behavioral Counseling Strategies

Behavioral counseling strategies used in treating addictions include: 1) "bibliotherapy" that assigns a client to read key educational literature. Other behavioral counseling strategies used in treating addictions include: 2) Activity scheduling that supports behavioral change via assigned activities (AA meetings, family interactions, etc.); 3) behavior modeling demonstrates a specific behavior and encourages client imitation; 4) behavior rehearsal practices new behaviors in a safe setting; 5) contingency contracting defines and records behavioral expectations, time frames, and rewards for accomplishments; 6) counter-conditioning is anxiety reduction via rehearsal of opposing emotions (e.g., relaxation), perhaps via guided imagery, music therapy, or breathing exercises; 7) goal setting selects goals and identifies strategies and time frames; 8) journaling is writing to organize thoughts, enhance memory, and work through issues; 9) physical exercise is for stress reduction (with doctor approval); 10) self-monitoring is tracking thoughts and/or behaviors to understand and change prior habits.

Collaborative Behavioral Training

Aggressive confrontation and demeaning attitudes and interactions create defensive resistance, and merely limiting access only postpones a return to the addiction. Collaborative Behavioral Training techniques are typically much more effective. Frequently used treatment methods include: 1) self-control training (emphasizing self-monitoring and behavioral change); 2) contingency management (environmental manipulation to produce necessary rewards or punishments for substance abuse behaviors); 3) stress management, assertion, relaxation, and social skills training; 4) education regarding decision making and problem solving; 5) couples and family therapy and group counseling; 6) vocational and career counseling; 7) cognitive restructuring (revised self-image and environmental perceptions); aversion approaches (real or imagined aversive conditioning); 8) lifestyle and recreational planning; 9) education regarding burdens of substance abuse; 10) self-help organization referrals (AA, NA, etc.). In addition, alternate motivational sources may be appropriately added to a treatment plan, such as joining an exercise program, attending religious services, returning to school, or joining a club—every reasonable source of meaningful change should be incorporated.

Key Developmental Tasks Identified by Kinney and Leaton

Kinney and Leaton (1983) have identified four key developmental tasks faced during adolescence: 1) understanding and responding to biological changes; 2) becoming at ease with sexual preference (moving from same-sex preferences to opposite sex attraction, especially if same-sex preferences persist); 3) finding an occupational identity (exploring work options and part-time employment, etc.); and 4) reconciling a need for autonomy and independence. Some researchers note another task: 5) developing a personal identity (ie, a personal style, set of standards, goals).

Positive adolescent development can also be divided into five key areas: 1) values (life's rules of conduct); 2) thinking (learning to grasp and apply logic, make decisions, and anticipate consequences); 3) emotions (ideally coping via thinking, applied values, and resultant positive choices); 4) physicality (coping with biological changes); with all culminating in 5) positive behavior (actions). Inadequate development in any area can lead to poor self-esteem and decreased self-efficacy, which can predispose to drug experimentation and abuse. Thus, positive growth is crucial.

Adolescent Drug Abuse

The initial drug use stage is described as the "experimental stage." Of those who use (particularly boys), most will become regular users. Positive drug experiences reinforce the need to continue. The second stage is the "social use stage." Social users formulate personal guidelines for use and adhere to them. Those most at risk of entering more compromised stages are the 20% who have struggled to develop a coherent value system, and for whom drugs present as "the best thing" available. The third stage is the "preoccupation stage." Here, an increasing amount of thought, time, energy, and money is devoted to obtaining and using drugs. Legal or family issues may result in brief periods of abstinence (weeks), leading youths to believe they could stop. However, they are increasingly unable to control their use. The fourth stage is the "dependency stage." As an addict, the only important thing in life is using drugs—at the cost of friends, achievements, self-image, and even health.

Overall, escalating drug use in the 1960s resulted in a significant increase in drug use among adolescents in the 1970s. This was aided in part by a persistent myth that drugs were not harmful. Popular drugs in the 1960s were psychedelic drugs (e.g., LSD, marijuana, psilocybin mushrooms), while adolescents in the '70s gravitated toward marijuana and stimulants (e.g., amphetamines, cocaine). By the early 1980s, some 16% of high school seniors had tried cocaine, 60% had smoked marijuana, and 70% had ingested alcohol within the past month. An explosion in young damaged lives followed. In just accidents alone, drivers aged 16 to 24 years accounted for 48% of all fatal automobile crashes, with substance abuse a key element in most. Finally, virtually all alcoholics and drug addicts started using as adolescents, making this a pivotal period in the addictive process. This is especially true for adolescents experiencing a tumultuous upbringing (e.g., chaotic home lives, poor parental support).

Professional Practice Issues

CONFIDENTIALITY

Confidentiality fundamentals: 1) information shared in a counseling setting must not be divulged in any way that could identify the patient. Anything further requires the patient's full knowledge regarding the purpose, and written authorization. Group members may be encouraged to role play and determine consequences for breaking confidentiality. "Privileged communication" only exists where membership in a state-recognized professional organization exists. Confidentiality must be abridged where a clear and imminent danger to the client or others arises, and where a child (and sometimes dependent adult) has been or will be abused. Patients must be informed in advance of these limitations. Confidentiality levels: First level: basic professional use of information. Second level: information shared for the client's welfare, requiring a written release; dilemmas arise when significant others with a primary concern appear inadequately informed. Third level: constructing confidentiality to allow for shocking/disturbing revelations. This requires advance discussion and preparation to ensure the client feels adequate confidence to fully disclose.

Review Video: Confidentiality
Visit mometrix.com/academy and enter code: 250384

ETHICAL PROFESSIONAL CONDUCT

Working to benefit a client. The term most used is "beneficence," which refers to promoting the well-being, health, and welfare of those involved. "Iatrogenic" harm is that caused by a treatment or procedure, rather than by natural processes. Where asymmetric knowledge and insight are held by the counselor, a "fiduciary relationship" exists, meaning one is obliged to look after another who is not in a position to fully secure his or her own best interests by means of independent knowledge and judgment. A proper relationship must include an understanding of "boundaries" (ie, client-professional), including: 1) a zone of safety (wherein actions are engaged that are always acceptable), 2) a zone of vulnerability (in areas such as attachment and disengagement, where some actions would not be acceptable), and 3) a zone of abuse (recognizing actions that would never be acceptable).

Key challenges: 1) comprehensive ethical guidelines do not yet exist; 2) ethical obligations may overlap; 3) group work limits counselor control over what is said, lending to ethical concerns. The National Association of Alcoholism and Drug Abuse Counselors had no formal code of ethics until 1987. Fundamentally, the needs and welfare of all individuals must be protected and respected at all times. To this end, counselors must act in accordance with patient rights, professional ethical standards, and the fundamental moral standards and values (both individual and cultural) that are extant in the life of each patient.

Ethical obligations exist whenever professional and private conduct meet. If private conduct (e.g., immoral or illegal behavior) threatens the reputation of your agency and your own professional reputation, it enters the "nexus" of overlap. Other ethical issues include misrepresenting one's credentials, or practicing outside the scope of one's training. Maintaining professional-client boundaries is particularly important in addiction counseling, where relapse issues are not uncommon. Most therapeutic codes define a formal relationship as existing for at least 2 years following closure, and many include family members in that scope. Address with clients how they may want to handle accidental public encounters (How do we say we know each other?). Dual relationships are not permitted (counseling family members, past relationships, etc.) as they compromise objectivity. Sexual relationships are always violations. Self-disclosures to clients are often problematic, and should at least be brief and limited to avoid shifting the focus of counseling.

Zones of Vulnerability

There are seven zones of vulnerability. Specifically, they include 1) personal conduct; 2) business conduct; 3) nonclinical professional conduct; 4) conduct with clients and families; 5) peer relationship conduct; 6) conduct related to safety threats; and 7) ethics in the course of special roles and functions (e.g., training, research, prevention). Three steps to ethical analysis are: 1) Who is expected to benefit and who may be harmed? 2) What cultural or universally accepted values may apply? 3) What existing codes, laws, regulations, policies, and/or standard practices apply? The NAADAC Code of Ethics offers 12 principles: 1) nondiscrimination; 2) responsibility (including integrity and objectivity); 3) competence; 4) legal and moral standards; 5) public statements; 6) credit in publication; 7) client welfare; 8) confidentiality/privacy; 9) proper client relationships; 10) proper interprofessional relationships; 11) remuneration; and 12) societal obligations.

Therapist-Client Boundary Drift

Over-engagement by a counselor with a client. Signs of boundary drift include: 1) possessiveness or preoccupation with a client; 2) avoiding a necessary referral away; 3) protracted or overly frequent sessions; 4) sexualized discussions; 5) inappropriate self-disclosure; 6) increased touching; 7) client dependency; 8) avoiding supervision; 9) contact outside a professional setting; 10) courtship activities (grooming, dress, gifts). "Under-engagement" or "disengagement" may result from personal frustration or depletion, and may constitute client abandonment, often due to the stressful nature of addictive processes (relapses, denial, resistance, etc.). Signs include: 1) poor preparation; 2) attention drift during sessions; 3) aversion to seeing a client(s); 4) avoiding phone contacts; 5) shortened sessions; 6) superficial sessions; 7) disrespect; 8) adversarial contacts; 9) client depersonalization (e.g., use of negative labels); 10) abrupt terminations.

Kickback Remuneration for Client Referrals

Report the coworker to the proper agency administrators. The National Association of Alcohol and Drug Abuse Counselors (NAADAC) Code of Ethics, Principle 2 requires the reporting of unethical conduct, and it is not the counselor's duty to determine the veracity of what was shared before reporting. The more frequent professional peer ethical conflicts include: 1) unethical conduct; 2) impairment; 3) intra-agency confidentiality issues; 4) inter- and intra-agency conflicts; 5) fee-splitting (kickbacks for referrals); 6) supervisory power abuses; 7) dual relationship issues; and 8) whistle-blowing. Maintain ethical standards by: 1) effective self-care; 2) attend ethics trainings; 3) seek mentors; 4) self-monitor vigilantly; 5) seek consultations and help; 6) share and document issues in any "zone of vulnerability" to ensure all is appropriate, and known openly in advance; 7) always ensure that no harm is done.

Prevalence of Substance Use Disorder

If defined as having "had at least one experience in which they abused drugs," the prevalence of drug use approaches 100% of the adult population. If one considers the rate at which adults have experienced or will experience any problem with substance abuse, either personally or with someone they love at some point in their lives, it is virtually 100%. Alcohol consumption has occurred since Paleolithic times, and it remains the single most abused drug and causes by far the greatest number of substance use disorder problems. Functionally, a person is chemically dependent if they "continue to use mood-altering chemicals, despite the problems that their usage causes." Thus, chemical dependency is "chronic, progressive, and often fatal" (34.5 of every 36 will die from it). Once chemically dependent, the disorder persists indefinitely and the individual remains forever subject to relapse. A key feature of chemical dependence is continually excusing the abuse, versus taking personal responsibility and stopping the behavior.

Costs of Substance Use Disorder

Alcohol abuse is involved in over 10% of all US deaths, and is the leading cause of death among those between the ages of 16 to 24 years. Approximately 68% of drowning deaths, 50% of deaths from falls, and 50% of deaths from fires involved alcohol. Suicide rates are 30 times higher among alcoholics. According to US data from 1934 to 1987, a consumption increase of 1 liter of alcohol per capita brings an increase in the divorce rate of about 20% (*J Stud Alcohol.* 1999). Reduced inhibitions and impulse control lead to family violence, and verbal, emotional, and sexual abuse (especially incest). Alcohol is involved in 38% of all child abuse cases. Some 50% of all police officer deaths occur responding to family disputes, virtually all of which involve alcohol, and 50% of all arrests involve substance abuse. Health problems (for both substance users and their families), accidents, lost productivity and employment, legal costs, and other collateral burdens make the costs of substance abuse astronomical.

Substance Use Disorder Myths

Numerous substance use disorder–perpetuating myths exist, including the following: 1) "It's only beer" to excuse heavy drinking; 2) homeless persons are all alcoholics (less than half have drinking problems); 3) alcoholics are homeless (just 3% to 5% of alcoholics are vagrants; most are employed, married, and seem normal); 4) inebriation is humorous (incapacity is rarely comedic); 5) women rarely become alcoholics (the ratio of men to women is narrowing, and some believe it to be nearly equal now); 6) alcohol is a stimulant (disinhibition merely gives an appearance of liveliness, but alcohol depresses the central nervous system); 7) illegal drugs are the biggest social problem (alcohol problems dwarf those of illicit drug use); 8) only heavy drinkers are alcoholics (it's not the quantity consumed, but rather continued use in spite of serious consequences that best characterizes alcoholism); 9) black coffee will sober up someone (it won't); 10) a couple of drinks helps you relax (it frequently produces problematic disinhibition).

Common Drugs of Abuse

Pharmacological classes of drugs of abuse include the following: 1) alcohol (beer, wine, liquor); 2) cannabis (marijuana, hashish); 3) tranquilizers (benzodiazepines such as *Equanil*, *Librium*, *Miltown*, and *Valium*); 4) sedative/hypnotics (barbiturates such as amobarbital, butabarbital, pentobarbital, and secobarbital); 5) hallucinogens (LSD, mescaline/peyote, and PCP); 6) narcotics (heroin, methadone, opium); 7) stimulants (amphetamines, cocaine, MDMA/"ecstasy"); and 8) solvents/inhalants (e.g., glue, gasoline, aerosol sprays). In 1914, the Harrison Narcotic Act erroneously classified cocaine as a narcotic (i.e., grouped with opium-derived depressants). This legal designation was never revised. However, pharmaceutically and psychoactively, cocaine is a stimulant. Cocaine, in its various forms, is the most common illicitly used drug in the United States. Typically called simply "coke," other street names include flake, snow, toot, blow, nose candy, lady, liquid lady (cocaine and alcohol), speedball (cocaine and heroin), and, in freebase form for smoking, it may also be called crack, rock, and base.

Predominant Historical Perspectives

Historically, substance use disorders have been seen as a moral failing, a "sin," and as evidence of a weak character. Negative labels such as "drunkard," "pot head," and "dope fiend," among others, were popularized, and "treatment" was primarily punitive and socially ostracizing in nature (e.g., "drunk tanks" to get inebriated individuals off the streets to sober up, flop houses to isolate the problem persons). Medically, substance abuse gradually became to be seen as a condition that could not be directly treated as it was a symptom of an underlying problem, such as depression, anxiety, or character disorder, which could be treated. While more progressive, this resulted in treatment success rates of approximately 5%. Late in the 1950s, the American Medical Association finally labeled alcoholism a disease with a variety of contributing genetic, biochemical, endocrinological, and environmental factors that all needed attention in the treatment process. Since that time recovery rates have risen to 60% to 80%.

Categories of Drinking Described by E.M. Jellinek

Jellinek's five categories of drinking are 1) "alpha alcoholism": solely psychological drinking to relieve physical or emotional pain, with minimal physiological symptoms (some remain alpha drinkers for 30 to 40 years; 25% to 50% of AA members are alpha drinkers); 2) "beta alcoholism": marked by the onset of physical deterioration (e.g., cirrhosis, gastritis, neurological compromise), but without psychological or physiological alcohol use disorder (ie, no withdrawal symptoms), and potentially culture-driven if heavy drinking is a common cultural norm; 3) "gamma alcoholism": loss of control, tolerance, and withdrawal symptoms emerge, with the progression from psychological to physiological dependence (Jellinek's four phases of alcohol addiction are actually phases of gamma alcoholism); 4) "delta alcoholism": hidden, often culturally approved alcoholism where alcohol is constantly in the bloodstream and abstinence for even 1 to 2 days is not possible because of withdrawal symptom onset; and 5) "epsilon alcoholism": periodic "binge" drinking (ie, unable to stop once starting) followed by weeks to months of abstinence.

Jellinek's Four Phases of Alcohol Addiction

Jellinek's four phases are: 1) "prealcoholic" phase: evolving from social drinking to drinking for emotional relief and deliberately seeking out drinking situations; 2) "prodromal" phase (prodromal = disease warning): first alcoholic amnesic episode ("blackout"), where standard inebriation cannot be recalled the next day, often followed by a "trial abstinence," a retreat to social drinking, or intensified "need-based" drinking (e.g., sneaking/gulping early drinks; lasting 6 months to 4 to 5 years and terminating with "loss of control"); 3) "crucial" phase: chain-drinking, where alcohol can still be refused but controlled drinking is no longer possible (any cover-up ends, replaced by rationalization and outward efforts of control (e.g., temporary abstinence, changing drinking patterns and/or forms of alcohol); and 4) the "chronic" phase: alcohol dominates life (cravings at roughly 4-hour intervals), and jobs, marriages, and social relationships are lost, binge "benders" occur, tremors and health changes emerge, and the emotional bottom is hit (barring death or organic brain damage).

Categories of Alcoholism Progression by R.L. George

George suggests there are as many as 50 to 60 signs and symptoms of substance use disorder progression. In the "early" stages, substances are abused to obtain relief from worry, emotional, and/or physical pain. The "middle" stages are characterized by "classic" symptoms (e.g., poor work performance, absenteeism, escalating family and finance problems, deteriorating ethical/moral conduct). These stages are optimal for treatment, as physical damage (e.g., brain damage, pre-lethal liver and other changes, outright death) has not yet limited or proscribed treatment options. Only after years of substance abuse (e.g., 20 to 25 years of alcohol abuse) is the "chronic" stage reached, with few people actually living to that hitting bottom point, or being able to recover from it. Recognition of the impact of substance abuse on the physical status, personality, cognition, and motivation of the individual is necessary before proper understanding of the disease nature of the problem can be properly appreciated and accepted.

Nace's Six Constructs of Substance Abuse and Alcoholism

Nace's six constructs are as follows: 1) "psychological dependence" (key thinking changes): unfolding over some 5 years prior to physical dependence and persisting long after any detoxification, characterized by: a) *psychological primacy* (evolution from substance pleasure to demand); b) *self-doubt* (feeling the substance is necessary to cope); c) *sense of loss* (grief-like dread of relinquishing the substance); d) *inability to abstain* (abstinence failures producing a fear they can't quit); 2) "craving": needing the experience of relief (less than the actual drug euphoria = "positive reinforcement"), exacerbated by withdrawal symptoms (ie, avoiding unpleasant feelings and experiences = "negative reinforcement"); key components are affective (dysphoric moods), cognitive (euphoric recollections), compulsive (obsessive thoughts), and physical (sensation-based desires); 3) "loss of control": unpredictable usage; 4) "personality regression": reduced maturity and protective defenses (e.g., poor impulse control, inability to delay gratification, exaggerated grandiosity, impatience, undue passivity), potentially covering preexisting personality pathology; 5) "denial": a primary defense reinforced by cognitive distortions; and 6) "conflicted behaviors": rejecting important relationships, etc.

Substance Use Disorders Among Elderly Persons

Although drug and alcohol use disorder rates tend to decline with aging, alcohol remains a significant problem for some. Drinking for men drops off most dramatically in their mid-70s (50s to 60s is the steepest period of decline for women). Approximately 1% to 2% of women are problem drinkers in their 60s, compared with 5% to 12% of men. The most frequently abused drugs in elderly persons are nicotine and caffeine, followed by over-the-counter pharmaceuticals. Negative experiences from greater cognitive impairment, dysphoria, and other physical symptoms cause older individuals to self-limit illicit drug use. Other major factors of decreased use include the following: 1) early mortality (many drug users don't reach old age); 2) spontaneous recovery (simply deciding to abstain); and 3) underdiagnosis (elderly users appear less socially deviant, and drug abuse symptoms may be accounted for by dementia and/or depression, etc.). Precipitants for continue abuse, among others; include loneliness and isolation, serial losses, health changes, and loss of emotional supports.

Pharmacological Classes of Drugs of Abuse

Drugs of abuse may be grouped into pharmacological "classes," as follows: 1) alcohol (beer, wine, liquor); 2) cannabis (marijuana, hashish); 3) depressants (benzodiazepines, barbiturates); 4) hallucinogens (LSD, mescaline/peyote); 5) narcotics (heroin, methadone, opium); 6) stimulants (amphetamines, MDMA/"ecstasy"); 7) inhalants (solvents, aerosols, and gases). The proper pharmacological category for cocaine (including the freebased form, crack cocaine) is "stimulant." In 1914, with the Harrison Narcotic Act, cocaine was erroneously classified as a "narcotic" (i.e., grouped with opium-derived depressants; see also the Controlled Substances Act of 1970). However, pharmaceutically and psychoactively, cocaine is a stimulant. Cocaine, in its various forms, is currently the most common illicitly used drug in the United States. Typically called simply "coke," street names include flake, snow, toot, blow, nose candy, lady, liquid lady (cocaine and alcohol), speedball (cocaine and heroin), and, in freebase form for smoking, crack, rock, hard, iron, cavvy, and base.

Narcotic

A narcotic is any psychoactive drug that dulls the senses, has anesthetic properties, induces sleep, and in excess produces stupor, coma, or death. The term is commonly associated with the opioids (e.g., morphine, heroin), and is often used by law enforcement and others to refer to any government-controlled psychoactive substance. However, neither of these definitions is sufficient. Common high-potency (and usually injected) narcotics include heroin, morphine, fentanyl, and meperidine (*Demerol*), while low-potency prescription medications, such as codeine, propoxyphene, and oxycodone (*OxyContin*; or combined with acetaminophen, some trade names are *Endocet, Percocet, Roxicet*, or *Tylox*), come primarily in pill form. All are used to treat pain. In situations of overdose, the opiate antagonist naloxone (*Narcan*) can be used to displace narcotic drugs from receptor sites, and reverse the potentially lethal respiratory suppressant effects common to opiates.

Standard Portions of Beer, Wine, and Distilled Spirits

Standard portions of alcoholic beverages are arranged so as to provide roughly equal amounts of total alcohol in each drink. Beer contains approximately 3.5% to 9% alcohol, table wines range from 9% to 12%, dessert ("fortified") wines range from 16% to 20%, and distilled ("hard") liquor averages from 40% to 50% and up to 80% in "fortified" distillates. Once ingested, approximately 20% of the alcohol is absorbed through the stomach, and 80% in the intestines. However, greater concentrations of alcohol and beverages that are carbonated will accelerate absorption, and food in the stomach will reduce the rate of absorption. Elimination of alcohol from the system is accomplished via the kidneys (5%), the lungs (5%), and the liver (90%).

Rate at Which the Liver Can Metabolize Alcohol

The liver breaks down alcohol by "oxidization" into acetic acid. On average, the liver of a 150 lb person can oxidize about 7 grams of pure alcohol per hour. This is the equivalent of 7¾ to 8 ounces of beer, 2½ ounces of wine, and ¾ ounce of distilled spirits. The effects of alcohol intoxication (imbibing faster than the body can metabolize the alcohol) include early symptoms of impaired judgment and decreased inhibition; moderate symptoms (0.01% to 0.3% blood alcohol): reduced control over movement, speech, and vision; more severe symptoms (0.15% to 0.35% blood alcohol): impaired balance, coordination, and reflexes. Blood alcohol concentration (BAC, usually reported as grams of ethanol per 100 grams of blood) of 0.08% is considered intoxicated in most states. A blood alcohol of 0.35% and above can result in death, depending upon the body's level of developed tolerance. Impaired reaction time, motor control, and sensory processing are all factors that contribute to the dangers of drunk driving (killing about 16,000 people each year).

Organ Systems Commonly Damaged by Alcohol

Excessive alcohol consumption can damage virtually every organ system in the human body. While high levels of alcohol consumption can lead to respiratory depression, respiratory arrest, and suffocation due to emesis (vomitus) aspiration, chronic alcoholism is not a leading cause of pulmonary disease. However, alcohol use disorder is the number one cause of liver-related deaths in the United States. Cirrhosis (fibrous scarring) of the liver routinely occurs with chronic alcoholism. Women are particularly prone to injury when more than 2 to 3 drinks a day are consumed. Alcohol is metabolized by two liver enzymes: alcohol dehydrogenase (which converts alcohol to acetaldehyde) and acetaldehyde dehydrogenase (which converts acetaldehyde to acetic acid). Hepatic encephalopathy (compromised brain function from high levels of toxins in the blood due to poor liver function) can also occur. Acute alcohol toxicity can also damage heart muscle (cardiomyopathy), inflame the pancreas (pancreatitis), induce gastrointestinal ulcers and bleeding, produce a 10-fold risk of esophageal cancer, predispose other kinds of cancer, and may lead to hypertension. Alcohol is the leading cause of cardiomyopathy in the United States.

Physical Dependence, Tolerance, and Addiction

The presence of withdrawal symptoms indicates that the individual has developed a physical dependence on the drug. Physical dependence indicates only that the body has integrated a drug in such a way that withdrawal symptoms will result from cessation, a reduced dose, or with administration of an antagonist drug. By contrast, addiction is a psychoneurobiological disease, and typically involves physical dependence on a drug, as well as one or more of the following: 1) an inability to control use of the drug; 2) compulsive use of the drug; 3) continued use of the drug in spite of mental, physical, and/or social harm; and/or 4) a craving for the drug. In addition to pain medications, many other legal drugs can produce physical dependence, including corticosteroids, beta-blockers, antidepressants, and alcohol. Drug tolerance refers to a drug's lessened effectiveness as the body adapts to and overcomes the influence of the drug; sensitization occurs when a drug's effects are magnified with continued use.

Statistics Relevant to Alcohol Use Disorder in the United States

Alcoholism occurs twice as often in males than in females. While alcoholism afflicts people of all demographic categories, those who beginning drinking at 14 years of age or younger are much more likely to develop alcoholism. One in every 13 US adults is alcohol dependent or abuses alcohol. Alcohol abusers drink about half of all the alcohol consumed in the United States, and the socioeconomic and health costs have reached $100 billion annually. In terms of preventable diseases, alcoholism ranks third in the United States, and 5% of all deaths in the United States are due to alcohol use disorder (about 100,000 people annually).

Tolerance to Psychoactive Substances

The two main types of tolerance are: 1) "metabolic tolerance" (the liver's increased production of the enzyme alcohol dehydrogenase, causing rapid alcohol metabolism); and 2) "functional tolerance" (reduced sensitivity to alcohol's effects). Alcohol abuse refers to any harmful use of alcohol. Irregular abusers may not have symptoms of tolerance or dependence.

Sedative-Hypnotic Drugs

Three major categories of sedative-hypnotics: 1) barbiturates; 2) nonbarbiturate sedatives; and 3) the minor tranquilizers (principally, benzodiazepines). Some are used in the treatment of seizure disorders (e.g., pentobarbital [*Nembutal*], phenobarbital [*Luminal*], and secobarbital [*Seconal*]), and some have anesthetic properties. Sedative-hypnotics are abused for their intoxicating, tension-relieving, anxiolytic, and hypnotic (sleep-inducing) effects. Undesirable short-term (15 hours or less) effects include emotional lability, loss of simple body functions, slurred speech, and cognitive and memory impairment. Long-term effects include loss of coordination, vertigo, chronic fatigue, sexual dysfunction, impaired reflexes, breathing disturbances, and menstrual irregularities. Continued use induces both physiological dependence and tolerance, as well as psychological dependence (use in order to "function and cope"). Withdrawal symptoms include anxiety, insomnia, agitation, seizures, and even death.

Benzodiazepines

Benzodiazepines and the newer imidazopyridine drugs are commonly used for treatment of anxiety and insomnia. Fortunately, they also have a "ceiling effect" (as they can only augment gamma-aminobutyric (GABA) neurotransmitter activity, rather than mimicking it outright as others do) and thus present limited danger of fatal overdose. Benzodiazepines with substantial sedating qualities (ie, estazolam, triazolam [*Halcion*]) are frequently prescribed for brief treatment of sleep disorders. Higher doses produce a sense of euphoria, but tolerance readily develops over time. As CNS depressants, benzodiazepines promote the action of the neurotransmitter GABA. Typical effects include changes in emotion, personality, muscle tone, the level of consciousness, and coordination. Long-term use leads to depression, personality changes, aggression, and feelings of fatigue, along with cognitive changes (impaired memory; mostly problems creating and accessing long-term memory), psychomotor impairment (problems driving), personality changes, and passivity.

Cocaine

Cocaine powder (cocaine hydrochloride) can be inhaled into the nasal passages (called "snorting" or "sniffing"), where it is rapidly assimilated into the bloodstream. When dissolved in water, it can be injected intravenously. When heated to free the pure cocaine from the hydrochloride base, the end product has a much lower burning point than cocaine in its "salt" form (ie, cocaine hydrochloride). Thus, when burned, the cocaine will sublimate (transform directly from a solid to a gas, as opposed to a liquid to gas transition) into vapor, which can then be inhaled. Intravenous injected and smoked cocaine each enter the bloodstream virtually at the same rate, and can produce a "high" in less than 10 seconds.

Freebase cocaine (a basic, or nonacidic "alkaloid") is less stable than cocaine hydrochloride (a chemical salt), and it is also more corrosive—both of which make it harder to transport and store. However, it is also more pure, offering a more intense "high" to the user. There are two forms of freebase cocaine (though the term "freebase" usually refers only to the purer version of the two). When cocaine hydrochloride is mixed with baking soda (sodium bicarbonate) and water, and then heated to free the pure cocaine from the hydrochloride base, the end product is called "crack" cocaine. When ammonia and ether are used, the result is a much purer product commonly called "freebase cocaine" because one contains residual baking soda, while the other has no such residue. Both crack and freebase cocaine have much lower burning points than cocaine hydrochloride. Consequently, when heated, the cocaine vapor can be inhaled. Crack is less expensive to produce and buy, intensely addictive, and was particularly popular in the mid-1980s.

The longest high occurs via sniffing or "snorting" the drug: 15 to 30 minutes. Smoked or injected cocaine offers only a 5- to 10-minute high. Intramuscular and subcutaneous injections range between these two. Using greater amounts or more frequently reduces both intensity and duration. The duration is inversely related to the intensity—a shorter high is much more intense than a longer high. When the drug is assimilated more quickly, it produces a greater "rush" that also ends more quickly. When alcohol and cocaine are consumed together, the liver synthesizes "cocaethylene," which intensifies the high but increases the risk of sudden death. Cocaine's stimulant effects induce vascular constriction, rapid heart rate, and fever, with risks of chest pain, cardiac arrest, stroke, seizures, and respiratory failure. Other common symptoms are headaches, abdominal pain, and nausea. Regular users may experience anxiety, irritability, depression, aggression, paranoia, restlessness, panic attacks, loss of appetite, and malnutrition. Prolonged snorting damages mucous membranes and may lead to nasal septum collapse. Needle users may contract HIV/AIDS during needle sharing.

Amphetamines

Street names for amphetamines include speed, cross tops, dexies, pep pills, uppers, bennies, black beauties, bumble bees, co-pilots, footballs, and hearts. Among the most commonly used prescription amphetamines are *Ritalin*, *Cylert*, and *Adderall*, which are used to treat attention deficit hyperactivity disorder in children, adolescents, and adults. The first synthesis of amphetamines (Benzedrine) occurred in 1887, but they were not marketed until 1932. Initially, they were prescribed as inhalers for relief from the symptoms of asthma and for nasal congestion due to colds and hay fever. Later, they were prescribed for obesity, attention deficit disorder, and narcolepsy. However, abuse became commonplace. Amphetamines became particularly popular during World War II, when soldiers were given the drug to fight fatigue and improve morale. Hitler's medical records show that he received eight injections a day of methamphetamine, in spite of the paranoia and unpredictable behavior that accompanies such dosages.

Methamphetamines

Street names include crystal, ice, batu, chalk, shabu, zip, amp, CR, go, glass, pink glass, red rock, tweak, poor man's coke, etc. More commonly, the drug is called simply "meth" or "crystal meth." A derivative of amphetamine, methamphetamine was first discovered in Japan in 1919. It is more potent than amphetamine. In crystalline form, the powder is soluble in water and is easily injected.

It is still legally produced in the United States as *Desoxyn*. Most of the illicit methamphetamine is produced using the phedrine/pseudoephedrine reduction method. Most domestic large-scale production is centered in California, although it is increasingly smuggled into the United States following production in Mexico.

Ice comes in crystal-shaped chunks—much like rock candy, chunks of ice, or broken glass. Ice is high-purity methamphetamine hydrochloride. Methamphetamines are also sold as pills, capsules, and in powder form. The crystalline power is white in color, bitter tasting, and odorless. It can be easily dissolved in water or alcohol. When mixed with water it can readily be injected, or applied to tobacco or marijuana in order to be smoked. Vaporizing easily when heated, the fumes can be inhaled for rapid intoxication. Methamphetamine can be smoked, sniffed ("snorted"), injected, or taken orally. Smoked, it is known as a "cool" smoke (while crack cocaine is known as a "hot" smoke). Ten to fifteen "hits" can be obtained from a single gram of substance. The intoxicating euphoric effects via "snorting" can be felt in approximately 5 minutes, while about 20 minutes are required if the drug is taken orally. If smoked or injected, a more intense "flash" or "rush" occurs lasting only a few minutes.

Formication

A visual hallucinatory disorder in which the abuser believes bugs are crawling on or under the skin—technically referred to as "formication" or "delusional parasitosis." The sensation is caused when profuse sweating (due to the drug use) washes away the skin's natural oils, and the toxins in the drug seek to escape through the skin. Nerve endings under the overdried skin produce the sensation of bugs crawling on the body or under the skin. Psychologically compromised persistent abusers often feel they "see" the "bugs" and dig and pick at themselves (typically on the face and arms), seeking to free the infesting insects. Dirty fingernails and the gouging routinely results in dermal infections, leaving permanent scars much like those from severe chickenpox. Street terms for the disorder include speed bumps, meth sores, and crank bugs.

Mescaline and Hashish

The hallucinogenic mescaline is extracted from the peyote cactus plant (*Lophophora williamsii*). Hashish is a sticky resin harvested from the flowering tops of the female marijuana plant (where the THC is most concentrated). It is most frequently smoked, although it can also be eaten. Marijuana is derived from the hemp plant (*Cannabis sativa*), and is the most frequently abused illicit drug in the United States. Tetrahydrocannabinol (THC) is the active chemical in the plant that produces the psychotropic effects. Via selective germination, THC levels today are far higher than in the past (3% to 5% in leaves; 6% to 12% in the "sinsemilla" or flowering tops; 9% to 20% in "hash oil"). The parts of the plant that are smoked are the plant's leaves, flowers, seeds, stems, and buds. Users smoke the plant as a "joint," or as a "blunt" (a cigar hollowed out and filled with the drug), or through a "bong" (a "water pipe" used to filter, cool, and collect the smoke).

Marijuana

The question of addiction is frequently debated, depending upon the definitions used. Some experts argue that there is no clear withdrawal syndrome, and thus they contend that the term addiction cannot be properly used. Others point to the low but measurable rate of drug dependency that results from prolong usage, as well as certain withdrawal-like symptoms. The US Drug Enforcement Administration (DEA) cites extensive literature and clearly states that THC is addictive. Many other researchers agree. The active ingredient in marijuana (THC) induces the release of dopamine within the brain, producing the intoxicating effects of the drug. Psychoactive properties of this nature can produce an addiction. THC binds to the "cannabinoid receptors" found on various neurons, particularly in areas such as the basal ganglia (involving control over movement), the cerebellum (involving balance and coordination), the cerebral cortex, and the hippocampus (controlling elements of learning and memory).

Medical Cannabis (Marijuana)

While marijuana has been touted as a treatment for a great variety of health problems, it is most commonly used to treat chronic pain, mood disorders, post-traumatic stress syndrome, anorexia, some gastrointestinal problems, and the nausea and vomiting associated with chemotherapy for cancer. Cannabis use tends to stimulate the appetite, so it has also been used in some situations to stimulate the appetite of individuals with failing intake due to various medical and/or health conditions. However, treatment may be complicated by the long half-life of the drug; daily users remain chronically intoxicated (which likely accounts for the "amotivational syndrome" often seen in these users) and memory, coordination, and cognitive functions can also remain impaired.

Hallucinogens

This class of drugs is referred to as hallucinogens. The term entheogens has been proposed for this class of drugs, but is not in routine pharmacological use. The term "psychotics" does not directly refer to a class of medications; hallucinogens can induce psychotic thinking and behavior. Hallucinogens can be derived from natural plant sources, or they can be synthesized via chemical processes in laboratory settings. Although the psychological distortions and other effects of this class of drugs can be problematic in many ways, among the most dangerous effects are impaired judgment and altered perceptions and thinking. Under the influence of hallucinogenic drugs, individuals may think they can undertake dangerous behaviors with impunity (e.g., leaping out of a window to fly, running in front of a train they believe they can control).

Lysergic acid diethylamide (LSD) was first synthesized in 1938 by a Swiss chemist seeking a respiratory and circulatory stimulant, and later explored as a treatment for schizophrenia. In the 1960s Harvard Professor Dr. Timothy Leary referred to LSD as an elixir of psychiatric and creative benefit. Users are particularly drawn to the visual hallucinatory images that follow ingestion of 50 to 150 micrograms of the drug (often 2 to 3 drops of the drug absorbed into a small piece of paper or in a minicapsule or very tiny pill). Intoxication experiences range from simple illusions (e.g., a sense of unreality) to pseudohallucinations (where the user knows the hallucinations are not real) and outright hallucinatory sensations. Currently there is no condition that can be appropriately treated with LSD, even under medical supervision. Since 1966, LSD has been classified as a controlled substance in California, and in 1970 it was included in the US Controlled Substances Act as a Schedule I substance (a drug highly prone to abuse).

After ingestion, the effects typically last about 12 hours; the onset of effects after ingestion emerge in about 30 to 90 minutes. LSD is a slightly bitter, odorless, and colorless substance that induces extremely unpredictable effects, many of which are dependent on the dosage, surrounding environment, mood, personality, and expectations of the user. Although the drug is not deemed addictive, users can develop a tolerance (requiring higher doses over time for the same effect). The hallucinatory and delusional effects can be compelling, such as "crossover" sensations (e.g., hearing colors and seeing sounds). However, fear, anxiety, and terror-inducing experiences are not uncommon. Persistent anxiety and lingering psychoses (e.g., schizophrenia symptoms, severe depression, long-term flashbacks, other mental health problems) may endure long after the drug has been cleared from the body. Physical effects routinely include anorexia (loss of appetite) insomnia, xerostomia (dry mouth), tachycardia, hypertension, and diaphoresis (sweating). Deaths typically arise from panic, psychotic, delusional, and paranoid reactions leading to self-destructive events.

Psychotic episodes may include experiences such as flashbacks, though the term psychosis is not the best description for flashbacks. Delusions are false beliefs retained in spite of evidence to the contrary. Psychiatric distortions come in many varieties, of which flashbacks are only one kind. Users of the powerful hallucinogen LSD (lysergic acid diethylamide) are particularly prone to flashbacks, which can occur without warning days to over a year after exposure to the drug. Immersive flashbacks (as opposed to the simpler recollection-based flashbacks) can be particularly disturbing, as there is a transient loss of proper orientation to both time and place. If the original hallucinatory experience was deeply disturbing and/or distressing, the flashbacks can be decidedly debilitating.

Ecstasy is a "designer drug" synthesized in a laboratory setting, while psilocybin is naturally derived from mushrooms ("magic mushrooms" or "shrooms"), which are typically eaten or smoked. Psilocybin's effects are fully felt within 1 to 2 hours of ingestion, and fully subside within 6 to 7 hours. Peyote is a small cactus plant with hallucinogenic properties. The top of the cactus can be cut away and dried. The dried buttons are chewed or boiled in water to produce an extremely bitter, typically nausea-inducing, psychoactive tea. Effects are fully felt within 1 to 2 hours of ingestion, and fully subside within 6 to 10 hours (some reports say as much as 14 hours). To avoid the bitter, nauseous effects, the dried peyote may be powdered and put in capsules. Mescaline, an alkaloid, is the active hallucinatory substance found in peyote. Regular users develop a tolerance lasting for a few days, and will develop a cross-tolerance with LSD and other psychedelic substances. Peyote and mescaline are illegal in the United States except for ceremonial use in certain religious groups such as the Native American Church.

Symptoms of anxiety and paranoia are the most frequent symptoms of negative experience, typically referred to by users as a "bad trip." Flashbacks (an involuntary, unexpected return to the effects of the substance weeks or even months later) are relatively uncommon, but can occur. Schizophrenic symptoms (e.g., persistent auditory hallucinations and delusions) may emerge during use of the drug, and may linger with any use. However, lingering symptoms tend to be limited to those with preexisting psychiatric conditions. Delusions (false beliefs) of a negative nature can occur during any "trip," but are not among the most common symptoms. The risk of accidental injury also exists during any intoxication experience, but is much higher when the hallucinations and emotional sensations induced by the drug are particularly frightening and negative. Panic attacks and feelings of terror can also occur during any negative intoxication experience, and/or may follow it some time later, but these symptoms are not among those most common to a bad trip.

Most users hope to experience elation, awe, bliss, mystical or spiritual feelings, and connectedness with others and the universe. Substance abusers seeking an increased sense of power, energy, and excitement tend to take stimulants rather than hallucinogenics. Hallucinogenic (or psychedelic) substances are typically used to enhance sensory experiences of a pleasant nature. They are also used by specific groups (such as Native Americans) in pursuit of spiritual enlightenment and to draw closer to nature and the universe. In this context, both psilocybin and mescaline are considered "entheogens," producers of spiritual experiences. Low doses usually induce positive changes in thought, emotions, and sensations, often characterized as euphoria, bliss, and awe (yet most frequently without loss of connectedness to basic reality). Higher doses induce more intense hallucinations that eclipse the normal sense of reality. At these higher doses, negative experiences, anxiety, paranoia, fear, and even feelings of terror are more likely to occur and more likely to create problems that may persist after the influence of the drug has subsided.

Psychoactive Inhalants

The term "inhalant," in the context of substance use disorder, refers to household and commercial products that can be abused by drawing the product's fumes into the lungs by inhaling via the mouth ("huffing") or nose ("sniffing"). The inhaled vapors induce a form of intoxication when exposed in sufficient quantities over an adequate length of time. Volatile solvents are among the substances most commonly abused, along with fluorocarbons and butane-like gases (e.g., cleaning solutions, correction fluid, adhesives, lighter fluids, gasoline, paint products). The products may be inhaled directly from the container, or via a plastic bag or saturated cloth. Some inhalants must first be released by heating. Inhalants depress the CNS, much like alcohol, causing feelings of euphoria and excitement, and a sense of "floating" and increased power.

Intoxication usually occurs quite rapidly (within 5 minutes), and lasts 5 to 30 minutes. To stay high, users may abuse for prolonged periods. The low cost of inhalants makes them easily available to the poor and children (ages 6 to 16). About 10% to 20% of those aged 12 to 17 have tried inhalants, peaking between the seventh and ninth grades. Signs of intoxication include vertigo (dizziness); nystagmus (rapid, involuntary, side-to-side eye movements); slurred speech; poor coordination and an unsteady gait; lethargy; psychomotor retardation; tremors; weakness; blurred or double vision; and euphoria (feeling giddy). Serious problems include stupor or coma, sickness, and death. Abusers may become unable to control of their body for 15 to 45 minutes after sniffing, and can severely damage the brain, heart, liver, and kidneys. Finally, "Sudden Sniffing Death" can occur during or right after abusing inhalants, as the heart beats rapidly but unevenly, leading to cardiac arrest. Even first-time abusers can die.

Review Video: Inhalants
Visit mometrix.com/academy and enter code: 926725

Anabolic and Androgenic Steroids

Anabolic and androgenic steroids are abused in the effort to quickly gain and maintain muscle mass. The term "androgenic" refers to male characteristics, and "anabolic" refers to muscle building. These forms of steroids are intended to enhance male characteristics and add muscle. With more than 100 forms of steroids available, patterns of use emerge. Cycling refers to starting and stopping steroids for set time periods over several weeks or months. Pyramiding refers to the slow escalation of steroid usage (including the dose, frequency, and time) to a mid-cycle peak, and then tapering back to a point of terminating the cycle. Stacking refers to the combination of several different kinds of steroids in an attempt to maximize their effectiveness (ideally, synergistically).

One side effect of anabolic-androgenic steroid abuse is stunted growth in adolescents. Other potential consequences of abuse include hypertension, cardiac disease, blood cholesterol imbalance, liver tumors and liver cancer, and HIV and hepatitis infection from needle sharing. Men may experience testicular withering, low sperm count and infertility, acne, baldness, gynecomastia (breast development), and a greater risk for prostate cancer. Women may experience disrupted menstruation, clitoral enlargement, a lowered voice range, facial hair growth, and male-pattern baldness. All users may develop mood swings, manic-like symptoms that tend toward violence, and poor judgment due to feelings of invincibility. Cessation of the drugs can result in withdrawal symptoms of severe depression, lethargy, anorexia, insomnia, poor sex drive, paranoid jealousy, delusions, and marked irritability.

Designer Drugs

Designer drugs are laboratory preparations that closely copy a controlled substance. Another term for designer drug is analog because the designer version is an analog of, or closely analogous to, the drug it is designed to mimic. Although designer drugs are synthesized in laboratory settings, not all synthesized drugs are designer drugs. In many cases, designer drugs are significantly more potent that the drugs they were designed to resemble. For example, some designer drugs are easily twice as powerful as heroin or cocaine, yet often cost much less to produce. Places where designer drugs are likely to be encountered are raves and nightclubs. Currently, the most frequently abused designer drug is 3,4-methylendioxymethamphetamine (ecstasy).

Ecstasy

The designer drug ecstasy is an "empathogen/entactogen," as it readily produces a sense of "bonding" and emotional connection. Ecstasy (also known as MDMA, XTC, DOM, and MMDA) is derived from the amphetamine family. MDA (methylenedioxyamphetamine) is a closely related empathogen/entactogen. Ecstasy has both stimulant and sensory distortion properties, but it is not a true hallucinogen. Users do not experience frank hallucinations, but rather marked distortions in time and perception. The drug is produced in both tablet and capsule forms for oral ingestion, but others may snort or inject ecstasy. When orally ingested, the effects of the drug last about 4 to 6 hours. The actual effects of ecstasy may vary widely, as ecstasy tablets or capsules often contain other undisclosed ingredients, including cocaine, ephedrine, caffeine, methamphetamine, and/or dextromethorphan.

Dopamine, norepinephrine, and serotonin are all stimulated for neuronal release by ecstasy (acetylcholine, however, is not stimulated). Serotonin, in particular, is released in large amounts, even as its synthesis is inhibited. The result can be an enduring depletion of serotonin over time. As serotonin aids in the regulation of appetite, emotions/mood, pain, and sleep, this depletion may be the cause of the persistent behavioral problems that moderate to high abusers of this drug often experience. While abusers often take ecstasy to boost energy at parties and dances, the long-term effects can be devastating. Already a highly idiosyncratic drug (effects vary widely from person to person), the drug also has a wide range of problematic effects (including amnesia, hallucinations, paranoia, and even death—sometimes even with the first use). Ecstasy can cause brain damage and has been implicated in numerous subsequent psychiatric disorders, including severe anxiety and depression, obsessions, paranoia, and sleep disruption, to name a few.

Ketamine

Ketamine has been around for more than 30 years, and is used medically as an anesthetic. It may be used for premedication, sedation, and induction and maintenance of general anesthesia. It may also be used for the treatment of chronic pain as it is a potent analgesic, either by itself or combined with other potent analgesics. More recently, it has been used as an antidepressant for treatment-resistant symptoms. Initially used only in veterinary medicine, over the past two decades its general anesthetic, analgesic (pain relieving), and sedative properties became more widely known. Structurally related to PCP (a drug known for inducing vivid hallucinations), ketamine has a tendency to produce a feeling of an out-of-body experience. However, also like PCP, the effects it produces are highly unpredictable and potentially dangerous. For years, ketamine was not a controlled substance, but in 1999 was placed under Schedule III of the Controlled Substances Act by the Drug Enforcement Administration.

Gamma-Hydroxybutyrate (GHB)

Gamma-hydroxybutyrate (GHB) has no accepted medical use. A certain form of GHB (sodium oxybate; trade name: *Xyrem*) is used to treat narcolepsy (a chronic sleep disorder). However, the use of *Xyrem* is very tightly restricted. Those who abuse GHB (primarily body builders and party attendees) claim that it is, variously, a strength enhancer, a euphoriant, and an aphrodisiac. It has also gained notoriety as a "date rape drug" because of its amnesia-inducing effects.

Pharmacologically, GHB is a CNS depressant, and it can be lethal if used with alcohol or other depressants. Street names include blue nitro, cherry meth, easy lay, gamma g, liquid ecstasy, and poor man's heroin.

GHB can easily be slipped into drinks and food because it has no color (it looks exactly like water) and no smell. It does, however, have a slightly salty taste, but that may be easily masked or explained away. Even a very small amount of GHB may cause a person to experience "retrograde amnesia" (forgetting events prior to ingestion) or to "black out" (become unconscious). The risk of overdose is high, as the difference between the dose to get "high" (or subdue a date) and a life-threatening dose is very small, and mixing the drug with alcohol is extremely dangerous. A sedative-hypnotic, at low doses, the drug causes users to feel very euphoric and relaxed. The effects are felt in 10 to 15 minutes and may last for 2 to 3 hours. At higher doses, users may experience dizziness, nausea and vomiting, disorientation, seizures, respiratory depression, severe drowsiness, unconsciousness, and even coma or death.

Rohypnol (Flunitrazepam)

From the benzodiazepine class of drugs, *Rohypnol* (flunitrazepam) is sometimes used medically to treat insomnia. It is also a powerful sedative, anticonvulsant, anxiolytic, amnesic, and muscle relaxant. It is 7 to 10 times stronger than *Valium*, with primary effects evident some 15 to 20 minutes after ingestion and lasting about 4 to 6 hours. Residual effects may persist for 12 hours or more. It has been a Schedule IV controlled substance since 1984 because of its high potential for abuse. Once dissolved in a beverage it has no color, odor, or taste, and it readily induces amnesia, making it a classic date rape drug. It will also enhance the high of heroin and ease the crash following cocaine use. *Rohypnol* (flunitrazepam) is most commonly abused via oral ingestion. However, it may also be snorted as a powder by crushing the tablets. It is frequently combined with alcohol, whereupon both enhance the other's toxic effects. Used with marijuana, users may experience a "floating" sensation. When combined with cocaine, it produces a fast hit followed by a mellow state. *Rohypnol* may cause gastrointestinal problems, confusion, drowsiness, dizziness, slurred speech, and loss of coordination and motor control. Consequently, it greatly impairs reaction time and driving skills. Higher doses may produce respiratory depression. Persistent use can cause physical dependence, and abrupt cessation may lead to a withdrawal syndrome. Street names include date rape drug; forget pill; Mexican valium; roachies; roofies; and ruffies.

Levels of Controlled Substances

Drugs that may be abused are regulated by the US Drug Enforcement Administration (DEA) via the Controlled Substances Act (CSA), Title II of the Comprehensive Drug Abuse Prevention and Control Act of 1970, and the Controlled Substances Act of 1990. Schedule I: no recognized medical use; high abuse and dependency potential. Special licensing is required, primarily for research. Examples include mescaline, LSD, heroin, and marijuana. Schedule II: recognized medical utility; high potential for abuse and dependency. Examples: morphine, cocaine, pentobarbital, oxycodone, and methadone. Schedule III: recognized medical utility; moderate risk of abuse and dependency. Examples include glutethimide and various codeine-based analgesics. Schedule IV: high medical utility; limited risk of abuse and dependency. Examples include chloral hydrate, meprobamate, and oxazepam. Schedule V: recognized medical utility; low abuse/addiction potential. Examples include prescribed medications with minimal codeine or diphenoxylate. Schedule V drugs vary greatly by state. Some states have a Schedule VI, covering substances of abuse with little or no potential for addiction (e.g., glue, ibuprofen, penicillin).

Various Ideologies Driving the Diagnosis and Treatment of Substance Use Disorder

Biological, behavioral, and psychological perspectives can shape substance use disorder treatment. A biologically oriented clinician might focus on the biological processes underlying substance use disorder and utilize a medical intervention, for example, naltrexone hydrochloride (marketed as *Revia*, *Depade*, and *Vivitrol* in an extended-release formulation) is an opiate antagonist that decreases alcohol cravings and blocks the effects of opioid medications and street drugs, and disulfiram (marketed as *Antabuse*) creates unpleasant symptoms when alcohol is ingested. A behavioral clinician might focus on the use of alcohol and/or opioids to cope with physical pain and malaise, and adopt a behavioral intervention. A psychological orientation could focus on a history of post-traumatic stress from a military tour of duty, in which the substances used are an attempt to mask emotional pain and distressing recollections. The most effective treatment approach, however, would incorporate all three ideologies, to address all issues and maximize the potential for success.

Evolution of Popular Views

In the past, excessive use of any substance was seen as a mark of poor character, deficient self-control, and a lack of meaningful values. Later, "biological" models propagated the ideas of addiction being: 1) an illness or disease; 2) neurobiological regulatory problems resulting in impulse control problems; 3) genetic predispositions ("biogenetic vulnerability"); and 4) neuroadaptation and reward system deficiencies. "Psychological" models include: 1) behavioral excess (social pressure and reinforcement contingencies); 2) poor judgment (naiveté and a failure to understand consequences); and 3) psychological deficits (emotional and personality problems leading to self-medication); 4) psychodynamic neuroticism (intrapsychic conflicts with problematic developmental roots); and 5) flawed thought patterns (e.g., misunderstanding indices of risk and probability). "Social" models include: 1) psychosocial (social and moral) constraints that induce addictive issues; and 2) a public health perspective (addiction arises in the social context and the shared societal costs are the focus).

Addiction

Addiction is characterized by the following: a) a sense of craving or compulsion for an associated "high"; b) a loss of personal control over the behavior/substance used; and c) continuation of the behavior in spite of negative consequences. Currently there is no "gold standard" for producing a diagnosis of addiction, as confusion still exists around myths of mental illness and simple intemperate behaviors that produce adverse consequences. Further, clinician biases also remain significant. The *DSM-5* provides a classification/organizational scheme, but the clinician is the one who must make an actual diagnosis. Biopsychosocial formulations include: 1) biological components (ie, tolerance and/or withdrawal symptoms); 2) psychological components (e.g., loss of control, post-abuse distress); and 3) social components (adverse social consequences, such as DWI arrests, or loss of jobs and/or relationships).

Addiction Syndrome

Initiation is the first stage, including primary prevention programs focused on education and information about long-term consequences. Second stage: Positive consequences, requiring secondary prevention (e.g., further education and counseling to emphasize costs and poor outcomes). Third stage: Part I: Negative experiences (without awareness = pre-contemplation), requiring awareness enhancement and overcoming resistance, due to unawareness that addiction is the source of the negative experiences. Part II: Adverse consequences (awareness begins = contemplation), requiring tertiary prevention (outpatient counseling, self-help groups to prepare for change, and acute inpatient services if a crisis erupts). Fourth stage: Turning point(s), including preparation and orientation to change (outpatient/inpatient services: self-help, 12-step, partial care, and detoxification as needed). Fifth stage: Active quitting (all as in stage 4, and chemical substitutions, counseling, and residential care if required). Sixth stage: Relapse prevention and maintenance (self-help, 12-step, outpatient, and residential care if no/limited social support).

Behavioral Conditioning Influences in the Development of Addiction

The removal of a stimulus that increases the likelihood of a response that will remove the stimulus again is known as "negative reinforcement." The opposite, or "positive reinforcement," occurs when the presentation of a stimulus increases the likelihood of a response that will engage the stimulus again. In situations of drug-seeking behavior, classical (Pavlovian) conditioning can be observed when the appearance of related but previously neutral stimuli (e.g., the presence of drug-use paraphernalia, drug-using friends, a drug-abuse environment) come to evoke a decidedly positive or negative behavioral response. A functional understanding of conditioned stimuli can play a significant role in either drug avoidance or relapse. Drug-induced euphoria, when paired with a distinctive environment, can produce a "conditioned place preference" (or, with a negative experience, a "conditioned place aversion").

Brain Pathway Most Relevant to Drug Abuse

The medial forebrain bundle is the brain pathway most relevant to drug abuse. Various other areas of the brain (e.g., the hindbrain and midbrain) have "projections" that connect to one or more parts of this nerve bundle pathway, which is integral to behavior motivation and various rewarding neural stimuli. A particular subset of "projections" is known as the "mesocorticolimbic dopamine pathway," which connects to the midbrain's "ventral tegmental area" (VTA) and the "nucleus accumbens" (NA), where dopamine release (and the associated reward stimulus) becomes elevated with exposure to numerous drugs of abuse. Other less significant areas of the brain that nevertheless contribute meaningfully to the reward system via dopamine release include the frontal cortex, the limbic cortex, and the amygdala. Additional neurotransmitters such as serotonin, GABA, and glutamate also augment and enhance the brain's reward system. In particular, the interaction of multiple neuronal and neurotransmitter systems serves to activate the "extended amygdale," which produces common (natural and drug reward) neural substrates for numerous aspects of the brain's reward system.

Neurotransmitters with Increased Synaptic Availability from the Use of Stimulant Drugs

The neurotransmitters are Serotonin, Dopamine, and Norepinephrine. Indirect sympathomimetics, such as cocaine, ecstasy (MDMA [3,4-methylenedioxymethamphetamine]), methamphetamine, and amphetamine, are all "psychomotor stimulants" that readily induce physical activity and euphoria, and decease feelings of hunger and fatigue. Cessation, however, leads to an initial "crash" characterized by irritability, low energy, and disrupted sleep. Following the crash, a withdrawal syndrome is experienced involving feelings of dysphoria, anxiety, apathy, and a craving for more of the drug. The primary reinforcing effects of psychomotor stimulants are directly due to increased dopamine availability within the mesolimbic system. In contrast to these, GABA (gamma-aminobutyric acid) is an inhibitory neurotransmitter that is directly affected by the presence of the central nervous system depressant alcohol.

Opioid Receptor Antagonists

It decreases heroin use. Heroin is an opioid drug. Opioid drugs are naturally derived from the opium poppy, and provide opium, morphine, and codeine. Synthetically (laboratory) created opioids include meperidine, methadone, and oxycodone, among others. Heroin is a semisynthetic opioid, as it is an altered version of morphine (diacetylmorphine). The name "heroin" was a trademark of Bayer Drug Company, who marketed the product as an alternative cough suppressant to morphine in 1895. All opioid drugs have analgesic (pain relieving), antitussive (cough suppressing), and euphoria-inducing properties. They interact with both opioid and dopamine receptors to produce reward and reinforcement outcomes. In addition, nicotine, alcohol, and THC (tetrahydrocannabinol, the primary psychoactive compound in marijuana) can also access the opioid reward system in varying degrees.

Nicotine

Nicotine is a stimulant. Nicotine's stimulant effects include decreased appetite and fatigue, anxiolysis (reduced anxiety), enhanced alertness, and increased physical activity. Nicotine also indirectly activates transmission and release of dopamine via the mesolimbic system. Dopamine release is very rapid, and has an extremely rapid dopamine-reward reinforcement response in the brain. Nicotine addiction treatment medications such as *Chantix* (varenicline) and *Zyban* (bupropion) are, respectively, a dopamine receptor antagonist and a dopamine reuptake inhibitor—both of which can reduce the desire for nicotine. Nicotine withdrawal symptoms include depressed mood, irritability, headaches, and nicotine craving. Nicotine relapse is common because of issues of dependence, habituation rituals, and conditioned place and time preferences, and because nicotine is a direct acetylcholine receptor agonist; it stimulates both the dopamine and endogenous opioid peptide systems.

Endogenous Neurotransmitter System(s) That Play a Role in the Behavioral Effects of Alcohol

All three are influenced by alcohol and contribute to the behavioral effects. Research reveals that there are multiple neurochemical substrates (systems) that are involved in effectuating the intoxicating effects of sedative-hypnotic drugs, such as alcohol, benzodiazepines, and barbiturates. The intoxicating effects of these drugs include anxiolysis, disinhibition, hypnosis, mild euphoria, and sedation. Cessation results in "hangover" symptoms such as blurred vision, dysphoria, headache, nausea, sleep disruption, and tremors. Neurotransmitter systems involved include GABA (via antagonists at the $GABA_A$ receptor subtype), glutamate (by blocking receptors and thereby increasing serotonin transmission), and opioid peptide neurotransmitters (which act as endogenous agonists that are essential to achieve an opiate reward).

Psychoactive Ingredient in Marijuana

THC (delta-9-tetrahydrocannabinol). The cannabinoid receptors are activated by a neurotransmitter called anandamide. Cannabinoid receptors are scattered in varying densities throughout the brain. As with many drugs of abuse, THC also activates the mesolimbic dopamine transmission system and produces similar effects. These include a lowered threshold to the brain's reward system, a predisposition to continued use, and the development of conditioned place preferences. More than 80 forms of THC are known, and coupled with varying modes of entry (eating vs smoking), the effects can vary. Mild cannabis intoxication typically makes the user feel euphoric, relaxed, sociable, and hungry. Some users become uninhibited, talkative, or giggly, while the hallucinogenic properties can heighten color and sound awareness. Negative effects may include acute anxiety and paranoia. Addiction occurs in 9% to 25% or more of users, depending on age of initiation and frequency of use. Withdrawal symptoms include irritability, sleeplessness, decreased appetite, anxiety, and drug craving. Long-term use is associated with anxiety, depression, and a greater likelihood of schizophrenia.

Chronic Drug Intake

Chronic drug use induces numerous neurological changes. First, intracellular signaling pathways may become "upregulated" (ie, increasing in numbers and/or capacity), resulting in changes in brain activity. Second, neurogenesis (the production of new neurons) in the hippocampus is decreased, potentially leading to altered brain structure and function. Third, the morphology (shape and appearance) of neuronal dendrites (the branching arms receiving signals between neurons) becomes altered (shrinking with opiate use and overgrowing with stimulants), dramatically altering neural function and capacity. In rodents, all these changes appear to persist for 4 or more months, with changes that reflect withdrawal and cessation effects (e.g., fatigue, lethargy, dysphoria) and tend toward drug use relapse for symptom relief. Fifth, drug use and withdrawal produce stress responses and biochemical changes in ways that predispose to drug use.

Influences That Motivate Progression from Recreational Drug Use to Substance Use Disorder

Key mediating influences that motivate progression from recreational drug use to substance use disorder dependence include: a) alleviation of emotional and/or physical distress; b) habitual stimuli associations (place, people, etc.); and c) escalating pleasure-seeking needs. The "Opponent Process Theory" suggests that positive affective/intoxication "A-Processes" (activation of neurological rewards) wane via neuroadaptation (e.g., tolerance) even as aversive "B-Processes" such as withdrawal symptoms and/or hyperalgesia (increased sensitivity to pain) increase along with escalating stress- and anxiety-inducing CRF pathways in the brain. The shift to compulsive use is complete once the "hedonic set point" is breeched, when A-Processes are low and B-Processes are high, requiring ever more frequent use and higher doses. Processes of "allostasis" (the body's attempt to retain balance by way of change) may sometimes produce a protracted withdrawal configuration, making efforts to abstain more difficult and the need for compulsive intake more insistent.

Physiologically Addictive Substances

Three key features of physiologically addictive substances are: 1) they have similar mechanisms of action (ie, tending to stimulate the brain's reward system by increasing synaptic dopamine in mesolimbic projections, and targeting drug reinforcement areas of the brain, such as the mesocorticolimbic system and/or extended amygdala); 2) they alter behavioral motivation via adaptive biological changes in neural circuitry; and 3) those who use them tend to exhibit similar use/abuse patterns. Compulsively abused drugs largely are only alcohol, nicotine, marijuana, certain sedative-hypnotics, and the psychomotor stimulants (e.g., amphetamines, cocaine). The route of administration can predispose to addiction (ie, routes with a more rapid and stronger "highs" are more likely to induce addiction), while slow-release drugs such as ADHD-treating methylphenidate and long-acting methadone are rarely abused. Although all addictive drugs stimulate brain reward and dopamine release (some directly and others indirectly), they may act through different brain areas and/or neural receptors.

Withdrawal

During withdrawal from opiates, sedative-hypnotics (including alcohol), and psychostimulants (including nicotine), the brain's reward threshold is increased. This indicates a persistent dysphoric state that other normal rewards cannot readily penetrate. By contrast, these same drugs abnormally lower the reward threshold when acutely administered. Prolonged usage alters the brains "internal landscape" profoundly, not only in areas of the brain that are directly affected biochemically, but in collateral systems recruited to restore homeostasis. Mesolimbic neurochemistry is explicitly affected. Drug-induced increases in extracellular levels of neurotransmitters such as dopamine, serotonin, and norepinephrine are followed by drops to subnormal levels following drug cessation. The result is particularly profound dysphoria with cessation.

Both drug use and withdrawal will activate the stress response, including activation of the sympathetic nervous system and the endocrine (hormone) system, and reduced immune function and insulin sensitivity. These changes may predispose a return to drug use. For example, alcohol, nicotine, opioids, THC, and psychostimulants induce stress by activating the pituitary glands release of corticotropin-releasing factor (CRF), which elevates anxiety and stress. Secondarily activated "anti-reward" systems in the brain (e.g., dopamine-inhibiting dynorphin, and reductions in the natural anxiolytic NPY) also result in lost pleasure and increased anxiety. Stress also sensitizes various mesolimbic neurotransmitters and hormones (e.g., dopamine, glutamate, CRF), which reinforce drug use via enhanced positive reinforcing effects and facilitate negative effects. Although some biological changes may be transient, with chronic use, behavioral sensitization (the functional predisposition to relapse) develops and lasts up to a year. Cross-sensitization between psychosocial stressors and drugs may predispose relapse for much longer periods.

Calming and Anxiety-Reducing Effects of Alcohol

The primary action of alcohol in the brain involves enhancement of the agonist function of the GABA (gamma-aminobutyric acid) inhibitory neurotransmitter. Potentiation of GABA-mediated brain inhibition results in the anxiolytic and sedative effects of ethanol on the brain. However, the more addictive properties of alcohol use arise from its stimulation of the brain's reward system. As the level of alcohol rises in the blood, it enters the brain and stimulates a commensurate rise in dopamine. This is the reward paradigm described as "feeling a buzz." Alcohol also interferes with glutamate receptor function, and when reaching behaviorally relevant concentrations, ataxia and memory and learning problems become evident. Withdrawal peaks at 2 to 3 days after cessation, with symptoms including tremors, anxiety, hyperactivity, insomnia, and agitation. Severe withdrawal may demonstrate "delirium tremens" symptoms, with the added symptoms of rapid heart and respiratory rates and elevated blood pressure. Withdrawal symptoms wane in 4 to 5 days, but cravings may persist from weeks to years.

Psychomotor Stimulants

Psychomotor stimulants are best known for the sense of euphoria, well-being, and energy that they produce, but also for their weight-loss (anorexia) and sleep-fighting (insomnia) properties. All psychomotor stimulants also increase attention, heart rate, blood glucose, and blood pressure, and dilate the pupils and bronchioles in the lungs. Psychomotor stimulants can have legitimate uses; even cocaine is used for its local anesthetic and vasoconstrictive properties, such as in the treatment of attention-deficit hyperactivity disorder (ADHD). Of the stimulants, methylphenidate enters the bloodstream more slowly, and other stimulants used medically are typically produced in a time-release form to limit issues of abuse and dependence.

Quickest Route of Stimulant Administration to Achieve Intoxication

Injection (needles). However, time to intoxication from smoking is essentially equal to injection. Snorting provides a slower and less intense "high" that lasts longer. Ingestion of cocaine (coca leaves) provides a particularly slow intoxication rate that is mild in nature, as bioavailability is very low. Smoked or intravenously injected cocaine produces an intense intoxication almost immediately, but it lasts only 20 to 30 minutes (half-life, 30 to 40 minutes). When methamphetamine is smoked, it also peaks virtually immediately, but the half-life is 8 to 10 hours. Methylphenidate peaks very slowly, with effects persisting 3 to 6 hours in a "regular" preparation, and up to 8 hours in sustained-release form.

Anorexia

Because tolerance to the appetite-suppressant properties of stimulants tends to develop early on, these drugs are of limited value in the treatment of obesity. Psychomotor stimulants all work similarly, increasing the synaptic availability of the monoamine neurotransmitters (dopamine, norepinephrine, and serotonin). Cocaine blocks their reuptake equally, while amphetamines displace them, and methylphenidate has both blocking and releasing actions. All make dopamine more available, and thus can be addicting. Methylphenidate, however, is very slow acting and the intoxication is not as comparatively intense. Thus, it is not as likely to produce addiction. Indeed, where used properly, to treat ADHD for example, children using this medication are actually less likely to become drug users when compared with the population on the whole. Overdose of psychomotor stimulants can lead to hallucinations (e.g., formication) and schizophrenia-like symptoms, and severe overdose can be lethal, from seizures (amphetamines or cocaine), hyperthermia (amphetamines), or cardiovascular events (via both drugs), such as stroke or heart attack.

Principal Medical Use for Narcotics

Pain control. While narcotic (opiate) drugs, such as morphine, are primarily used to treat pain, they are abused for the euphoric "dreamy" state they induce. All narcotics have respiratory depressant effects, which is the most common cause of death in overdose. They also slow gastrointestinal motility (inducing constipation), cause ciliary body constriction in the eye (causing pinpoint pupils), have antitussive (cough suppressant) properties, and may cause pruritus (itching). Heroin, a pseudo-synthetic opiate, differs from morphine largely in the rate in which it enters the brain (faster). A fully synthetic opiate, fentanyl treats breakthrough pain not otherwise easily controlled. It comes as a pain-relieving injectable or sustained-release skin patch. Buprenorphine and methadone are partial and full opiate agonists, respectively. They also have analgesic properties, as well as withdrawal-suppressing effects for those being treated for opiate addiction. Codeine is an isomer of methylated morphine, and as a low-efficacy analgesic it is typically used for the treatment of mild pain and cough suppression.

Nonaddictive Opiate Drug

Both loperamide and diphenoxylate have no analgesic properties and are considered nonaddictive opiates. Both are marketed primarily as antidiarrheals. However, the use of stronger, dependency-producing narcotics is very much acceptable in certain medical situations, particularly at or near the end of life. Even so, in most situations, it is preferable to use narcotics with low addictive properties and long-acting pharmacology. Methadone provides both of these, as it does not readily induce a "high" and is extremely long-acting (18 to 24 hours). Narcotic use in medical settings to treat pain may produce transient dependence (ie, withdrawal symptoms if stopped abruptly, requiring a "weaning" process), but virtually never produces addictive cravings in anyone but former drug abusers. The recent popularity of addictive oxycodone (*OxyContin*) emerged when it was discovered that biting down on a time-release capsule could produce a rapid drug release and a "high." The drug had been used more frequently to control pain in situations where codeine was poorly effective.

Introduction of the Term Alcoholism

Dr. Magnus Huss used the term in 1849 to describe the cluster of common alcohol abuse symptoms. However, the popular term of the day was "inebriety" (e.g., opium inebriety, alcohol inebriety). Although "sober houses" were proposed by Dr. Benjamin Rush in 1790, it was not until 1857 that the first "inebriate home" was opened in Boston (and in Chicago in 1863). They utilized voluntary stays and subsequent involvement in support groups. The first "inebriate asylum" opened in 1864, offering the first medically oriented treatment in the United States. It relied upon coercion for patients (multiyear legal commitments). The American Association for the Study and Cure of Inebriety was the first professional association of addiction treatment providers and was established in New York City in 1870, and by 1876 the association began publication of the "Quarterly Journal of Inebriety." Inebriety treatment was soon a profit-making endeavor, and the first of more than 120 Keeley Institute franchises was founded in 1879 by Dr. Leslie Keeley.

Cause of the Collapse of Most Addiction Treatment Programs Between 1900 and 1920

Key causes included: 1) exposés of ethical abuses; 2) ideological treatment schisms; 3) leadership attrition due to death and economic downturns; 4) a lack of treatment efficacy studies; and 5) public pessimism. Concurrent with the "for-profit" expansion of treatment in the 1870s and 1880s, home "addiction cures," urban religious "missions," "inebriate colonies," and city hospital "inebriate wards" began to be established. However, an addiction "cure" exposé in 1905 to 1906 revealed that most over-the-counter treatments for alcohol and drug inebriety actually contained high concentrations of alcohol, cannabis, cocaine, and morphine. Public cynicism and pessimism ensued, and programs began closing in the following years. People with addictive problems were soon shunted into "foul wards" in urban hospitals, insane asylums, and inebriate penal colonies. What few treatment efforts continued often resulted in profound iatrogenic damage to those suffering with addiction. Indiscriminate sterilization, serum and bromide therapies, chemical and electroconvulsive therapies, psychosurgery, LSD, amphetamines, barbiturates, as well as anti-anxiety and tranquilizing agents, were commonly and ineffectively used.

First Clinic Model for Outpatient Substance Use Disorder Counseling

The Emmanuel Church of Boston's clinic was established in 1906. While individual alcoholic abusers in wealthy families could turn to private sanatoria and elite hospitals (such as the Charles B. Towns Hospital for the Treatment of Alcoholic and Drug Addictions) for help in the early 20th century, it was not until the first clinic model for outpatient counseling was established in 1906 that treatment became more affordable and more widely available. The clinical model was based on the early work of the Washingtonian Movement of 1840, the sobriety-based Fraternal Temperance Societies, the Ribbon Reform Clubs, on through to the Business Men's Moderation Society of 1879. These mutual aid societies of the 19th century largely collapsed when the inebriate homes and other alcohol and drug programs were lost in the early years of the 20th century. However, the void was filled in 1935 with the establishment of Alcoholics Anonymous (AA).

Alternative to Alcoholics Anonymous

Women for Sobriety. Established in 1975, it uses principles similar to those of Alcoholics Anonymous. AA was founded in 1935 by Bill Wilson and Dr. Bob Smith ("Bill W" and "Dr. Bob") in Akron, Ohio. In conjunction with other early members, Wilson and Smith developed the "Twelve Steps" used in AA, and the "Twelve Traditions," including anonymity, altruism, and inclusion of all who want to stop drinking. In addition, the Traditions encourage AA groups try to avoid politics, hierarchies, and other organizational and public issues. Wilson, a stockbroker from New York, had traveled to Akron, Ohio, for a shareholders' meeting and proxy fight that turned out badly. Desperate to maintain sobriety, his first thought was, "I've got to find another alcoholic." Asking around, he met an Akron surgeon, Dr. Smith, who also struggled with a drinking problem. The effect of their meeting was profound, as the lent each other mutual support. This led to the founding of AA in an upstairs room at Dr. Bob's home. The two men began helping other alcoholics, one person at a time.

National Prohibition

1919 to 1933. National Prohibition was preceded by the ratification of the 18th Amendment to the Constitution, and inaugurated with the passage of the Volstead Act in 1919, which provided for law enforcement and penalties. Initially, alcohol problems were substantially reduced, but the robust emergence of an illicit alcohol trade eroded the effectiveness of the law, and National Prohibition formally ended in 1933 with the ratification of the 21st Amendment, which repealed the 18th. Drug laws began in 1875, in San Francisco, with a local ordinance aimed at curbing the proliferation of Chinese opium dens in that area. Other ordinances soon followed, addressing cocaine and morphine as well. By the turn of the century, the policy of having physicians control the use and distribution of primary drugs of abuse was emerging in law. The Pure Food and Drug Act of 1906 was the first federal law covering psychoactive substances beyond alcohol and tobacco. Among other things, it required that all medicines containing alcohol, cocaine, and/or opiates be labeled as such.

Harrison Narcotic Act of 1914

The federal Harrison Narcotic Act of 1914 stipulated that cocaine and opiates could only be dispensed/sold by a physician or a pharmacist with specific authorization by a physician. The US Supreme Court heard several arguments related to this Act, the most significant of which was the Webb v. United States decision, which indicated that physicians could be legally punished if they maintained addicts on opiates. The Narcotic Drugs Import and Export Act of 1922 prohibited the import of processed cocaine and morphine. The Heroin Act of 1924 prohibited the importing of opium for purposes of manufacturing heroin. The Marijuana Tax Act of 1937 prohibited the possession and sale of cannabis. The Opium Poppy Control Act of 1942 required licensure in order to grow and harvest opium poppies. The 1951 Boggs Amendment to the Harrison Act began the mandatory minimum sentencing of drug offenders. The Narcotic Control Act of 1956 introduced increased penalties and the first death penalty provision in drug legislation.

Changes in National Drug Policy During the Richard Nixon Presidential Years

During the Richard Nixon presidential years, national drug policy became prevention oriented. In 1966, the Narcotic Addicts Rehabilitation Act (NARA) was passed, allowing treatment as an alternative to incarceration. The 1970s saw further liberalization, primarily in recognition that youthful experimentation was increasingly common. The 1980s saw a backlash arising from escalating drug-related violence and escalating cocaine addiction. President Reagan presided over a shift in the national drug control budget, creating a budget allocation that was inverse to what had previously existed. Now, two-thirds went to law enforcement and one-third to prevention and treatment. The prison population went from 1 in 15 incarcerated for drug charges to 1 in 3 (with 85% imprisoned for solely possession charges). As of year 2000 statistics, 60% of those in the federal prison system are there for drug-related charges.

Racial Group Currently Most Likely to Be Prosecuted for Drug Possession/Use

African Americans. Issues of racial disparity have been a continuing focus in drug debates. It has been noted that African Americans represent 60% of those in state prisons, even though they constitute only 15% of illicit drug users. Further, African American mothers prenatally testing positive for illicit substances are 10 times more likely to be reported. Defenders of the system note that African American drug use is highest among all demographic groups, except Native Americans (where sociocultural groupings and reservation legal systems may limit systemic arrests). Further, crime rates are highest in low income areas, and minority representation tends to be high in these same areas. According to the 2006 National Survey on Drug Use and Health, the highest rate of current (past month) illicit drug use was among American Indian/Alaska Natives (13.7%), followed by Blacks/African Americans (9.8%), persons reporting two or more races (8.9%),

Whites/Caucasian Americans (8.5%), Native Hawaiian/other Pacific Islander Americans (7.5%), and Hispanic Americans (6.9%). The lowest rate was among Asian Americans (3.6%).

Five Kinetic Ideas That Formed the Core of the Modern Alcoholism Treatment Movement

Developed by Dwight Anderson and Marty Mann, the Five Kinetic Ideas are as follows: 1) alcoholism is a disease; 2) the alcoholic is, therefore, a sick person; 3) the alcoholic can be helped; 4) the alcoholic is worth helping; and 5) alcoholism is our #4 public health problem, and our public responsibility" (Mann, 1944). The modern alcoholism movement involved pioneering approaches in treatment and improved public attitudes during the 1940s and 1950s. The following institutions were collectively responsible: Alcoholics Anonymous; the Research Counsel on Problems of Alcohol; the Yale Center of Studies on Alcohol; and the National Committee for Education on Alcoholism. Due to their combined efforts, the view that alcoholism is a disease rose from 6% in 1947 to 66% in 1967, aided by statements from groups such as the American Medical Association, the American Hospital Association, the American Public Health Association, and the American Psychiatric Association.

Year When the National Council on Alcoholism First Developed Diagnostic Criteria

The year was 1972. There have recently been three stages in the field of addiction treatment. During the first stage, there was the development of effective diagnostic criteria (aided by research organizations such as the National Institute on Alcohol Abuse and Alcoholism [NIAAA], founded in 1970); professional training systems to properly educate treatment personnel; establishment of the "profession" (founding of the National Association of Alcoholism Counselors and Trainers, precursor to the National Association of Addiction Counselors founding in 1972); research in core competencies that supported certification programs; the establishment of national accreditation and state licensure standards; the integration of alcoholism and drug abuse treatment programs (1975 to 1985); and declarations of recovery by many prominent Americans such as First Lady Betty Ford. The second stage involved the growth of available treatment programs, handicapped in part by ethical abuses of inappropriate marketing, unnecessary admissions, and undue lengths of stay. The third stage involved integration with other social programs (e.g., public health, criminal justice) and the acceptance of multimodal approaches necessary for treatment success.

Drug Use Trajectory

The term "drug use trajectory" refers to individual drug use patterns over the lifespan. Lifespan research suggests that all behaviors, including drug use, have multiple origins, changes, and transitions arising from related biological, psychological, and social contributions. Thus, drug use research extends from embryological genetics, through the development of personality, and on through the life course in terms of related sociocultural and psychological influences, and changes in use through aging, etc. An individual's pattern of use throughout the lifespan may be referred to as his or her drug trajectory and use pattern. Recent advances in genetics research has aided in better understanding how genes versus family origin contribute to the decision to use illicit drugs and how addiction may subsequently develop.

Drug Classification Systems

Researchers may use one or more classification schema in attempting to understand the processes of drug abuse in individual and social contexts. The behavioral perspective tends to focus on how a drug makes one feel, move, and interact with others, along with methods and motivations for use, sociological and environmental impacts, and costs. A biological perspective tends to focus on drug interactions within the body in terms of intoxicating effects, neurological pathways, metabolism, and elimination of the drug from the body. A chemical perspective addresses a drug's composition, mechanisms of action, chemical combinations, and secondary products. These perspectives must also be viewed in the context of social norms, societal attitudes and beliefs, legal ramifications, and political changes in order to fully understand the patterns and persistence of various forms of drug use in any given society. Consequently, all drug use behaviors are also "bio-psycho-social" in nature.

"Q/F UT" FORMULA

The "q/f ut" formula refers to how much (quantity), how often (frequency), and how long (units of time). This formula is used by researchers to explore patterns of drug abuse in terms of dosage changes, frequency changes, and intoxication periods, in order to evaluate the impact of any given drug on an individual's life. The formula can assist in determining when an individual has moved past recreational use to habitual use, and/or into addictive compulsion. However, it remains difficult to determine thresholds for each transitional phase, particularly as various drugs of abuse may have different use patterns, and the various use patterns may have markedly different impacts on the lives, health, and outcomes for each user. Further, where multi-substance abuse occurs, the clinical picture becomes far more complex. Answers about whether use of one drug predisposes progression into the use/abuse of another (the "gateway hypothesis") are also difficult to determine.

TRANSITIONAL PROCESS MODEL

The first period in the Transitional Period Model is the "acquisition period." It includes the "priming phase" (information and exposure to drugs and drug users prior to actual use); the "initiation phase" (early drug use experiences); and the "experimentation phase" (where drug use becomes a repeated behavior). The second period is the "maintenance period." It includes the "habit formation phase" (where drug use becomes routine or habituated); the "dependence phase" (with drugs used to sustain homeostasis and to avoid dysfunction); and the "obsessive-compulsive phase" (ie, the entrenchment of dependence, and where even using the drug may not sustain homeostasis). The final period is the "control period." It consists of a "problem awareness phase" (as the consequences of continued drug use begin to accrue); the "interruption or suspension phase" (where the user attempts to cap or even reduce drug use in an effort to secure control); and the "cessation phase" (where drug use may be stopped for a short or even long period of time).

THREE STAGE MODEL

Researchers have identified a prototypical sequence in the trajectory of substance initiation and use. In Stage One, legal substances (alcohol and tobacco) are initiated; in Stage Two marijuana is initiated; and in Stage Three cocaine and then heroin are initiated. While tobacco use may lead directly to marijuana use, alcohol tends to be an intermediate step. Likewise, cocaine tends to precede heroin use. Other pathways are possible, such as marijuana leading to hallucinogenic substance abuse, or alcohol directly to prescription drug use. The concept of gateway drugs is an oversimplification, as causation is not in evident. Certainly, delaying drug-use onset is highly significant for fewer problems, as drug use may be avoided altogether, and the younger a person starts, the more difficult the problems tend to become.

GENERIC LEARNING

This concept notes that prior experiences with specific drugs may generically influence future experimentation with other drug forms. However, this concept will most likely be a subconscious factor in further drug experimentation, as it is more or less an unconscious motivator or de-motivator (ie, prior positive drug experimentation may predispose further experimentation, and negative events may discourage further experimentation). Perceptions about potential risks and benefits, however, have a more direct cognitive bearing on future experimentation, as both help to develop and sustain potential expectancies about drug use in general. Further, ideas about "soft" versus "hard" drugs may influence future drug experimentation. For example, many see marijuana as a relatively "soft" illicit drug, and may therefore be much more willing to experiment with it than with a "hard" drug like heroin. Peer pressure for or against also plays a significant role. Finally, the more intensively prior drugs were used/abused has direct bearing on future drug use.

Drug Abuse Research and Findings Reporting

Researchers have identified specific factors that either predispose or protect an individual from experiencing drug/alcohol problems in life. Many of the factors identified can constitute or indicate enhanced "risk factors" or "protective factors," depending upon the state of the factor identified. These factors can be further divided into "markers," "modifiers," and "mediators." Markers are sometimes called "surface indicators" and include gender, availability of drugs and use among peers, being a child of a known user, etc. Modifiers are considered augmenting or amplifying factors that either increase or decrease relative risk, and may include both environmental and collateral genetic risk factors that affect the risk for abuse (e.g., greater sensitivity to a substance). Mediators are actual causal mechanisms of drug use susceptibility and related outcomes and phenomena. Delineation between each may sometimes be confusing, as "familial history," for example, can act as a marker, modifier, or mediator (mechanism), depending upon the perspective being taken.

Risk Factor Categories in a Classification Schema

Major biological risk factors include genetics, neurocognitive and sensory deficits, affective disorders (e.g., anxiety, depression), and impulse disorders (e.g., conduct disorder, antisocial personality), either personally and/or by family history, and substance use in the family. Major psychological/behavioral risk factors include personality history (sensation seeking, risk taking, nonconformist), emotional makeup, coping skills (self-regulation), personal capacity (behavioral competence), compelling life experiences (positive or negative), and attitudes, beliefs, and values as related to substance use. Major social/environmental factors include family support systems/structure, parenting styles, basic competency models, peers, educational/economic opportunities, prosocial institution availability (schools, centers, employers), and social norms and morays about substance use.

Multidisciplinary Team

The makeup of the multidisciplinary team can greatly influence the nature and forms of roles assumed by an addiction counselor. Ideally, a team will consist of psychiatrists, clinical nurse specialists/mental health nurses, psychologists, social workers, and vocational and occupational therapists, potentially joined by other disciplines such as counselors, drama therapists, art therapists, advocacy workers, and care workers. Often, the social worker is seen as the default case manager, helping to pull together all of the necessary elements of care needed by the client. However, this role may also pass to the addiction counselor when resources are limited. The primary role of the addiction counselor is to formulate and implement the addiction treatment plan, aided by the psychiatrist (focused on medication management) and nurse (focused on health and relapse symptoms). Vocational, occupational, and educational counselors endeavor to help the client develop or regain independent living skills and training. Others may help with recreation, stress relief, and activities management. Being able to assume broader tasks and to work within a multidisciplinary team can greatly help facilitate positive client outcomes.

The benefits of a multidisciplinary team are manifold. Clients benefit from the unique skills of every team member, and each one of the team members is able to draw upon the training and insights of every other team member. The overall result is far more effective treatment, with the best of each discipline contributing to positive outcomes. The challenges are also multidimensional. For example, in a multidisciplinary team environment, it can be easier for a client to get "lost" in the disciplinary milieu, with no one discipline taking overall responsibility for the client's welfare and outcomes. Further, interdisciplinary overlap can sometimes lead to friction among team members because each one may feel that others are usurping their traditional functions and/or eroding their professional boundaries. To compensate, it is essential for team members to clearly understand their roles and responsibilities in advance and for a clearly established team coordinator and/or case manager to be recognized by all involved.

Countertransference

In 1991, Henry N. Blansfield, M.D. coined the term "addictophobia" to refer to the tendency to negatively view those struggling with substance abuse. Often referred to as "junkies" and "addicts," those who abuse substances are frequently seen as "lying, manipulative, aggressive people who lack motivation" (Carroll, 1993). However, multiple studies have revealed that negative attitudes, particularly among treatment staff and important support persons, will impede treatment, result in premature termination of treatment, and generate self-fulfilling expectations that prevent success. It has been noted that "[punitive attitudes] do not have a place in a caring profession" (Carroll, 1993, p 710). It is important to recognize addiction as a disease needing treatment, rather than a personal character failure to be stigmatized and punished. Common countertransference reactions include anger, apathy, withdrawal, boredom, inadequacy, rescuing, advice giving, and impulsive acting out in retaliation.

Reasons People Become Substance Use Disorder Counselors

First, to help others, usually because of past personal experiences with the devastation of substance use disorder (their own or via codependency experiences). Problems arise if the individual has a lingering need to work out unresolved personal issues, or when he/she assumes all others have issues/feelings similar to their own. Second, the person had a positive counseling experience when chemically dependent. This transference is problematic as helping others is far more demanding than being helped. Third, to exert control and power over others, leading to harsh and polarizing tactics designed to build their own egos. Fourth, to resolve past guilt, moving the focus from others to the self. Counselors need to have worked through their past issues, as successful chemically dependency counselors will perceive others as capable of change, dependable, friendly, and self-revealing. In short, they are able to find positive traits in their clients, and then help them to live up to higher expectations.

Burnout

Chemically dependent clients live chaotic, problem-strewn lives. Addressing their issues professionally can be draining and exhausting. This is evident in the high turnover rate of counselors. Some symptoms include isolation and withdrawing from colleagues and others, an increase in critical and complaining expressions, depression, and work avoidance. Strategies to avoid burnout include: 1) ensuring a rich and supportive personal life; 2) avoiding work overload (either in numbers of clients or in the off-hours time devoted to meeting their needs); 3) ensuring adequate treatment planning and evaluation time to more effectively meet client needs; 4) continuing education; 5) adequate consultation resources; 6) joining Al-Anon to cope with the stressors of exposure to chemically dependent individuals in much the same way that family members and significant others must discover ways to cope.

Labeling and Stereotyping

It has long been seen that negative labeling of and attitudes toward chemically dependent clients will negatively impact their treatment progress (Reichelt and Christensen, 1990). Even spouses and children of chemically dependent individuals can suffer, often being prematurely labeled as codependent, enabling, and psychologically impaired based on inadequate assessments and assumptions. In a study involving both peers and mental health professionals, Burk and Sher (1990) revealed that videotaped actors labeled as children of alcoholics and spouses of alcoholics were deemed to have significantly greater psychopathology than nonlabeled videotaped actors. Thus, not only does stereotyping further damage those who struggle with chemical dependency, but the prejudice extends to their families as well. Regardless, it is detrimental to the treatment and recovery process.

Master Addiction Counselor (MAC) License

To maintain the Master Addiction Counselor (MAC) credential, every counselor is required to participate in at least 100 hours of continuing education every five years. Of the required 100 hours, at least 25 must be centered on the following seven key content areas: 1) drug information and terminology (updates and expansions in new and ongoing changes in drug information, nomenclature, and terminology); 2) theories of addiction (with relevance to practice and application, as well); 3) medical and psychosocial aspects of addiction (pharmacological, psychological, and model-based changes in practice and theory); 4) addiction assessment (skills, domains, and instrument revisions); 5) issues in the treatment of addiction (ensuring up-to-date knowledge and skills in current treatment trends and practices); 6) addiction group counseling (ensuring current skills in group counseling techniques); and 7) family addiction counseling (ensuring up-to-date knowledge and skills in current treatment trends and practices).

Key Competencies

Key competencies include the following: 1) psychodynamics of denial and dependence; 2) the relationship between chemical dependency and dysfunctional behavior, lifestyles, and value system; 3) alcohol consumption patterns and societal values and attitudes; 4) the impact of chemical dependency on society, family, and employment/education, and the implications of each on recovery; 5) the impact of chemical dependency on human growth/development, family dynamics and dysfunction, and other important psychosocial and sociocultural implications; 6) the physiological effects of common mood-altering substances (both individually and in common combinations); 7) the physiological elements of addiction and withdrawal; 8) core features of problems (physiological, medical, and psychological) arising from chemical dependency; 9) signs and symptoms that indicate the need for further assessment and/or intervention (medical, psychological, and/or social in nature); 10) evaluation criteria for the stages, progression, treatment, and rehabilitation; 11) key counseling approaches, philosophies, methods, objectives, and functional applications; and 12) the need for continuing education.

Supervision

Clinical supervision serves to educate the counselor, protect client welfare, and ensure clinical service integrity. This involves issues of professional standards, practice, cultural competence, and ethics. Quality clinical supervision should always include direct observation.

Common models of clinical supervision include the following: 1) competency-based, focusing on the supervisees' learning needs, skill development, and goal setting. Key strategies involve social learning principles (e.g., role playing, role reversal, and practice), demonstrations, teaching, and consulting. 2) Treatment-based, directed toward a specific theoretical approach and practice adaptation to the theoretical model (i.e., cognitive–behavioral therapy, motivational interviewing, etc.). 3) Developmental, centered on the counselor's stages of development, allowing for changes in assignments, populations, and setting. 4) Integrated, articulating a model of treatment and incorporating skills and best practices, competency development, and affective issues. All models must account for cultural and diversity factors.

Supervision should be sought out by a counselor in a variety of situations. These include the following: 1) when a client's adherence to a treatment plan cannot be maintained (the client's relapsing or behaviors move outside the parameters of services that the agency can provide or when a client's conduct threatens program discontinuance); 2) when presenting problems are complex and multifaceted (particularly when they move beyond the clinician's immediate experience and skill development); 3) when issues of policy need clarification (to ensure that treatment interventions remain within the scope of the agency and/or professional service and practice domains); 4) in situations of ethical dilemmas (e.g., boundaries, mandated responses, etc.); 5) when legal and liability issues arise, making it unclear how to protect a client's well-being and the integrity of the agency and professional practice; 6) when issues of culture and ethnicity require further exploration; 7) when the safety of a client and/or others begins to present as compromised (e.g., suicidal and/or homicidal); and 8) in any situation in which the counselor feels unsure of his or her professional practice or competence.

PRACTICE EFFICACY EVALUATION

Counselors have an obligation to ensure they are using effective tools and intervention strategies. Key evaluative designs include: 1) Formative evaluation (similar to "process evaluation") uses ongoing data collection regarding treatment efficacy, with continuous revisions to meet clients' unmet needs. Although highly subjective, it can deliver important improvements to the unfolding treatment experience. 2) Summative evaluation (similar to "outcome evaluation") uses concluding analysis for treatment efficacy. Underlying decisions include time frames during which adequate intervention will occur, with definitions and measures of initial success, relapse rates, etc. The field has done too little of this, and stricter measures are profoundly needed.

Master Addiction Counselor Practice Test

1. Heroin is commonly abused in all but one of the following ways:

a. Sniffing/snorting
b. Swallowing
c. Smoking
d. Injection

2. Common health conditions associated with heroin abuse include all but one of the following:

a. Vascular collapse; abscesses
b. Respiratory and cardiac depression
c. HIV infection (with needle sharing); heart infections; liver disease
d. Retinopathy and glucose absorption impairment

3. Drugs of abuse may be grouped into pharmacological classes such as: 1) alcohol (beer, wine, liquor); 2) cannabis (marijuana, hashish); 3) depressants (benzodiazepines, barbiturates); 4) hallucinogens (LSD, mescaline/peyote); 5) narcotics (heroin, methadone, opium); and 6) stimulants (amphetamines, MDMA/Ecstasy). Please indicate below the proper pharmacological category for cocaine (including the free-based form, crack cocaine):

a. Depressant
b. Hallucinogen
c. Narcotic
d. Stimulant

4. The most correct definition of a narcotic is:

a. Any psychoactive drug that dulls the senses, has anesthetic properties, induces sleep, and, in excess, produces stupor, coma, or death
b. Any legally restricted psychoactive drug, whether physiologically addictive and narcotic or not
c. A group of strong pain medications that block opioid pain receptors
d. A class of depressant drugs derived from opium or compounds related to opium

5. Opiates are able to rapidly cross the blood-brain barrier to produce a euphoric rush, and physical dependence develops rapidly when opiates are used regularly. Withdrawal symptoms include all but one of the following:

a. Nausea and diarrhea
b. Aphasia and echolalia
c. Irritability and restlessness
d. Diaphoresis and chills ("cold sweats")

6. Opiates are central nervous system (CNS) depressants, as is alcohol (ethanol or ethyl alcohol, as opposed to rubbing alcohol, i.e., isopropanol or isopropyl alcohol). All of the following entries identify CNS depressants except one:

a. Chloral hydrate and glutethimide
b. Barbiturates and methaqualone
c. Nandrolone and stanozolol
d. Anxiolytics and benzodiazepines

7. Standard portions of the alcoholic beverages, beer, wine, and distilled spirits, as expressed in ounces (oz) are, respectively:

a. 10 oz, 4 oz, and 1 oz
b. 12 oz, 5 oz, and 1.5 oz
c. 16 oz, 6 oz, and 2 oz
d. 18 oz, 7 oz, and 3 oz

8. The liver breaks down alcohol by oxidization into acetic acid. On average, the liver of a 150-pound person can oxidize about 7 grams of pure alcohol per hour. This is the equivalent of how many ounces of beer, wine, and distilled spirits, respectively?

a. 4.75–5 oz, 1 oz, 0.25 oz
b. 15.75–16 oz, 5.75 oz, 2 oz
c. 11.5–12 oz, 4.5 oz, 1.25 oz
d. 7.75–8 oz, 2.5 oz, 0.75 oz

9. Excessive alcohol consumption can damage virtually every organ system in the human body. Alcoholism is a major cause of all but one of the following:

a. Pulmonary disease
b. Hepatic disease
c. Cardiac disease
d. Pancreatitis

10. The use of some drugs (whether legal or illegal) can produce withdrawal symptoms if the dosage is stopped or reduced too quickly. The presence of withdrawal symptoms indicates that the individual has developed one of the following:

a. An addiction to the drug
b. A physical dependence on the drug
c. A tolerance for the drug
d. An aversion to the drug

11. Alcohol abuse and alcoholism tend to be most prevalent in which of the following groups?

a. College students
b. Teenagers
c. People in poverty
d. Men, as opposed to women

12. The need to drink increasing amounts of alcohol to obtain a "buzz" (i.e., feel intoxicated) is referred to as:

a. Abuse
b. Dependence
c. Addiction
d. Tolerance

13. Identify the entry that is not a behavioral sign of alcoholism:

a. Focusing on a single brand or type of alcoholic beverage and drinking increasing amounts to obtain the same effect
b. Being aware of a compulsion or craving for alcohol; determining to quit drinking, but not being able to stop; drinking to reduce a hangover or to stop motor tremors
c. Drinking only hard spirits
d. Experiencing withdrawal symptoms after a short period of abstinence; limiting friends and social activities to those that involve alcohol

14. All of the following are categories of sedative-hypnotic drugs except one:

a. Anticonvulsants
b. Barbiturates
c. Minor tranquilizers
d. Nonbarbiturate sedatives

15. All of the following are sedative-hypnotic drugs with the exception of one:

a. Pentobarbital
b. Ethanol (alcohol)
c. Diethylpropion
d. Triazolam

16. Benzodiazepines are routinely prescribed for all but one of the following conditions:

a. Malingering
b. Anxiety
c. Acute stress reactions
d. Panic attacks

17. The class of frequently abused drugs that produces feelings of euphoria, dramatically boosts self-confidence, and generates a feeling of super strength is called:

a. Hallucinogens
b. Stimulants
c. Inhalants
d. Performance enhancers

18. The euphoric high experienced by cocaine users is the result of:

a. The release of neurotransmitters that stimulate the brain's pleasure center
b. A cascade of neuro-synaptic linkages in the brain triggered by cocaine
c. The adrenalin rush experienced when natural epinephrine is released by cocaine
d. The prolonged presence of dopamine in the brain when reabsorption is prevented by cocaine

19. Cocaine, in either a powder form (cocaine hydrochloride salt) or in a free-base form is commonly taken into the body in all but one of the following ways:

a. Intranasally (sniffing/snorting)
b. Sublingually (placed under the tongue)
c. Intravascularly (by needle injection)
d. Pulmonarily (by smoking)

20. What does the term "free-base" mean when used in reference to cocaine?

a. A more unstable form of the drug
b. A more corrosive form of the drug
c. A more pure form of the drug
d. All of the above

21. The longest lasting high, or intoxication period, occurs when cocaine is taken:

a. By intramuscular injection
b. By subcutaneous injection
c. By smoking or intravascular injection
d. By sniffing or snorting

22. Cocaethylene is the chemical name for one of the following drug combinations:

a. Cocaine and heroin
b. Cocaine and methamphetamine
c. Cocaine and alcohol
d. Cocaine and barbiturates

23. Bennies, black beauties, bumblebees, copilots, footballs, and hearts are all street names for:

a. Amphetamines
b. Barbiturates
c. Hallucinogens
d. Benzodiazepines

24. Crystal, ice, batu, chalk, shabu, and zip are all street names for:

a. Date rape drugs
b. Psychedelics
c. Hallucinogenics
d. Methamphetamines

25. The shape and/or appearance of methamphetamine called ice is:

a. Crystalline power
b. Crystal-shaped chunks
c. Clear capsules
d. Pill-shaped

26. Methamphetamine's primary action involves interaction with one of the following in the body:

a. Epinephrine
b. Norepinephrine
c. Dopamine
d. Adrenalin

27. The term "formication" refers to one of the following conditions:

a. A delusional disorder (during intoxication)
b. A hallucinatory disorder (during intoxication)
c. Vascular collapse (due to chronic intravenous abuse)
d. Atrophy of neural tissue (from stimulant abuse)

28. Methamphetamine may directly induce all but one of the following psychiatric symptoms:

a. Depression
b. Hallucinations
c. Paranoia
d. Aggression

29. Only one of the following products is not derived from the hemp plant (*Cannabis sativa*):

a. Marijuana
b. Hashish and hashish oil
c. Tetrahydrocannabinol (THC)
d. Peyote

30. Medical cannabis (marijuana) is used to treat all but one of the following conditions:

a. Pain
b. Obesity
c. Glaucoma
d. Nausea

31. Does prolonged marijuana use lead to physiological addiction?

a. Absolutely
b. Never
c. Frequently
d. Rarely

32. The health risks of prolonged marijuana use include all but one of the following:

a. Heart disease
b. Memory loss
c. Diabetes
d. Lung cancer

33. Drugs that stimulate the brain to produce distorted visual and auditory sensations and that alter emotions, awareness of self, and cognitive function are most formally referred to as:

a. Psychotics
b. Hypnotics
c. Hallucinogens
d. Entheogens

34. A recurrence of an earlier hallucinatory experience or perceptual distortion caused by a drug that involuntarily recurs sometime after the original exposure to the drug is best known as:

a. A flashback
b. A psychotic episode
c. A delusion
d. A distortion

35. Lysergic acid diethylamide (LSD) is medically used to treat:

a. Schizophrenia
b. Depression
c. Autism
d. Nothing

36. The effects of lysergic acid diethylamide (LSD) typically last for about:

a. 12 hours
b. 6 hours
c. 1 hour
d. 30 minutes

37. All of the following are natural sources for hallucinogenic substances except one:

a. Psilocybin
b. Ecstasy
c. Peyote
d. Mescaline

38. For users of psilocybin (mushrooms), peyote, or mescaline, the most common symptoms of a "bad trip" are:

a. Anxiety and paranoia
b. Flashbacks and schizophrenic symptoms
c. Delusions and accidental injury
d. Panic attacks and terror

39. Users of psilocybin (mushrooms), peyote or mescaline ingest these substances in order to experience certain specific effects, including all but:

a. Elation, awe, and bliss
b. Mystical or spiritual feelings
c. Increased power, energy, and excitement
d. Connectedness with others and the universe

40. The term "huffing" refers to abuse of one of the following substances:

a. Crack
b. Steroids
c. Stimulants
d. Inhalants

41. The high obtained from inhalants typically lasts for approximately:

a. 4–6 hours
b. 2–4 hours
c. 30–60 minutes
d. 5–30 minutes

42. All but one of the following patterns are seen in the abuse of anabolic-androgenic steroids:

a. Stacking
b. Alternating
c. Cycling
d. Pyramiding

43. Anabolic-androgenic steroids are used to treat all but one of the following conditions:

a. Delayed puberty
b. Certain forms of impotence
c. Stunted post-puberty growth
d. Chronic "wasting" as seen in AIDS patients

44. The term "designer drug" refers to which of the following?

a. A drug that closely copies a controlled substance
b. A drug synthesized in a laboratory setting
c. A specific drug prepared to order
d. A fashionable "yuppie" drug

45. Pharmacologically, Ecstasy (3,4-methylendioxymethamphetamine) has the properties of:

a. A psychedelic
b. An empathogen/entactogen
c. A hallucinogen
d. Both stimulant and hallucinogenic properties

46. Ecstasy stimulates the activity levels of all but one of the following neurotransmitters:

a. Norepinephrine
b. Acetylcholine
c. Dopamine
d. Serotonin

47. Ketamine has been available for more than 30 years and is used medically as:

a. An anesthetic
b. A sedative
c. A stimulant
d. An expectorant

48. Ketamine is primarily abused for its ability to produce the following effect(s):

a. Pain relief
b. High energy
c. Hallucinations
d. Euphoria

49. GHB (gamma-hydroxybutyrate) is medically used to treat:

a. Insomnia
b. Depression
c. Anorexia
d. Nothing

50. GHB (gamma-hydroxybutyrate) is used as a date rape drug because of the following properties:

a. It is colorless.
b. It is odorless.
c. It is an amnesiac.
d. All of the above.

51. Rohypnol® (flunitrazepam) is medically used to treat:

a. Angina
b. Insomnia
c. Depression
d. Nothing

52. What is the most common way to abuse Rohypnol®?

a. Needle injection
b. Skin patch
c. Oral ingestion
d. Snorting

53. Drugs that can be abused are regulated by the U.S. Drug Enforcement Administration (DEA) under provisions of the Controlled Substances Act (CSA), Title II of the Comprehensive Drug Abuse Prevention and Control Act of 1970, and the Controlled Substances Act of 1990. The legislation places all drugs into the following number of schedule categories:

a. Six
b. Five
c. Four
d. Three

54. The term "addiction" is currently used to describe:

a. Physical dependence on a drug or other substance such that withdrawal symptoms occur with abrupt cessation
b. An obsessive preoccupation with a drug, substance, or behavior to the extent that it is pursued without regard to negative consequences
c. A compulsive behavior that produces distress if not carried out, in spite of any negative consequences that may result
d. An intense attachment to or dependence on any substance, idea, thing, or person that avoids reality and is pursued in spite of the consequences

55. The best definition for the term "neuroadaptation" is:

a. The psychological accommodation that arises through repeated events
b. Automatic behaviors carried out without immediately conscious thought
c. The body's tolerance and withdrawal reactions to chemical substances
d. The body's ability to accommodate physiological change

56. Historically, the term "addiction" was used in reference to:

a. Alcohol dependence
b. Pharmaceutical drug dependence
c. Irrational commitment
d. Surrender to a master

57. An individual who continues to utilize an illicit drug can best be described as:

a. A drug abuser
b. A drug-addicted user
c. A dependent drug user
d. A drug user

58. The term "process addiction" is used to refer to:

a. Recreational drug use
b. Activity-based addiction
c. Neuroadaptive addiction
d. Psychological addiction

59. One class of neurotransmitters that has been implicated in the development and sustaining of addictive behaviors is:

a. Dobutamine
b. Serotonin
c. Dopamine
d. Norepinephrine

60. Reward deficiency syndrome results from dysfunction in one of the following systems:

a. Dopamine
b. Glutamate
c. Epinephrine
d. Norepinephrine

61. The neurotransmitter system primarily affected by alcohol ingestion is:

a. The GABA system
b. The glutamate system
c. The serotonin system
d. The norepinephrine system

62. Obsessive-compulsive disorders can be distinguished from addictions by:

a. Behavioral patterns
b. Ego-syntonic qualities
c. Ego-dystonic qualities
d. None of the above

63. The current model of addiction is characterized by the presence of all but one of the following:

a. A sense of craving or compulsion for an associated high
b. A loss of personal control over the behavior/substance used
c. Escalation in the frequency/amount of the behavior/substance used
d. Continuing the behavior in spite of negative consequences

64. Various ideologies can drive the diagnosis and treatment of substance abuse. The use of naltrexone to treat alcohol and/or opioid abuse is an example of which of the following treatment ideologies?

a. Behavioral
b. Biological
c. Psychological
d. None of the above

65. The "self-medication hypothesis" is a psychodynamic model of substance abuse that frames substance use/abuse as an effort to self-regulate where deficits in all but one of the following exist:

a. Interpersonal relationships
b. Affective dysfunction
c. Self-care/self-esteem
d. Cognitive capacity

66. The earliest perspective on addictive disorders proposed addiction to be a problem of:

a. Public health
b. Reward deficiency
c. Moral turpitude
d. Poor thought patterns

67. Addiction is best viewed as a syndrome with a largely identifiable course and predictable stages, the first of which is called:

a. Onset
b. Initiation
c. Activation
d. Origination

68. The central nervous system (CNS) includes all but one of the following structures:

a. The sympathetic nervous system
b. The spinal cord
c. The cerebrum
d. The cerebellum

69. Neurons are the basic cells that make up the functional part of brain and nerve tissue. All of the following are parts of a neuron except one:

a. Axon
b. Synapse
c. Dendrite
d. Soma

70. The study of drug interactions with biological organisms is known as:

a. Pharmacy
b. Pharmacokinetics
c. Pharmacodynamics
d. Pharmacology

71. The removal of a stimulus that increases the likelihood of a response that will remove the stimulus again is known as:

a. Behavioral adaptation
b. Positive reinforcement
c. Classical conditioning
d. Negative reinforcement

72. The brain pathway most relevant to drug abuse is called the:

a. Basal forebrain
b. Medial forebrain bundle
c. Hindbrain
d. Midbrain

73. Stimulant drugs increase the synaptic availability of all but one of the following neurotransmitters:

a. GABA (gamma-aminobutyric acid)
b. Serotonin
c. Dopamine
d. Norepinephrine

74. The introduction of opioid receptor antagonists into the body affects the utilization of heroin in the following way:

a. Reduces heroin withdrawal symptoms
b. Decreases heroin use
c. Increases heroin use
d. Has no effect on heroin use

75. Nicotine (e.g., from tobacco ingestion (chewing), inhalation (snuff), or smoking) is biochemically a:

a. Sedative
b. Depressant
c. Stimulant
d. Hypnotic

76. Alcohol is classified among other sedative-hypnotic drugs such as barbiturates and benzodiazepines. Identify the endogenous neurotransmitter system(s) that play a role in the behavioral effects of alcohol:

a. Glutamate
b. GABA (gamma-aminobutyric acid)
c. Opioid peptides
d. All of the above

77. THC (delta 9-tetrahydrocannabinol) is the psychoactive ingredient in marijuana. The cannabinoid receptors are activated by a neurotransmitter called:

a. Aspartate
b. Adenosine
c. Acetylcholine
d. Anandamide

78. Animal studies involving intracranial self-stimulation (ICSS) reveal that during drug withdrawal the brain's reward threshold:

a. Remains unchanged.
b. Is increased
c. Is decreased
d. Varies dramatically

79. All but one of the following neurological responses may follow chronic drug intake:

a. Upregulation of intracellular signaling pathways
b. Homeostatic trends in intracellular neuronal activities
c. Decreased neurogenesis in the hippocampus
d. Changes in dendritic morphology

80. Which of the following is acute drug use most likely to precipitate?

a. An acute stress response with drug use
b. An acute stress response with drug withdrawal
c. Limited stress with use; increased stress with withdrawal
d. Both A and B

81. The progression from recreational drug use to dependence may be mediated by all but one of the following:

a. Identification of a drug of choice
b. Habitual stimuli associations (place, people, etc.)
c. Escalating pleasure seeking
d. Alleviation of emotional and/or physical distress

82. Identify which of the following are the names of two physiologically addictive drugs or substances:

a. LSD and heroin
b. Morphine and mescaline
c. Ecstasy and cocaine
d. Alcohol and methamphetamine

83. Identify the ethnic group with a genetic variation predisposing to prolonged intoxication:

a. Asians
b. Caucasians
c. American Indians
d. Africans

84. The calming and anxiety-reducing effects of alcohol are primarily a result of interaction with one of the following neurotransmitters:

a. Glutamate
b. Adenosine
c. GABA (gamma-aminobutyric acid)
d. Serotonin

85. All but one of the following can play a role in the development of alcoholism:

a. Rearing environment
b. Birth order
c. Family history
d. Genetics

86. The class or category of drugs known as psychomotor stimulants is comprised of all but one of the following:

a. Barbiturates
b. Methylphenidate
c. Amphetamines
d. Cocaine

87. The quickest route of stimulant administration (introduction to intoxication) is:

a. Oral (swallowing)
b. Nasal (snorting)
c. Injection (needles)
d. Inhalation (smoking/huffing)

88. Psychomotor stimulants are most likely to produce tolerance to which of the following effects first?

a. Euphoria
b. Anorexia
c. Insomnia
d. Bronchodilation

89. The principal medical use for narcotics is for the treatment of:

a. Anorexia
b. Weight gain
c. Insomnia
d. Pain

90. Identify the nonaddictive opiate from the following list:

a. Codeine
b. Darvon® (propoxyphene)
c. Loperamide
d. Hydrocodone

91. When was the term "alcoholism" introduced?

a. 1849
b. 1868
c. 1922
d. 1947

92. What was the primary cause of the collapse of most addiction treatment programs between 1900 and 1920?

a. Exposés of ethical abuses and ideological schisms
b. Leadership attrition due to death and economic downturns
c. A lack of treatment efficacy studies and public pessimism
d. All of the above

93. The first clinic model for an outpatient counseling program established was founded by:

a. The Fraternal Temperance Society
b. The Washingtonian Movement
c. The Emmanuel Church of Boston clinic
d. The Charles B. Towns Hospital

94. The first alternative to Alcoholics Anonymous especially for women was called:

a. Women's Temperance Group (WTG)
b. Women's Suffrage Society (WSS)
c. Women's Alcoholics Anonymous (WAA)
d. Women for Sobriety (WFS)

95. National Prohibition in the United States was the law during what period?

a. 1916–1928
b. 1919–1933
c. 1921–1934
d. 1923–1935

96. Name the law that required any opiates and/or cocaine to be dispensed only by a physician:

a. The Narcotic Control Act
b. The Harrison Anti-Narcotic Act
c. The Boggs Amendment
d. The Opium Poppy Control Act

97. During the presidency of Richard Nixon (1969–1974), national drug policy became:

a. Sidelined politically
b. Harsher in terms of penalties
c. Permissive in terms of penalties
d. Prevention/treatment oriented

98. Identify the racial group currently most likely to be prosecuted for drug possession/use:

a. Hispanic Americans
b. African Americans
c. Asian Americans
d. Caucasian Americans

99. Who developed the Five Kinetic Ideas that formed the core of the modern alcoholism treatment movement?

a. Smith and Wilson of AA
b. The Yale Center of Studies on Alcohol
c. Anderson and Mann
d. The National Committee for Education on alcoholism

100. When did the National Council on Alcoholism first develop diagnostic criteria?

a. 1954
b. 1965
c. 1972
d. 1983

Answer Key and Explanations

1. B: Swallowing. Although oral ingestion of heroin will produce a psychoactive effect, the bioavailability is only about 35%, and the protracted period of assimilation will not produce the intense "rush" valued by abusers. Until recently, injecting heroin into a vein ("mainlining") was the most common method of abuse, with subcutaneous injections ("skin-popping") and intramuscular injections used if veins collapsed, etc. Now, with increased drug purity, the drug is more commonly smoked (as "black tar" heroin) and snorted (in crystalline powdered form). Irregular, recreational heroin use (called "chipping") typically occurs via "snorting."

2. D: Retinopathy and glucose absorption impairment. Although primary health changes brought about by heroin abuse may lead to a great variety of secondary ailments (including those presented here), these two conditions are not normally associated primarily (i.e., proximally) with heroin abuse. Illicitly obtained heroin is often "cut" (diluted) with other substances. When the cutting agent is insoluble, clots and occlusions may result. Withdrawal symptoms may set in within hours, peak within 48–72 hours, and last about a week and include muscle and bone pain, restlessness, cravings, and vomiting. Overdose is characterized by respiratory and/or cardiac depression, convulsions, coma, and death.

3. D: Stimulant. In 1914, with the Harrison Drug Act, cocaine was erroneously classified, in the eyes of the law, as a narcotic (i.e., grouped with opium-derived depressants; see also the Controlled Substances Act of 1970). This legal designation was never revised, thus, identifying cocaine as a narcotic would be legally correct. However, pharmaceutically and psychoactively, cocaine is a stimulant; therefore, this would be the most correct answer, from an abuse and rehabilitation perspective. Cocaine in its various forms is currently the most common illicitly used drug in the United States. Typically called simply "coke," street names include: flake, snow, toot, blow, nose candy, lady, liquid lady (cocaine combined with alcohol), speedball (cocaine combined with heroin), and, in free-base form for smoking, it may be called crack, rock, hard, iron, cavvy, and 'base).

4. A: Any psychoactive drug that dulls the senses, has anesthetic properties, induces sleep, and, in excess, produces stupor, coma, or death. Although the term is commonly associated with the opioids (morphine, heroin, etc.) and is often used by law enforcement and others to refer to any government-controlled psychoactive substance, neither of these definitions is sufficient. Many experts suggest that the term remains ineffectually defined. Common high-potency (and usually injected) narcotics include heroin, morphine, fentanyl, and meperidine (Demerol®), while low-potency prescription medications such as codeine, propoxyphene, and oxycodone (OxyContin® or—when coformulated with acetaminophen—Endocet ®, Percocet®, Roxicet®, Tylox®, etc.) come primarily in pill form. All are used to treat pain. In case of overdose, the opiate antagonist naloxone (Narcan®) can be used to displace narcotic drugs from receptor sites, thereby reversing the potentially lethal respiratory-suppressant effects common with opiates.

5. B: Aphasia and echolalia—meaning, respectively, the inability to use and/or understand language and the involuntary repetition of words just spoken by others. Other withdrawal symptoms include: anxiety, piloerection ("goosebumps," causing hair to stand up), insomnia, convulsions, tremor, difficulty urinating, constipation, dizziness, mood changes, blood disorders, rashes, abdominal cramps, blurred vision, and vomiting. The excess ingestion of opiates can result in cardiac irregularities (chiefly bradycardia—slowed heart rate) and/or respiratory depression (bradypnea—reduced breathing rate). Significant overdose, or combining opiates with other central nervous system (CNS) depressants such as alcohol, can ultimately lead to asystole (cessation of the heart beat) and/or outright apnea (cessation of breathing) and death.

6. C: Nandrolone and stanozolol, which are both performance-enhancing anabolic-androgenic steroids. Pharmaceutical depressants have long been called "downers," due to their calming down effects. Prescription uses include the relief of tension, anxiety, and irritability. The potential for abuse is high if used regularly, as physiological tolerance often quickly develops. Moderate overdose can result in poor motor coordination, slurred speech, and impaired judgment, whereas more toxic levels may result in respiratory failure, coma, and death.

7. B: 12 oz, 5 oz, and 1.5 oz. Standard portions of alcoholic beverages are arranged so as to provide approximately equal amounts of total alcohol in each type of drink. Beer contains approximately 3.5–9% alcohol, table wines range from 9% to 12%, dessert ("fortified") wines range from 16% to 20%, and distilled ("hard") liquor averages 40–50% and up to 80% in fortified distillates. Once ingested, approximately 20% of the alcohol is absorbed through the stomach and 80% through the intestines. However, greater concentrations of alcohol and carbonated beverages accelerate absorption, and food in the stomach will reduce the rate of absorption. Alcohol is eliminated from the system via the kidneys (5%), the lungs (5%), and the liver (90%).

8. D: 7.75–8 oz, 2.5 oz, .75 oz. The effects of alcohol intoxication (imbibing faster than the body can metabolize the alcohol) include the earliest symptoms: impaired judgment and decreased inhibition; moderate symptoms (0.01–0.30% blood alcohol): reduced control over movement, speech, and vision; more severe symptoms (0.15–0.35% blood alcohol): impaired balance, coordination, and reflexes. Blood alcohol concentration (BAC, usually given as g%, or grams of ethanol per 100 grams of blood) of 0.08% is considered intoxicated in most states. A blood alcohol of 0.35% and above can result in death, depending upon the body's level of developed tolerance. Impaired reaction time, motor control, and sensory processing are all factors that contribute to the dangers of drunk driving (which kills about 16,000 people each year in the United States).

9. A: Pulmonary disease. Although high levels of alcohol consumption can lead to respiratory depression, respiratory arrest, and suffocation due to emesis (vomit) aspiration, chronic alcoholism is not a leading cause of pulmonary disease. However, alcohol abuse is the number-one cause of liver-related deaths in the United States. Cirrhosis (fibrous scarring) of the liver routinely occurs with chronic alcoholism. Women are particularly prone to injury when more than 2–3 drinks a day are consumed regularly. Alcohol is metabolized by two liver enzymes: alcohol dehydrogenase (which converts alcohol to acetaldehyde) and acetaldehyde dehydrogenase (which converts acetaldehyde to acetic acid). Hepatic encephalopathy (compromised brain function from high levels of toxins in the blood due to poor liver function) can also occur. Acute alcohol toxicity can also damage heart muscle (cardiomyopathy), inflame the pancreas (pancreatitis), induce gastrointestinal ulcers and bleeding, produce a 10-fold greater risk of esophageal cancer, predispose an individual to other kinds of cancer, and may lead to hypertension. Alcohol is the leading cause of cardiomyopathy in the United States.

10. B: A physical dependence on the drug. Physical dependence indicates only that the body has integrated a drug in such a way that withdrawal symptoms will result from cessation, a reduced dose, or administration of an antagonist drug. By contrast, addiction is a psychoneurobiological disease and typically involves physical dependence on a drug as well as one or more of the following: 1) inability to control use of the drug; 2) compulsive use of the drug; 3) continued use of the drug in spite of mental, physical, and/or social harm; and/or 4) craving for the drug. In addition to pain medications, many other legal drugs, including corticosteroids, beta blockers, antidepressants, alcohol, etc., can produce physical dependence. Drug tolerance refers to a drug's lower effectiveness as the body adapts and overcomes the influence of the drug; sensitization occurs when a drug's effects are magnified with continued use.

11. D: Men, as opposed to women. Alcoholism occurs twice as often in males as in females. Although alcoholism afflicts people of all demographic categories, those who begin drinking at age 14 or under are much more likely to develop alcoholism. One in every 13 U.S. adults is alcohol dependent or abuses alcohol. Alcohol abusers drink approximately half of all the alcohol consumed in the United States, and the socioeconomic and health costs have reached $100 billion annually. In terms of preventable diseases, alcoholism ranks third in the United States, and 5% of all U.S. deaths are due to alcohol abuse (about 100,000 people annually).

12. D: Tolerance. The two main types of tolerance are: 1) metabolic tolerance (the liver's increased production of the enzyme alcohol dehydrogenase, causing rapid alcohol metabolism); and 2) functional tolerance (reduced sensitivity to alcohol's effects). Alcohol abuse refers to any harmful use of alcohol. Irregular abusers may not have symptoms of tolerance or dependence. The American Psychiatric Association refers to alcoholism as alcohol dependence—defined as a 12-month period during which one or more of the following is evident: 1) the abuse impairs home, occupational, and/or educational obligations; 2) the use occurs in physically hazardous situations (such as driving); 3) the use resulted in legal problems; 4) the use continues in spite of recurring social or interpersonal problems related to alcohol use.

13. C: Drinking only hard spirits. Many individuals conclude that they do not have a drinking problem because they only drink beer or low-alcohol table wines. However, even low-alcohol drinks can induce dependence and tolerance and can result in withdrawal symptoms at times when alcohol is not imbibed. Therefore, a definition of alcoholism that focuses on only drinkers of hard (distilled) alcoholic beverages would fall far short of including all of the 14 million individuals who abuse and/or are dependent on alcohol.

14. A: Anticonvulsants. Although some sedative-hypnotic medications are used in the treatment of seizure disorders (e.g., pentobarbital (Nambutal®), phenobarbital (Solfoton®, Luminal®), and secobarbital (Seconal®), many anticonvulsants are not, as not all of them have effective anticonvulsant properties. Similarly, not all sedative-hypnotics have anesthetic properties, although many do. Sedative medications induce a slowing of activity, agitation, and excitement, whereas hypnotic medications are soporific, i.e., sleep-inducing. In truth, however, this distinction is rather arbitrary, as many drugs in this class are sedating at low doses and hypnotic at higher doses. Many sedative-hypnotics reduce anxiety (anxiolysis), and all can produce unconsciousness at sufficiently high doses. There are three major categories of sedative-hypnotics: 1) barbiturates, 2) nonbarbiturate sedatives, and 3) the minor tranquilizers (principally, benzodiazepines). Benzodiazepines and the newer imidazopyridine drugs are commonly used for treatment of anxiety and insomnia. Fortunately, they also have a "ceiling effect" (as they can only augment GABA (gamma-aminobutyric acid) neurotransmitter activity, rather than mimic it outright, as others do) and therefore present limited danger of fatal overdose.

15. C: Diethylpropion, an amphetamine (stimulant). Alcohol (ethanol) does fall in the sedative-hypnotic category. Sedative-hypnotic medications are abused for their intoxicating, tension-relieving, anxiolytic, and hypnotic (sleep-inducing) effects. Other undesirable short-term (15 hours or less) effects include: emotional lability, loss of simple body functions, slurred speech, and cognitive and memory impairment. Long-term effects include loss of coordination, vertigo, chronic fatigue, sexual dysfunction, impaired reflexes, breathing disturbances, and menstrual irregularities. Long-term use also induces not only physiological dependence and tolerance, but psychological dependence (a need for the drug in order to function and cope). Withdrawal symptoms include: anxiety, insomnia, agitation, seizures, and even death.

16. A: Malingering. Benzodiazepines with substantial sedating qualities (e.g., estazolam [ProSom®] or triazolam [Halcion®]) are frequently prescribed for brief treatment of sleep disorders. Higher doses produce a sense of euphoria, but tolerance readily develops over time. As CNS depressants, benzodiazepines promote the action of the neurotransmitter gamma-aminobutyric acid (GABA). Typical effects include changes in emotion, personality, muscle tone, level of consciousness, coordination, etc. Long-term use leads to depression, personality changes, aggression, and feelings of fatigue, along with cognitive changes (impaired memory; mostly problems creating and accessing long-term memory), psychomotor impairment (e.g., problems driving), personality changes, and passivity.

17. B: Stimulants. Hallucinogenic drugs are used for the enhanced sensorial effects they produce. Inhalants are used to induce euphoria, hallucinations, and fantasies. Performance enhancers build muscle. None of these provides all of the identified enhancements generated through the use of stimulants. Signs of stimulant intoxication include nervousness, hyperactivity, pressured speech, difficulty standing or sitting still, decreased inhibition, poor concentration, becoming easily confused, and poor ability to judge distance and time. The duration of intoxication may range from five minutes to several hours, depending upon the stimulant used.

18. D: The prolonged presence of dopamine in the brain when reabsorption is prevented by cocaine. Dopamine is a chemical messenger in the brain that functions in conjunction with the brain's reward system. Cocaine interferes with the process by which dopamine is reabsorbed and thereby prolongs and enhances pleasure. Chronic cocaine abusers lose the ability to feel the effects of natural reward stimulation in the brain (e.g., by food, sensory stimulation, sex, etc.) and must eventually rely on the drug to stave off depression and experience any sense of physiological reward.

19. B: Sublingually. Cocaine powder (cocaine hydrochloride) can be inhaled into the nasal passages (called snorting or sniffing), where it is rapidly assimilated into the bloodstream. When dissolved in water, cocaine powder can be injected intravenously. When heated to free the pure cocaine from the hydrochloride base, the end product has a much lower burning point than cocaine in its salt form (i.e., cocaine hydrochloride). Therefore, when burned, the cocaine will sublimate (i.e., transform directly from a solid to a gas, as opposed to a liquid to gas transition) into a vapor, which can then be inhaled. Intravenously injected and smoked cocaine each enters the bloodstream virtually at the same rate and can produce a high in less than 10 seconds.

20. D: All of the above. Free-base cocaine (a base, or nonacidic alkaloid) is less stable than cocaine hydrochloride (a chemical salt), and it is also more corrosive—both of which make it harder to transport and store. However, it is also more pure, offering the user a more intense high. There are two forms of free-base cocaine (although the term free-base usually refers only to the purer version of the two). When cocaine hydrochloride is mixed with baking soda (sodium bicarbonate) and water and is then heated to free the pure cocaine from the hydrochloride base, the end product is called crack cocaine. When ammonia and ether are used, the result is a much purer product commonly called free-base cocaine, because one contains residual baking soda, whereas the other has no such residue. Both crack and free-base cocaine have much lower burning points than cocaine hydrochloride. Consequently, when heated, the cocaine vapor can be inhaled. Crack is less expensive to produce and buy, is intensely addictive, and was particularly popular in the mid-1980s.

21. D: By sniffing or snorting the drug. When cocaine hydrochloride is introduced into the nasal passages, the high, or period of intoxication, can last 15–30 minutes. By contrast, smoked or injected cocaine offers only a 5–10 minute high. Intramuscular and subcutaneous injections offer durations of intoxication ranging between these two. Using the product in greater amounts or more frequently can shorten both the intensity and the duration of intoxication over time. Furthermore, the duration of intoxication is inversely related to the intensity of the drug's effect—a shorter high is much more intense than a longer high. This is because the drug is assimilated more quickly, thereby producing a greater rush that also ends more quickly.

22. C: Cocaine and alcohol (ethanol). When alcohol and cocaine are consumed together, the liver synthesizes cocaethylene, which intensifies the euphoric high. However, it also increases the risk of sudden death. The stimulant effects of cocaine alone typically induce vascular constriction, rapid heart rate, and spikes in body temperature. There are accompanying risks of chest pain, cardiac arrest, stroke, seizures, and respiratory failure. Other common symptoms include headaches, abdominal pain, and nausea. Regular users may experience anxiety, irritability, depression, aggression, paranoia, restlessness, panic attacks, loss of appetite, and malnutrition. Prolonged snorting damages mucous membranes and may lead to nasal septum collapse. Needle users may contract HIV infection during needle sharing.

23. A: Amphetamines. Other street names include: cross tops, dexies, pep pills, speed, uppers, etc. Among the most commonly used prescription amphetamines are Ritalin®, Cylert®, and Adderall®, which are used to treat attention deficit hyperactivity disorder (ADHD) in children, adolescents, and adults. The first synthesis of amphetamines (Benzedrine®) occurred in 1887, but they were not marketed until 1932. Initially, they were prescribed as inhalers for relief from the symptoms of asthma and for nasal congestion due to colds and hay fever. Later, they were prescribed for obesity, attention deficit disorder, and narcolepsy. However, abuse became commonplace. Amphetamines became particularly popular during World War II, when soldiers were given the drug to fight fatigue and improve morale. Hitler's medical records show that he received eight injections a day of methamphetamine, in spite of the paranoia and unpredictable behavior that accompany such dosages.

24. D: Methamphetamines. Other street names include: amp, C.R., go, glass, pink glass, red rock, tweak, poor man's coke, etc. More commonly, the drug is called simply meth or crystal meth. A derivative of amphetamine, methamphetamine. was discovered in Japan in 1919 and is still legally produced in the United States under the name Desoxyn®. It is more potent than amphetamine. In crystalline form, the powder is soluble in water and is therefore easily injected. Most illicit methamphetamine is produced using the ephedrine/pseudoephedrine reduction method. Most domestic large-scale production is centered in California, although it is increasingly smuggled into the United States following production in Mexico.

25. B: Crystal-shaped chunks—much like rock candy, chunks of ice, or broken glass—"ice" is high-purity methamphetamine hydrochloride. Methamphetamines are also sold as pills, as capsules, and in powder form. The crystalline powder is white in color, bitter tasting, and odorless. It can be easily dissolved in water or alcohol. When mixed with water, it can readily be injected or applied to tobacco or marijuana to be smoked. Vaporizing easily when heated, the fumes can be inhaled for rapid intoxication. Methamphetamine can be smoked, sniffed ("snorted"), injected, or taken orally. When smoked, it is known as a cool smoke, whereas crack cocaine is known as a hot smoke. Ten to 15 "hits" can be obtained from a single gram of methamphetamine. The intoxicating euphoric effects obtained by snorting can be felt in approximately five minutes, while about 20 minutes are required if the drug is taken orally. If smoked or injected, a more intense "flash" or "rush" lasting only a few minutes occurs.

26. C: Dopamine. Pharmacologically, methamphetamine causes high levels of the neurotransmitter dopamine to be released. The dopamine release produces pleasurable feelings, boosts mood, and increases the capacity for physical activity. These effects can persist for as long as 12 hours after the dose. However, methamphetamine is also neurotoxic and can damage the cells containing both dopamine and another neurotransmitter known as serotonin. As damage accumulates over time, abusers can develop movement disorders and symptoms like those found in individuals with Parkinson's disease.

27. B: A visual hallucinatory disorder in which the abuser believes "bugs" are crawling on or under the skin—technically referred to as formication or delusional parasitosis. The sensation is caused when profuse sweating (due to the drug use) washes away the skin's natural oils, and by the toxins in the drug try to escape through the skin. Nerve endings under the over-dried skin produce the sensation of bugs crawling on the body or under the skin. Psychologically compromised persistent abusers often feel or "see" the "bugs" and dig and pick at their skin (typically on the face and arms), seeking to free the infesting insects. Dirty fingernails and gouging routinely result in dermal infections, leaving permanent scars much like those from severe chickenpox. Street terms for the disorder include: speed bumps, meth sores, crank bugs, etc.

28. A: Depression. The intoxicating effects of methamphetamines can directly induce many psychiatric symptoms, but depression is not among them. Although withdrawal from the drug can precipitate depressive symptoms, intoxication would not produce that mood. Other symptoms induced by meth include: euphoria, restlessness, insomnia, reduced appetite, and hyperthermia, along with increases in respiratory rate, heart rate, and blood pressure, potentially inducing a hemorrhagic stroke. Potential central nervous system (CNS) changes could result in aggression, anxiety, confusion, paranoia, seizures, and tremors.

29. D: Peyote. Peyote (*Lophophora williamsii*) is a cactus plant, from which the hallucinogenic drug mescaline is extracted. Marijuana is derived from the hemp plant (*Cannabis sativa*) and is the most frequently abused illicit drug in the United States today. Tetrahydrocannabinol (THC) is the active chemical in the plant that produces the psychotropic effects. By way of selective germination, THC levels today are far higher than in the past (3–5% in leaves; 6–12% in the sinsemilla, or flowering tops; 9–20% in hashish oil). The parts of the marijuana plant that are smoked are the plant's leaves, flowers, seeds, stems, and buds. Hashish, a sticky resin harvested from the flowering tops of the female plant (where the THC is most concentrated) is most frequently smoked, although it can also be eaten. Users may smoke the plant as a "joint" (a home-made cigarette composed of marijuana rolled in smoking paper), or via a "blunt" (a cigar hollowed out and filled with the drug), or through a bong (a water pipe used to filter, cool, and collect the smoke).

30. B: Obesity. Cannabis use tends to stimulate the appetite, and therefore it is not a treatment for obesity. While marijuana has been touted as a treatment for a great variety of health problems, it is most commonly used to treat chronic pain, mood disorders, post-traumatic stress syndrome, anorexia, some gastrointestinal problems, and the nausea and vomiting associated with chemotherapy for cancer. It has also been used in some situations to stimulate the appetite of individuals with failing nutrition intake due to various medical and/or health conditions. However, treatment may be complicated by the long half-life of the drug—daily users remain chronically intoxicated (which likely accounts for the "amotivational syndrome" often seen in these users), and memory, coordination, and cognitive functions can also remain impaired.

31. D: Rarely. The question of addiction is frequently debated, depending upon the definitions used. Some experts argue that there is no clear withdrawal syndrome and therefore contend that the term "addiction" cannot be properly used. Others point to the low but measurable rate of drug dependency that results from prolonged use, as well as certain withdrawal-like symptoms. The U.S. Drug Enforcement Administration (DEA) cites extensive literature and clearly states that THC is addictive. Many other researchers agree. The active ingredient in marijuana (THC) induces the release of dopamine within the brain, producing the intoxicating effects of the drug. The THC then binds to the cannabinoid receptors found on various neurons, particularly in areas such as the basal ganglia (involving control over movement), the cerebellum (involving balance and coordination), the cerebral cortex, and the hippocampus (controlling elements of learning and memory).

32. C: Diabetes. There is no documented incidence of diabetes linked to marijuana use. However, there are many potential health pitfalls. The THC in marijuana can disrupt the function of the hippocampus in the brain, and prolonged disruption can result in lasting memory impairment. Marijuana smoke contains more tar and harmful substances than cigarette smoke, is held in the lungs longer, and is inhaled more deeply than cigarette smoke. These can greatly increase the odds of developing lung cancer for frequent marijuana smokers. Other potential problems include cognitive impairment, cardiovascular disease, a compromised immune system, and respiratory illness. Certainly the intoxicating effects of use can lead to a greater likelihood of accidents and injuries. Psychologically, persistent use can lead to depression, panic attacks and anxiety, irritability, personality problems, and decreased activity and motivation.

33. C: Hallucinogens. The term entheogen has been proposed for this class of drugs, but it is not in routine pharmacological use. Hypnotics are from the sedative class of medications. The term "psychotics" does not directly refer to a class of medications. Hallucinogens can be either derived from natural plant sources or synthesized via chemical processes in laboratory settings. Although the psychological distortions and other effects of this class of drugs can be problematic in many ways, among the most dangerous effects are impaired judgment and altered perceptions and thinking. Under the influence of hallucinogenic drugs, individuals may think they can undertake dangerous behaviors with impunity (e.g., leaping in front of a train they believe they can control, etc.).

34. A: A flashback. Although psychotic episodes may include experiences such as flashbacks, that term is not the best description of flashbacks. Delusions are false beliefs retained in spite of evidence to the contrary. Psychiatric distortions come in many varieties, of which flashbacks are only one kind. Users of the powerful hallucinogen LSD (lysergic acid diethylamide) are particularly prone to flashbacks, which can occur without warning days to more than a year after exposure to the drug. "Immersive" flashbacks (as opposed to the simpler recollection-based flashbacks) can be particularly disturbing, as there is a transient loss of proper orientation to both time and place. If the original hallucinatory experience was deeply disturbing and/or distressing, the flashbacks can be decidedly debilitating.

35. D: Nothing. Lysergic acid diethylamide (LSD) was first synthesized in 1938 by a Swiss chemist searching for a respiratory and circulatory stimulant, and it was later explored as a treatment for schizophrenia. Furthermore, in the 1960s Harvard professor Timothy Leary, PhD, regarded LSD as an elixir of psychiatric and creative benefit. Users are particularly drawn to the visual hallucinatory images that follow the typical ingestion of 50–150 micrograms of the drug (often 2–3 drops of the drug absorbed into a small piece of paper or in a minicapsule or very tiny pill. Intoxication experiences range from simple illusions (such as a sense of unreality), to pseudohallucinations (where the user remains aware that the hallucinations are not real), to outright hallucinatory sensations. Currently there is no health or psychiatric condition that can be appropriately treated with LSD, even under medical supervision. Since 1966, LSD has been classed as a controlled substance in California, and in 1970 it was included in the U.S. Controlled Substances Act as a Schedule I substance (i.e., a drug highly prone to abuse).

36. A: About 12 hours; the onset of effects after ingestion emerge in about 30–90 minutes. LSD is a slightly bitter, odorless, and colorless substance that induces extremely unpredictable effects—many of which are dependent on the dosage; surrounding environment; and mood, personality, and expectations of the user. Although the drug is not deemed addictive, users can develop a tolerance (requiring higher doses over time for the same effect). The hallucinatory and delusional effects can be compelling, such as cross-over sensations (i.e., "hearing" colors and "seeing" sounds, etc.). However, fear, anxiety, and terror-inducing experiences are not uncommon. Persistent anxiety, lingering psychoses (i.e., schizophrenia symptoms, severe depression, long-term flashbacks, and other mental health problems) may endure long after the drug has been cleared from the body. Physical effects routinely include: anorexia (loss of appetite) insomnia, xerostomia (dry mouth), tachycardia (rapid heartbeat), hypertension, diaphoresis (sweating). Deaths typically arise from panic, psychotic, delusional, and paranoid reactions leading to self-destructive events.

37. B: Ecstasy. Ecstasy is a "designer drug" synthesized in a laboratory setting. Psilocybin is derived from mushrooms ("magic mushrooms" or "'shrooms"), which are typically eaten or smoked. Effects are fully felt within 1–2 hours of ingestion and fully subside within 6–7 hours. Peyote is a small cactus plant with hallucinogenic properties. The top of the cactus can be cut away and dried. The dried buttons are chewed or boiled in water to produce an extremely bitter, typically nausea-inducing, psychoactive tea. Effects are fully felt within 1–2 hours of ingestion, and fully subside within 6–10 hours (some reports say as much as 14 hours). To avoid the bitter, nauseating effects, the dried peyote may be powdered and put into capsules. Mescaline, an alkaloid, is the active hallucinatory substance found in peyote. Regular users develop a tolerance that lasts for a few days and will develop a cross-tolerance with LSD and other psychedelic substances. Peyote and mescaline are illegal in the United States except for ceremonial use in certain religious groups such as the Native American Church.

38. A: Anxiety and paranoia. Symptoms of anxiety and paranoia are the most frequent symptoms of negative experience, typically referred to by users as a "bad trip." Flashbacks (an involuntary, unexpected return of the effects of the substance weeks or even months later) are relatively uncommon, but can occur. Schizophrenic symptoms (persistent auditory hallucinations and delusions, etc.) may emerge during use of the drug and may linger with any user. However, lingering symptoms tend to be limited to those with preexisting psychiatric conditions. Delusions (false beliefs) of a negative nature can occur during any "trip," but are not among the most common symptoms. The risk of accidental injury also exists during any intoxication experience but is much higher when the hallucinations and emotional sensations induced by the drug are particularly frightening and negative. Panic attacks and feelings of terror can also occur during any negative intoxication experience, and/or may follow it sometime later, but these symptoms are not among those most commonly associated with a "bad trip."

39. C: Increased power, energy, and excitement. Substance abusers seeking an increased sense of power, energy, and excitement tend to take stimulants rather than hallucinogens. These hallucinogenic (or psychedelic) substances are typically used to enhance sensory experiences of a pleasant nature. They are also used by specific groups (such as Native Americans) in pursuit of spiritual enlightenment and to draw closer to nature and the universe. In this context, both psilocybin and mescaline are considered "entheogens"—i.e., producers of spiritual experiences. Low doses usually induce positive changes in thought, emotions, and sensations, often characterized as euphoria, bliss, and awe (yet most frequently without loss of connectedness to basic reality). Higher doses induce more intense hallucinations that eclipse the normal sense of reality. At these higher doses, negative experiences, anxiety, paranoia, fear, and even feelings of terror are more likely to occur and are more likely to create problems that may persist after the influence of the drug has subsided.

40. D: Inhalants. The term "inhalant," in the context of substance abuse, refers to household and commercial products that can be abused by drawing the product's fumes into the lungs by inhaling through the mouth ("huffing") or nose ("sniffing"). The inhaled vapors induce a form of intoxication when exposed in sufficient quantities over an adequate length of time. Volatile solvents are among the substances most commonly abused, along with fluorocarbons and butane-like gases (cleaning solutions, correction fluid, adhesives, lighter fluids, gasoline, paint products, etc.). The products may be inhaled directly from the container, or from a plastic bag or cloth saturated with the substance. Some inhalants must first be released by heating. Inhalants depress the CNS, much like alcohol, causing feelings of euphoria and excitement and a sense of floating and increased power.

41. D: 5–30 minutes. Intoxication usually occurs quite rapidly (within five minutes) and lasts 5–30 minutes. To stay high, users may abuse for prolonged periods. The low cost of inhalants makes them easily available to the poor and children (ages six to 16). About 10%–20% of those aged 12–17 have tried inhalants—peaking between the seventh and ninth grades. Signs of intoxication include: vertigo (dizziness); nystagmus (rapid, involuntary, side-to-side eye movements); slurred speech; poor coordination and an unsteady gait; lethargy; psychomotor retardation; tremors; weakness; blurred or double vision; and euphoria (feeling giddy). Serious problems include stupor or coma, sickness, and death. Abusers may become unable to control their bodies for 15–45 minutes after sniffing and can severely injure themselves, suffering damage to the brain, heart, liver, and kidneys. Finally, "sudden sniffing death" can occur during or right after abusing inhalants, as the heart beats rapidly but unevenly, leading to cardiac arrest. Even first-time abusers can die.

42. B: Alternating. The term "alternating" is not a steroid abuse pattern. Anabolic and androgenic steroids are abused in the effort to quickly gain and maintain muscle mass. The term "androgenic" refers to male characteristics, and "anabolic" refers to muscle building. Thus, these forms of steroids are intended to enhance male characteristics and add muscle. With more than 100 forms of steroids available, patterns of use emerge. Cycling refers to starting and stopping steroids for set periods of time over several weeks or months. Pyramiding refers to the slow escalation of steroid usage (including the dose, frequency, and time) to a midcycle peak, and then tapering back to a point of terminating the cycle. Stacking refers to the combination of several different kinds of steroids in an attempt to maximize their effectiveness (ideally, synergistically).

43. C: Stunted post-puberty growth is not treated with anabolic-androgenic steroids. In fact, one side effect of anabolic-androgenic steroid abuse is stunted growth in adolescents. Other potential consequences of abuse include: hypertension, cardiac disease, blood cholesterol imbalance, liver tumors and liver cancer, and HIV and hepatitis infection from needle sharing. Men may experience testicular withering, low sperm count and infertility, acne, baldness, gynecomastia (breast development), and a greater risk of prostate cancer. Women may experience disrupted menstruation, clitoral enlargement, lowered voice range, facial hair growth, and male-pattern baldness. All users may develop mood swings—i.e., manic-like symptoms that tend toward violence—and poor judgment due to feelings of invincibility. Cessation of the drugs can result in withdrawal symptoms of severe depression, lethargy, anorexia, insomnia, poor sex drive, paranoid jealousy, delusions, and marked irritability.

44. A: A drug that closely copies a controlled substance. Another term for "designer drugs" is "analogs"—so called because the designer version is an analog of, or closely related to, the drug it is designed to mimic. Although designer drugs are synthesized in laboratory settings, not all synthesized drugs are designer drugs. In many cases, designer drugs are significantly more potent that the drugs they were designed to resemble. For example, some designer drugs are easily twice as powerful as heroin or cocaine, yet often cost much less to produce. Places where designer drugs are likely to be encountered include raves and nightclubs. Currently, the most frequently abused designer drug is 3,4-methylendioxymethamphetamine (Ecstasy).

45. B: An "empathogen/entactogen," as it readily seems to produce a sense of bonding and emotional connection. Ecstasy (also known as: MDMA, XTC, DOM, and MMDA) is derived from the amphetamine family. MDA (methylenedioxyamphetamine) is a closely related empathogen/entactogen. Although Ecstasy has stimulant properties, it is not a true hallucinogen—users do not experience frank hallucinations, but rather marked distortions in time and perception. The drug is produced in both tablet and capsule forms for oral ingestion, but others may snort or inject Ecstasy. When orally ingested, the effects of the drug last about 4–6 hours. The actual effects of Ecstasy may vary widely, as the tablets or capsules often contain other undisclosed ingredients, including cocaine, ephedrine, caffeine, methamphetamine, and/or dextromethorphan.

46. B: Acetylcholine. Although acetylcholine is a major neurotransmitter, it is not acted upon by Ecstasy. Dopamine, norepinephrine, and serotonin, however, are all stimulated for neuronal release by Ecstasy. Serotonin in particular is released in large amounts, even as its synthesis is inhibited. The result can be an enduring depletion of serotonin over time. As serotonin aids in the regulation of appetite, emotions/mood, pain, and sleep, this depletion may be the cause of the persistent behavioral problems that moderate to high abusers of Ecstasy often experience. While abusers often take Ecstasy to boost energy at parties and dances, the long-term effects can be devastating. Already a highly idiosyncratic drug (effects varying widely from person to person), the drug also has a wide range of problematic effects (including amnesia, hallucinations, paranoia, and even death—sometimes even with the first use). Ecstasy can cause brain damage and has been implicated in numerous subsequent psychiatric disorders, including severe anxiety and depression, obsessions, paranoia, and sleep disruption, to name a few.

47. A: An anesthetic. In clinical settings, ketamine may be used for premedication, sedation, and induction and maintenance of general anesthesia. It may also be used for the treatment of chronic pain, as it is a potent analgesic by itself, or it may be used with other potent analgesics. More recently, it has been used as an antidepressant for treatment-resistant symptoms. It was initially used only in veterinary medicine, but over the past two decades its general anesthetic, analgesic (pain-relieving), and sedative properties became more widely known. Structurally related to PCP (phencyclidine) (a drug known for inducing vivid hallucinations), ketamine has a tendency to produce a feeling of an out-of-body experience. However, also like PCP, its effects are highly unpredictable and potentially dangerous. For years, ketamine was not a controlled substance but was placed under Schedule III of the Controlled Substances Act by the U.S. Drug Enforcement Administration in 1999. Several states have also increased penalties for its possession and distribution.

48. C: Hallucinations. More specifically, ketamine is known for its dissociative, out-of-body psychedelic properties, as well as its anesthetic qualities. The drug has increasingly been associated with the dance culture, where its effects (including the near-death experience) are particularly desired. Street names include: "K," "Special K," and "Vitamin K." When injected, ketamine can induce profound analgesia, amnesia, respiratory depression, and cardiovascular stimulation. Even low doses can lead to memory impairment, poor attention, and reduced ability to learn. Extended abuse has been associated with considerable psychological addiction. Furthermore, individuals who frequently use ketamine develop tolerance to the drug, requiring higher doses for the same desired effect. Since 1999, ketamine has been a Schedule III drug under the Controlled Substances Act.

49. D: Nothing. Gamma-hydroxybutyrate (GHB) has no approved medical use. A certain form of GHB (sodium oxybate; brand name: Xyrem®) is used to treat narcolepsy (a chronic sleep disorder). However, the use of Xyrem is very tightly restricted. Those who abuse GHB (primarily body builders and party attendees) claim that it is, variously, a strength enhancer, a euphoriant, and an aphrodisiac. It has also gained notoriety as a date rape drug, due to its amnesia-inducing effects. Pharmacologically, GHB is a CNS depressant, and it can be lethal if used with alcohol or other depressants. Street names include: blue nitro, cherry meth, easy lay, gamma G, liquid ecstasy, and poor man's heroin.

50. D: All of the above. GHB can easily be slipped into drinks and food, because it has no color (it looks exactly like water) and no smell. It does, however, have a slightly salty taste, but that can be easily masked or explained away. Even a very small amount of GHB can cause a person to experience retrograde amnesia (forgetting events that happened before ingestion) or to black out (become unconscious). The risk of overdose is high, as the difference between the dose to get high (or subdue a date) and a life-threatening dose is very small, and mixing the drug with alcohol is extremely dangerous. A sedative-hypnotic, at low doses the drug causes users to feel very euphoric and relaxed. The effects are felt in 10–15 minutes and may last for 2–3 hours. At higher doses, users may experience dizziness, nausea and vomiting, disorientation, seizures, respiratory depression, severe drowsiness, unconsciousness, and even coma or death.

51. B: Insomnia. From the benzodiazepine class of drugs, Rohypnol® (flunitrazepam) is also a powerful sedative, anticonvulsant, anxiolytic, amnesic, and muscle relaxant. It is 7–10 times stronger than diazepam (Valium®), with primary effects evident some 15–20 minutes after ingestion and lasting about 4–6 hours. Residual effects may persist for 12 hours or more. It has been a Schedule IV controlled substance since 1984 due to its high potential for abuse. Once dissolved in a beverage, it has no color, odor, or taste, and it readily induces amnesia, making it a classic date-rape drug. It will also enhance the high of heroin and ease the crash following cocaine use.

52. C: Oral ingestion. It may also be snorted as a powder by crushing the tablets. It is frequently combined with alcohol, whereupon both enhance the other's toxic effects. Taken with marijuana, users may experience a floating sensation. When combined with cocaine, it produces a fast hit, followed by a mellow state. Rohypnol may cause gastrointestinal problems, confusion, drowsiness, dizziness, slurred speech, and loss of coordination and motor control. Consequently, it greatly impairs reaction time and driving skills. Higher doses may produce respiratory depression. Persistent use can cause physical dependence, and abrupt cessation may lead to a withdrawal syndrome. Street names include: date rape drug, forget pill, Mexican valium, roachies, Roofies, Ruffies, etc.

53. B: Five. Schedule I covers drugs or other substances with no recognized medical use, high potential for abuse and dependence, and lack of safety; special licensing is required to utilize Schedule I drugs (primarily for research); examples: mescaline, LSD, heroin, and marijuana. Schedule II drugs have recognized medical utility, but a comparatively high potential for abuse and dependence; examples: morphine, cocaine, pentobarbital, oxycodone, and methadone. Schedule III drugs have recognized medical utility and a comparatively moderate risk of abuse and dependency; examples: glutethimide and various codeine-based analgesics. Schedule IV drugs have high medical utility and a limited risk of abuse and dependency; examples: chloral hydrate, meprobamate, and oxazepam. Schedule V drugs have recognized medical utility and a comparatively low potential for abuse or addiction; examples: prescribed medications with minimal codeine or diphenoxylate. The drugs in Schedule V vary greatly from state to state. A few states (e.g., Massachusetts) have a

Schedule VI, covering abusable substances with little or no potential for addiction (e.g., glue, ibuprofen, penicillin, etc.).

54. D: An intense attachment to or dependence on any substance, idea, thing, or person that avoids reality and is pursued in spite of the consequences. Until recent years, the term "addiction" was used virtually exclusively to refer to substance abuse from which physiological dependence resulted. Currently, however, the idea of behavioral addictions has arisen, expanding the use of the term to include a great variety of persistent behaviors, such as gambling, shopping, stealing, etc. The term "addict," however, has fallen from use and is no longer allowed in many professional journals due to its pejorative connotations.

55. C: The body's tolerance and withdrawal reactions to chemical substances. With persistent use of a drug or other substance, the body attempts to create an accommodation for the continuous presence of the drug or substance. This may include the increased production and release of various hormones, neurotransmitters, and other mediating responses. The body's goal is to maintain functional equilibrium. When successful, the frequent result is tolerance, i.e., the need for increasing amounts of the drug or substance to achieve disequilibrium (the high). In some cases, the body's accommodation mechanisms result in severe feelings of illness if the drug or substance is withdrawn. This response is known as withdrawal. The term "neuroadaptation" encompasses both of these physiological phenomena.

56. D: Surrender to a master. The term "addiction" first appeared in a seventeenth-century (1625) reference to Roman law. It was used to refer to a formal surrender to a master due to a court sentence. By 1641, the term had been broadened to refer to devotion to specific pursuits or habits in daily life (agricultural activities, reading, etc.). The use of the term in connection with a compulsion or craving as related to the ingestion of a drug did not emerge until the eighteenth century. Scientists continue to link the term primarily with physiological dependence on a drug. However, there is an increasing body of research suggest that the root of many compulsions may lie with the brain's reward systems in ways similar to the neurological rewards resulting from substance abuse. Therefore, use of the term "addiction" is trending toward including compulsive behaviors that exhibit addictive features (i.e., gambling, where higher stakes are needed to induce excitement over time, and marked distress results when abstaining from the activity).

57. D: A drug user. In the absence of additional information, the proper term would be "drug user," as there is no information indicating adverse consequences, dependence, or addiction. A "drug abuser" encounters recurrent adverse consequences that are significant in terms of personal, legal, social, academic, and/or occupational functioning. Drug dependence involves a cluster of symptoms (behavioral, cognitive, and/or physiological) that drive an individual to continued involvement in spite of recurrent adverse consequences that are significant. Although the terms "dependent," "addict," and "abuser" tend to be used only in the context of drugs, there is an increasing body of research suggesting that the root of many compulsions may lie with the brain's reward systems in ways similar to the neurological rewards resulting from substance abuse. Thus, the use of these terms is trending toward the inclusion of other compulsive behaviors that exhibit similar use and abuse patterns.

58. B: Activity-based addiction. Process addictions, also known as "behavioral addictions," fall into the category of nondrug addictions that exhibit similar addictive qualities. Certain human activities are particularly likely to stimulate the release of natural psychoactive neurotransmitters in the brain, just as certain chemical substances stimulate the release of those same psychoactive substances. Whether the high is chemically stimulated by an ingested substance, induced by fiercely competitive computer games, or experienced through the intense experience of high-stakes gambling, there may a similar biological substrate for both. Thus, with any activity that profoundly and dependably produces positive emotional changes, there exists the possibility for an addiction to emerge (e.g., running, eating, gambling, computer gaming, pornography, shopping, etc.).

59. C: Dopamine. This neurotransmitter has a role in initiating and maintaining the brain's biochemical reward system. Other neurotransmitters primarily interact only with the dopamine reward system. Any activity that stimulates the brain's powerful reward system, such as sexual expression, can lead to addictive behaviors. The areas of the brain involved in the neurochemical reward system include the ventral tegmental area (VTA), which is found in the anterior ventral midbrain, along with the nucleus accumbens (NA), which is situated in the ventral forebrain. The brain regulates the production and release of dopamine through the mesolimbic dopamine system. The cells' bodies of the brain's dopaminergic neurons are found in the VTA, and the terminals of the neurons are found in the NA. Neuroimaging studies have revealed that the brain's reward system can be boosted by substances such as cocaine, opiates, and alcohol. However, anticipation of money, enhanced beauty, and other external nondrug stimuli can also activate a similar neurobiological pathway in the brain. Therefore, even reward-boosting thoughts and behaviors can produce similarly addictive results.

60. A: Dopamine. Reward deficiency syndrome occurs when the dopamine system is hypoactive/hypofunctional. The result is a low level of pleasure, which may induce greater participation in behaviors designed to stimulate the dopamine reward system. During drug use, the dopamine reward system may be chemically stimulated to a greater or lesser degree based upon the kind of psychoactive substance used and the route of administration. Thus, orally ingested cocaine stimulates the reward system to a lesser degree (although typically over a longer period) than injected cocaine, due to its slower entry into the blood stream. By contrast, injected or snorted (inhaled) cocaine will enter the blood stream quickly and will profoundly stimulate the dopamine reward system (but over a much shorter period of time). The quality and persistence of an addiction may therefore vary according to the substance utilized and the route of administration.

61. A: The GABA system. GABA (gamma-aminobutyric acid) is a key inhibitory neurotransmitter that is affected by alcohol. Normally, when GABA binds to its target receptor, neuronal cell activity is inhibited. In the presence of alcohol, that process of inhibition is further facilitated, accounting for the characteristic behavioral changes. All psychoactive substances interact with one neurotransmitter system or another—opiates via the endogenous opioid system, etc., and all ultimately interact with the brain's reward system in some way. Propensities to addiction (as well as certain compulsive and impulsive behaviors) appear to be a function of various genetic phenotypes, indicating that addictive tendencies may be related to an individual's genetic makeup.

62. C: Ego-dystonic qualities. Addictions tend to result in ego-syntonic feelings—i.e., a sense of well-being and relief of psychological stress, at least until after the fact (i.e., until after the high of gambling, shopping, taking drugs, etc., has waned). Thus, most addictions arise from what are perceived as positive experiences, and many people are unaware that they are developing an addiction until the addiction is well entrenched. By contrast, obsessive-compulsive behaviors (and other psychiatric illnesses) tend to be accompanied by marked ego-dystonic (ego-alien) thoughts and distress. There is a desire to be rid of or free of something that is in some way continuously troubling, distressing, or concerning. Consequently, there is no high involved, but only the transient relief of distress when obsessions or compulsions are indulged in one way or another.

63. C: Escalation in the frequency/amount of the behavior/substance used. While addictive patterns of substances and/or behaviors tend to increase over time, this is most frequently a function of tolerance—i.e., needing more of the substance or behavior to achieve a similarly high effect. Currently there is no gold standard for producing a diagnosis of addiction, as confusion still exists around myths of mental illness and simple intemperate behaviors that produce adverse consequences, and clinician bias remains significant. The *Diagnostic and Statistical Manual of Mental Disorders* (DSM) provides a classification/organizational scheme, but the clinician is the one who must make an actual diagnosis. Biopsychosocial formulations include: 1) biological components (i.e., tolerance and/or withdrawal symptoms); 2) psychological components (loss of control, postabuse distress, etc.); and 3) social components (adverse social consequences, such as DWI arrests, loss of jobs and/or relationships, etc.).

64. B: Biological. A clinician with a biological orientation/ideology will more likely focus on the biological processes underlying substance use, abuse, and dependence. Consequently, a medical intervention would most likely be attempted. A clinician with a behavioral orientation may well focus on the fact that the individual uses alcohol and/or opioids to cope with physical pain and malaise. A psychological orientation could lead a clinician to recognize that the client also has a history of post-traumatic stress from a military tour of duty and that the substances selected are an attempt to mask emotional pain and distressing recollections. Naltrexone hydrochloride (marketed as ReVia®, Depade®, and in an extended-release formulation called Vivitrol®) is an opiate antagonist. It decreases alcohol cravings and blocks the effects of opioid medications and street drugs—by contrast, disulfiram (Antabuse®) creates alcohol sensitivity and induces unpleasant symptoms when alcohol is ingested. However, the most effective treatment approach would incorporate all three ideologies, to address all issues and maximize the potential for success.

65. D: Cognitive capacity. Alcohol or other substance abuse is not related to cognitive capacity. Individuals from all intellectual levels may become involved in substance use or abuse. However, individuals with self-regulation deficits (especially when also combined with a genetic predisposition) are much more likely to develop a substance use disorder than those without such features. Therefore, an individual with bipolar disorder may use substances to modulate manic episodes; an individual with a social phobia may use substances to cope with social fears; and an individual with attention-deficit hyperactivity disorder (ADHD) may use substances to self-medicate feelings of agitation and distraction.

66. C: Moral turpitude. In years past, excessive use of any substance was seen as a mark of poor character, deficient self-control, lack of meaningful values, etc. Later biological models propagated the ideas of addiction being: 1) an illness or disease; 2) neurobiological regulatory problems resulting in impulse-control problems; 3) genetic predispositions (i.e., biogenetic vulnerability); and 4) neuroadaptation and reward system deficiencies. Psychological models include: 1) behavioral excess (social pressure and reinforcement contingencies); 2) poor judgment (naiveté and a failure to understand consequences); 3) psychological deficits (emotional and personality problems leading to self-medication); 4) psychodynamic neuroticism (intrapsychic conflicts with problematic developmental roots); and 5) flawed thought patterns (misunderstanding indices of risk and probability, etc.). Social models include: 1) psychosocial (social and moral constraints that induce addictive issues; and 2) a public health perspective (addiction arises in the social context, and the shared societal costs are the focus).

67. B: Initiation. Initiation is the <u>first stage</u>, including primary prevention programs focused on education and information of long-term consequences. <u>Second stage</u>: positive consequences, requiring secondary prevention (further education and counseling to emphasize costs and poor outcomes, etc.). <u>Third stage</u>: <u>Part I</u>: Negative experiences (without awareness = precontemplation), requiring awareness enhancement and overcoming resistance, due to unawareness that addiction is the source of the negative experiences. <u>Part II</u>: Adverse consequences (awareness begins = contemplation), requiring tertiary prevention (outpatient counseling, self-help groups to prepare for change, and acute inpatient services if a crisis erupts). Fourth stage: Turning point(s), including preparation and orientation to change (outpatient/inpatient services: self-help, 12-step, partial care, and detoxification as needed). Fifth stage: Active quitting (all as in stage 4, plus chemical substitutions, counseling, and residential care if required). Sixth stage: Relapse prevention and maintenance (self-help, 12-step, outpatient, and residential care if no/limited social support).

68. A: The sympathetic nervous system. The brain includes the cerebrum (basal forebrain, hindbrain, and cortical structures), the cerebellum, and the brainstem (midbrain, pons, and medulla). Below the brain is the spinal cord. Together, these structures comprise the CNS. The peripheral nervous system (PNS) consists of the autonomic nervous system (controlling nerves to organs) and the somatic nervous system (controlling glands and skeletal muscles). The autonomic nervous system can be further divided into the sympathetic division ("flight or fight" arousal states) and the parasympathetic division (the "rest and digest" energy conservation states). Stimulant drugs are sympathomimetic in nature and arouse agitation and activity. Parasympathomimetic (also called cholinergic) drugs mimic stimulation of parasympathetic nerves. The nervous systems endeavor to maintain homeostasis (unchanging balance), and drugs that influence the brain's reward balance can upset this and produce serious imbalances in the brain. Neuroadaptation is the nervous system's effort to regain homeostasis.

69. B: Synapse—the space between neurons. At the head of a neuronal cell are finger-like projections known as dendrites. Through these, signals enter the neural cell and are carried to the main body of the cell (the soma). Extending away from the soma is an elongated fiber known as the axon, which divides into several finger-like axonal projections. The axon transmits information away from the neuron to other neurons. Between each neuron is an extremely small space called a synapse. Neurotransmitter chemicals are used to relay signals across the synapses, with a myriad of other neurochemicals that receive, neutralize, and replenish the neurotransmitter chemicals. Neurotransmitters influenced by drug abuse include: acetylcholine, dopamine, GABA (gamma-aminobutyric acid), glutamate, and serotonin. Neuropeptide transmitters are also involved (e.g., corticotrophin releasing factor (CRF), dynorphin, neuropeptide Y (NPY), etc.). All must function smoothly together for nerve signals to be properly relayed.

70. C: Pharmacodynamics. A pharmacy is a location where prepared drug formulations are made available. Pharmacokinetics is the study of drug actions (solubility, metabolism, routes of administration, etc.). Pharmacology is an umbrella term referring to all studies that are specifically drug-related. Agonist drugs either mimic or boost the effects of naturally occurring (endogenous, i.e., within the body) chemicals such as neurotransmitters. Antagonist drugs block or attenuate these same neurotransmitters. Understanding the final form and effect of drugs in the body requires an understanding of pharmacokinetics, i.e., the drug's initial form, its route of administration, its interactions with blood and other body chemicals, enzymes, digestive and metabolic processes, hormones, etc.

71. D: Negative reinforcement. The opposite, or positive reinforcement, occurs when the presentation of a stimulus increases the likelihood of a response that will engage the stimulus again. In situations of drug-seeking behavior, classical (Pavlovian) conditioning can be observed when the appearance of related but previously neutral stimuli (e.g., the presence of drug use paraphernalia, drug-using friends, a drug-abuse environment, etc.) comes to evoke a decidedly positive or negative behavioral response. A functional understanding of conditioned stimuli can play a significant role in either drug avoidance or a relapse. Drug-induced euphoria, when paired with a distinctive environment, can produce a "conditioned place preference" (or, with a negative experience, a "conditioned place aversion").

72. B: Medial forebrain bundle. Various other areas of the brain (e.g., the hindbrain and midbrain) have projections that connect to one or more parts of this nerve bundle pathway, which is integral to behavior motivation and various rewarding neural stimuli. A particular subset of projections is known as the mesocorticolimbic dopamine pathway and connects to the midbrain's ventral tegmental area (VTA) and the nucleus accumbens (NA), where dopamine release (and the associated reward stimulus) becomes elevated with exposure to numerous drugs of abuse. Other less significant areas of the brain that nevertheless contribute meaningfully to the reward system via dopamine release include the frontal cortex, the limbic cortex, and the amygdala. Additional neurotransmitters such as serotonin, GABA, and glutamate also augment and enhance the brain's reward system. In particular, the interaction of multiple neuronal and neurotransmitter systems serves to activate the extended amygdala, which produces common (natural and drug reward) neural substrates for numerous aspects of the brain's reward system.

73. A: GABA (gamma-aminobutyric acid). GABA is an inhibitory neurotransmitter that is affected by the presence of alcohol, a CNS depressant. Indirect sympathomimetics such as cocaine, Ecstasy (MDMA, i.e., 3,4-methylenedioxymethamphetamine), methamphetamine, amphetamine, etc., are psychomotor stimulants that readily induce physical activity and euphoria and decrease feelings of hunger and fatigue. Cessation, however, leads to an initial crash characterized by irritability, low energy, and disrupted sleep. Following the crash, a withdrawal syndrome involving feelings of dysphoria, anxiety, apathy, and a craving for more of the drug is experienced. The primary reinforcing effects of psychomotor stimulants are directly due to increased dopamine availability within the mesolimbic system.

74. B: Decreases heroin use. Heroin is an opioid drug. Opioid drugs are derived from the opium poppy and can be used to produce opium, morphine, and codeine. Synthetically (laboratory) created opioids include meperidine, methadone, and oxycodone, among others. Heroin is a semisynthetic opioid, as it is an altered version of morphine (diacetylmorphine). The name heroin was originally a trademark of Bayer Drug Company, which marketed the product as an alternative cough suppressant to morphine in 1895. All opioid drugs have analgesic (pain-relieving), antitussive (cough-suppressing), and euphoria-inducing properties. They interact with both opioid and dopamine receptors to produce reward and reinforcement outcomes. Nicotine, alcohol, and THC (tetrahydrocannabinol, the primary psychoactive compound in marijuana) can also access the opioid reward system to varying degrees.

75. C: Stimulant. Nicotine's stimulant effects include decreased appetite and fatigue, anxiolysis (reduced anxiety), enhanced alertness, and increased physical activity. Nicotine also indirectly activates transmission and release of dopamine via the mesolimbic system. Dopamine release is very rapid and has an extremely rapid dopamine-reward reinforcement response in the brain. Nicotine addiction treatment medications such as Chantix® (varenicline) and Zyban® (bupropion) are, respectively, a dopamine-receptor antagonist and a dopamine-reuptake inhibitor—both of which can reduce the desire for nicotine. Nicotine withdrawal symptoms include depressed mood, irritability, headaches, and nicotine craving. Nicotine relapse is common, due to issues of dependence, habitualized rituals, conditioned place and time preferences, etc., and because nicotine is a direct acetylcholine receptor agonist (stimulating both the dopamine and endogenous opioid peptide systems).

76. D: All of the above. Research reveals that there are multiple neurochemical substrates (systems) that are involved in producing the intoxicating effects of sedative-hypnotic drugs such as alcohol, benzodiazepines, and barbiturates. The intoxicating effects of these drugs include anxiolysis, disinhibition, hypnosis, mild euphoria, and sedation. Cessation results in hangover symptoms: blurred vision, dysphoria, headache, nausea, sleep disruption, tremors, etc.

Neurotransmitter systems involved include GABA (via antagonists at the $GABA_A$ receptor subtype), glutamate (by blocking receptors and thereby increasing serotonin transmission), and opioid peptide neurotransmitters (which act as endogenous agonists that are essential to achieve an opiate reward).

77. D: Anandamide. Cannabinoid receptors are scattered in varying densities throughout the brain. High concentrations exist in the basal ganglia, cerebellum, and hippocampus, accounting for impairment of motor coordination and short-term memory, among other things. As with many drugs of abuse, THC also activates the mesolimbic dopamine transmission system and produces similar effects. These include: a lowered threshold to the brain's reward system, a predisposition to continued use, and the development of conditioned place preferences. More than 80 forms of THC are known, and, coupled with varying modes of entry (eating vs smoking), the effects can vary. Mild cannabis intoxication typically makes the user feel euphoric, relaxed, sociable, and hungry. Some users become uninhibited, talkative, or giggly, and the hallucinogenic properties can heighten color and sound awareness. Negative effects may include acute anxiety and paranoia. Addiction occurs in 9–25% or more of users, depending upon age of initiation and frequency of use. Withdrawal symptoms include irritability, sleeplessness, decreased appetite, anxiety, and drug craving. Chronic use is associated with anxiety, depression, and a greater likelihood of schizophrenia.

78. B: Is increased. During withdrawal from opiates, sedative-hypnotics (including alcohol) and psychostimulants (including nicotine), the brain's reward threshold is increased, indicating a persistent dysphoric state that other normal rewards cannot readily penetrate. By contrast, these same drugs abnormally lower the reward threshold when acutely administered. Prolonged usage alters the brain's internal landscape profoundly, not only in areas of the brain that are directly affected biochemically, but in collateral systems recruited to restore homeostasis. Mesolimbic neurochemistry is explicitly affected. Drug-induced increases in extracellular levels of neurotransmitters such as dopamine, serotonin, and norepinephrine are followed by drops to subnormal levels following drug cessation. The result is particularly profound dysphoria with cessation.

79. B: Homeostatic trends in intracellular neuronal activities. Homeostasis refers to an absence of change. However, chronic drug use induces numerous changes. Intracellular signaling pathways may become upregulated (i.e., increases in numbers and/or capacity), resulting in changes in brain activity. Neurogenesis (the production of new neurons) in the hippocampus is decreased, potentially leading to altered brain structure and function. The morphology of neuronal dendrites (the branching arms receiving signals between neurons) becomes altered (shrinking with opiate use and overgrowing with stimulants), dramatically altering neural function and capacity. In rodents, all these changes appear to persist for four or more months, with changes that reflect withdrawal and cessation effects (i.e., fatigue, lethargy, dysphoria, etc.) and thus tend toward drug use relapse for symptom relief. Drug use and withdrawal produce stress responses and biochemical changes in ways that predispose one to drug use.

80. D: Both A and B. Both drug use and drug withdrawal will activate the stress response—including activation of the sympathetic nervous system, the endocrine (hormone) system, and reduced immune function and insulin sensitivity. These changes may predispose an individual to return to drug use. For example, alcohol, nicotine, opioids, THC, and psychostimulants induce stress by activating the pituitary glands release of corticotrophin-releasing factor (CRF), which elevates anxiety and stress. Secondarily activated antireward systems in the brain (e.g., dopamine-inhibiting dynorphin and reductions in the natural anxiolytic, neuropeptide Y [NPY]) also result in lost pleasure and increased anxiety. Stress also sensitizes various mesolimbic neurotransmitters and hormones (e.g., dopamine, glutamate, corticotrophin-releasing factor [CRF], etc.), which reinforce drug use via enhanced positive reinforcing effects and facilitated negative effects. Although some biological changes may be transient, with chronic use, behavioral sensitization (the functional predisposition to relapse) develops and lasts up to a year. Cross-sensitization between psychosocial stressors and drugs may predispose to relapse for much longer periods.

81. A: Identification of a drug of choice. Having a preferred drug of choice does not in itself predispose to progression to dependency. The "opponent process theory" suggests that positive affective/intoxication "A-processes" (activation of neurological rewards) wane during neuroadaptation (tolerance, etc.) even as aversive "B-processes," such as withdrawal symptoms and/or hyperalgesia (increased sensitivity to pain), increase along with escalating stress- and anxiety-inducing CRF pathways in the brain. The shift to compulsive use is complete once the hedonic set point is breeched, when A-processes are low and B-processes are high, requiring ever more frequent use and higher doses. Processes of allostasis (i.e., the body's attempt to retain balance by way of change) may sometimes produce a protracted withdrawal configuration, making efforts to abstain more difficult and the need for compulsive intake more insistent.

82. D: Alcohol and methamphetamine. However, virtually any psychoactive substance can become addictive, even if only psychologically. Physiologically addictive substances tend to share three key features: 1) they have similar mechanisms of action (i.e., tending to stimulate the brain's reward system by increasing synaptic dopamine in mesolimbic projections, and targeting drug reinforcement areas of the brain, such as the mesocorticolimbic system and/or extended amygdala; 2) they alter behavioral motivation via adaptive biological changes in neural circuitry; and 3) those who use them tend to exhibit similar use/abuse patterns. Compulsively abused drugs primarily include only alcohol, nicotine, marijuana, certain sedative-hypnotics, and the psychomotor stimulants (amphetamines, cocaine, etc.). The route of administration can predispose to addiction (i.e., routes with a more rapid and stronger high are more likely to induce addiction), whereas slow-release drugs such as ADHD-treating methylphenidate and long-acting methadone are rarely abused. Although all addictive drugs stimulate brain reward and dopamine release—some directly and others indirectly—they may act through different brain areas and/or neural receptors.

83. A: Asians. Numerous individuals of Asian descent (50%) have one or more inactive copies of the liver enzyme acetaldehyde dehydrogenase necessary to metabolize acetaldehyde. As a result, they tend to require longer periods of time to metabolize alcohol out of the body. The genetic variant is evident by marked facial flushing and nausea in those carrying the inactive gene copies. For many, these negative associations cause them to self-limit their drinking, and rates of alcoholism are lower among Asians than among other groups. It is important to note, however, that affected individuals do not become intoxicated faster or experience higher blood alcohol proportionate to the alcohol consumed. Furthermore, not all Asian groups have similar alcohol abuse patterns. For example, Koreans and Korean-Americans have higher alcoholism rates than Chinese and Chinese-Americans. Although alcoholism rates are particularly high among Native Americans and Native Alaskans, there are no known genetic causative factors.

84. C: GABA (gamma-aminobutyric acid). The primary action of alcohol in the brain involves enhancement of the agonist function of the GABA inhibitory neurotransmitter. Potentiation of GABA-mediated brain inhibition results in the anxiolytic and sedative effects of ethanol on the brain. However, the more addictive properties of alcohol use arise from its stimulation of the brain's reward system. As the level of alcohol rises in the blood, it enters the brain and stimulates a commensurate rise in dopamine. This is the reward paradigm described as "feeling a buzz." Alcohol also interferes with glutamate receptor function, and when behaviorally relevant concentrations are reached, ataxia, memory, and learning problems become evident. Withdrawal peaks at 2–3 days after cessation, with symptoms including tremors, anxiety, hyperactivity, insomnia, and agitation.

Severe withdrawal may demonstrate delirium tremens symptoms, with the added symptoms of rapid heart and respiratory rates and elevated blood pressure. Withdrawal symptoms wane in 4–5 days, but cravings may persist for weeks to years.

85. B: Birth order. However, genetics plays a well-known role and is particularly likely among those who began drinking as teens and progressed quickly to alcohol abuse. By contrast, those who did not begin drinking until young adulthood were more likely to self-medicate for anxiety and progressed into alcoholism more slowly. Long-term heavy drinking can produce marked cognitive impairment, particularly evident in areas of both recent and remote memory. Cognitive problems are particularly common if the abuse involves episodes with high blood alcohol concentrations. Wernicke's syndrome occurs due to an alcohol-related thiamine deficiency. The encephalopathy is also significant for sixth nerve palsy and ataxia; all can be reversed with correction of the thiamine deficiency. Korsakoff's syndrome arises from the alcohol toxicity and is less reversible. Symptoms include profound recent memory amnesia, inability to learn, confabulation, hallucinations, deficits in abstract and conceptual reasoning, and visuospatial impairment. Finally, peripheral neuropathy (with numbness, tingling, and paresthesias) results in 5–10% of alcoholics.

86. A: Barbiturates, which are sedatives, not stimulants. Psychomotor stimulants are best known for the sense of euphoria, well-being, and energy that they produce, but also for their weight-loss (anorexia) and sleep-fighting (insomnia) properties, etc. All psychomotor stimulants also increase attention, heart rate, blood glucose, and blood pressure, as well as dilate the pupils and bronchioles in the lungs. All psychomotor stimulants—even cocaine, which is used for its local anesthetic and vasoconstrictive properties—have legitimate uses, such as the treatment of attention-deficit hyperactivity disorder (ADHD). Of the stimulants, methylphenidate enters the bloodstream more slowly, and other stimulants used medically are typically produced in a time-release form to limit issues of abuse and dependence.

87. C: Injection (needles). However, time to intoxication from smoking is essentially equal to injection. Snorting provides a slower and less intense but longer-lasting high. Ingestion of cocaine (coca leaves) provides a particularly slow intoxication rate that is mild in nature, as bioavailability is very low. Smoked or intravenously injected cocaine produces an intense intoxication almost immediately, but it lasts only 20–30 minutes (half life = 30–40 minutes). When methamphetamine is smoked, it also peaks virtually immediately, but the half-life is 8–10 hours. Methylphenidate peaks very slowly, with effects persisting 3–6 hours in a regular preparation, and up to 8 hours in sustained-release form.

88. B: Anorexia. Because tolerance to the appetite-suppressant properties of stimulants tends to develop early on, these drugs are of limited value in the treatment of obesity. Psychomotor stimulants work similarly, increasing the synaptic availability of the monoamine neurotransmitters (i.e., dopamine, norepinephrine, and serotonin). Cocaine blocks their reuptake equally, while amphetamines displace them, and methylphenidate has both blocking and releasing actions. All make dopamine more available and therefore can be addicting. Methylphenidate, however, is very slow-acting, and the intoxication is comparatively less intense. Therefore, it is not as likely to produce addiction. Indeed, when used properly, e.g., to treat ADHD, children using this medication are actually less likely to become drug users when compared with the population on the whole. Overdose of psychomotor stimulants can lead to hallucinations (formication, etc.) and schizophrenia-like symptoms, and severe overdose can be lethal—from seizures (amphetamines or cocaine), hyperthermia (amphetamines), or cardiovascular events (both amphetamines and cocaine), such as stroke, heart attack, etc.

89. D: Pain. Although narcotic (opiate) drugs such as morphine are primarily used to treat pain, they are abused for the euphoric, dreamy state they induce. All narcotics have respiratory-depressant effects, which is the most common cause of death in situations of overdose. They also slow gastrointestinal motility (inducing constipation), cause ciliary body constriction in the eye (leading to pin-point pupils), have antitussive (cough-suppressant) properties, and may cause pruritus (itching). Heroin is a pseudo-synthetic opiate and differs from morphine largely in the faster rate at which it enters the brain. A fully synthetic opiate, fentanyl, is used to treat break-through pain that is not otherwise easily controlled. It comes as a pain-relieving injectable or a sustained-release skin patch. Buprenorphine and methadone are, respectively, partial and full opiate agonists. They also have analgesic properties, as well as withdrawal-suppressing effects for those being treated for opiate addiction. Codeine is an isomer of methylated morphine, and as a low-efficacy analgesic it is typically used for the treatment of mild pain and cough suppression.

90. C: Loperamide. Both loperamide and diphenoxylate have no analgesic properties and are considered nonaddictive opiates. Both are marketed primarily as antidiarrheals. However, the use of stronger, dependency-producing narcotics is very much acceptable in certain medical situations, particularly at or near the end of life. Even so, in most situations it is preferable to use narcotics with low addictive properties and long-acting pharmacology. Methadone provides both of these, as it does not readily induce a high and is extremely long-acting (18–24 hours). Narcotic use in medical settings to treat pain may produce transient dependence (i.e., withdrawal symptoms if stopped abruptly, and therefore requiring a weaning process), but it virtually never produces addictive cravings in anyone but former drug abusers. The recent popularity of addictive oxycodone (OxyContin®) emerged when it was discovered that biting down on a time-release capsule could produce a rapid drug release and a high. The drug had been used more frequently to control pain in situations where codeine was poorly effective.

91. A: 1849, by Dr. Magnus Huss, who used the term to describe the cluster of common symptoms. However, the popular term of the day was "inebriety" (opium inebriety, alcohol inebriety, etc.). Although "sober houses" were proposed by Dr. Benjamin Rush in 1790, it was not until 1857 that the first "inebriate home" was opened in Boston (and in Chicago in 1863). They utilized voluntary stays and subsequent involvement in support groups. The first "inebriate asylum" opened in 1864, offering the first medically oriented treatment in the United States. It relied upon coercion for patients, with multiyear legal commitments. The American Association for the Study and Cure of Inebriety was the first professional association of addiction treatment providers and was established in New York City in 1870, and by 1876 the Association began publication of the *Quarterly Journal of Inebriety*. Inebriety treatment was soon a profit-making endeavor, and the first of more than 120 Keeley Institute franchises was founded in 1879 by Dr. Leslie Keeley.

92. D: All of the above. Concurrent with the for-profit expansion of treatment in the 1870s and 1880s, home addiction cures, urban religious missions, inebriate colonies, and city hospital inebriate wards began to be established. However, an addiction cure exposé in 1905–1906 revealed that most over-the-counter treatments for alcohol and drug inebriety actually contained high concentrations of alcohol, cannabis, cocaine, and/or morphine. Public cynicism and pessimism ensued, and programs began closing in the coming years. People with addiction problems were soon shunted into "foul wards" in urban hospitals, insane asylums, and inebriate penal colonies. The few treatment efforts that continued often resulted in profound iatrogenic damage to those suffering with addiction. Indiscriminate sterilization, serum and bromide therapies, chemical and electroconvulsive therapies, psychosurgery, LSD, amphetamines, barbiturates, as well as anti-anxiety and tranquilizing agents all were commonly and ineffectively used.

93. C: The Emmanuel Church of Boston clinic, established in 1906. Whereas individual alcohol abusers in wealthy families could turn for help to private sanatoria and elite hospitals (such as the Charles B. Towns Hospital for the Treatment of Alcoholic and Drug Addictions) in the early 20th century, it was not until the first clinic model for outpatient counseling was established in 1906 that treatment became more affordable and more widely available. The clinic model was based on the early work of the Washingtonian Movement of 1840, the sobriety-based Fraternal Temperance Societies, the Ribbon Reform Clubs, on through to the Businessmen's Moderation Society of 1879. These mutual aid societies of the 19th century largely collapsed when the inebriate homes and other alcohol and drug programs were lost in the early years of the 20th century. However, the void was filled in 1935 with the establishment of Alcoholics Anonymous (AA).

94. D: Women for Sobriety. Established in 1975, it uses principles similar to those of Alcoholics Anonymous. AA was founded in 1935 by Bill Wilson and Dr. Bob Smith ("Bill W" and "Dr. Bob") in Akron, Ohio. In conjunction with other early members, Wilson and Smith developed the Twelve Steps used in AA and the Twelve Traditions, including anonymity, altruism, and inclusion of all who want to stop drinking. In addition, the Traditions encourage AA groups to try to avoid politics, hierarchies, and other organizational and public issues. Wilson, a stock broker from New York, had traveled to Akron, Ohio, for a shareholders' meeting and proxy fight that turned out badly. Desperate to maintain sobriety, his first thought was, "I've got to find another alcoholic." Asking around, he met an Akron surgeon, Dr. Smith, who also struggled with a drinking problem. The effect of their meeting was profound, as they lent each other mutual support. This led to the founding of AA in an upstairs room at Dr. Bob's home. The two men began helping other alcoholics one person at a time.

95. B: 1919–1933. National Prohibition was preceded by the ratification of the 18th Amendment to the U.S. Constitution and was inaugurated with the passage of the Volstead Act in 1919, which provided for law enforcement and penalties. Initially, alcohol problems were substantially reduced, but the robust emergence of an illicit alcohol trade eroded the effectiveness of the law, and National Prohibition formally ended in 1933 with the ratification of the 21st Amendment, which repealed the 18th. Drug laws began in 1875, in San Francisco, with a local ordinance aimed at curbing the proliferation of Chinese opium dens in that area. Other ordinances soon followed, addressing cocaine and morphine as well. By the turn of the century, the policy of having physicians control the use and distribution of primary drugs of abuse was emerging in law. The Pure Food and Drug Act of 1906 was the first federal law covering psychoactive substances in addition to alcohol and tobacco. Among other things, it required that all medicines containing alcohol, cocaine, and/or opiates be labeled as such.

96. B: The federal Harrison Anti-Narcotic Act of 1914 stipulated that cocaine and opiates could only be dispensed/sold by a physician or by a pharmacist with specific authorization by a physician. The U.S. Supreme Court heard several arguments related to this Act, the most significant of which was the Webb v. U.S. Supreme Court decision, which indicated that physicians could be legally punished if they maintained addicts on opiates. The Narcotics Import and Export Act of 1922 prohibited the import of processed cocaine and morphine. The Heroin Act of 1924 prohibited the importing of opium for purposes of manufacturing heroin. The Marijuana Tax Act of 1937 prohibited the possession and sale of cannabis. The Opium Poppy Control Act of 1942 required licensure to grow and harvest opium poppies. The 1951 Boggs Amendment to the Harrison Act began the mandatory minimum sentencing of drug offenders. The Narcotic Control Act of 1956 introduced increased penalties and the first death penalty provision in drug legislation.

97. D: Prevention/treatment oriented. In 1966, the Narcotic Addicts Rehabilitation Act (NARA) was passed, allowing treatment as an alternative to incarceration. The 1970s saw further liberalization, primarily in recognition that youthful experimentation was increasingly common. The 1980s saw a backlash arising from escalating drug-related violence and escalating cocaine addiction. President Ronald Reagan presided over a shift in the national drug-control budget, creating a budget allocation that was inverse to what had previously existed. Now, two-thirds of the budget went to law enforcement and one-third to prevention and treatment. The prison population went from one in 15 incarcerated for drug charges, to one in three (with 85% imprisoned solely on possession charges). Year 2000 statistics indicated that 60% of inmates in the federal prison system are there for drug-related charges.

98. B: African Americans. Issues of racial disparity have been a continuing focus in drug debates. It has been noted that African Americans represent 60% of those in state prisons, even though they constitute only 15% of illicit drug users. Furthermore, African American mothers prenatally testing positive for illicit substances are 10 times more likely to be reported. Defenders of the system note that African American drug use is higher than all other demographic groups, (save Native Americans only, where sociocultural groupings and reservation legal systems may limit drug arrests). Furthermore, crime rates are highest in low-income areas, and minority representation tends to be high in these same areas. According to the 2006 National Survey on Drug Use and Health, the highest rate of current (past month) illicit drug use was among American Indian/Alaska Natives (13.7%), followed by Blacks/African Americans (9.8%), persons reporting two or more races (8.9%), Whites/Caucasian Americans (8.5%), Native Hawaiian/other Pacific Islander Americans (7.5%), and Hispanic Americans (6.9%). The lowest rate was among Asian Americans (3.6%).

99. C: Dwight Anderson and Marty Mann. The Five Kinetic Ideas were: 1) Alcoholism is a disease. 2) The alcoholic is therefore a sick person. 3) The alcoholic can be helped. 4) The alcoholic is worth helping. 5) Alcoholism is our #4 public health problem, and our public responsibility" (Mann, 1944). The modern alcoholism movement evolved as pioneering approaches in treatment and improved public attitudes during the 1940s and 1950s. The following institutions were collectively responsible: Alcoholics Anonymous, the Research Counsel on Problems of Alcohol, the Yale Center of Studies on Alcohol, and the National Committee for Education on Alcoholism. Due to their combined efforts, the view that alcoholism is a disease rose from 6% in 1947 to 66% in 1967, aided by statements from groups such as the American Medical Association, the American Hospital Association, the American Public Health Association, and the American Psychiatric Association.

100. C: 1972. There have recently been three stages in the field of addiction treatment. During the first stage, there was the development of effective diagnostic criteria (aided by research organizations such as the National Institute on Alcohol Abuse and Alcoholism [NIAAA], founded in 1970); professional training systems to properly educate treatment personnel; establishment of the profession (founding of the National Association of Alcoholism Counselors and Trainers, precursor to the National Association of Addiction Counselors' founding in 1972); research in core competencies that supported certification programs; the establishment of national accreditation and state licensure standards; the integration of alcoholism and drug abuse treatment programs (1975–1985); and declarations of recovery by many prominent Americans such as former First Lady Betty Ford. The second stage involved the growth in available treatment programs, handicapped in part by ethical abuses of inappropriate marketing, unnecessary admissions, and undue lengths of stay. The third stage involved integration with other social programs (public health, criminal justice, etc.) and the acceptance of multimodal approaches necessary for treatment success.

How to Overcome Test Anxiety

Just the thought of taking a test is enough to make most people a little nervous. A test is an important event that can have a long-term impact on your future, so it's important to take it seriously and it's natural to feel anxious about performing well. But just because anxiety is normal, that doesn't mean that it's helpful in test taking, or that you should simply accept it as part of your life. Anxiety can have a variety of effects. These effects can be mild, like making you feel slightly nervous, or severe, like blocking your ability to focus or remember even a simple detail.

If you experience test anxiety—whether severe or mild—it's important to know how to beat it. To discover this, first you need to understand what causes test anxiety.

Causes of Test Anxiety

While we often think of anxiety as an uncontrollable emotional state, it can actually be caused by simple, practical things. One of the most common causes of test anxiety is that a person does not feel adequately prepared for their test. This feeling can be the result of many different issues such as poor study habits or lack of organization, but the most common culprit is time management. Starting to study too late, failing to organize your study time to cover all of the material, or being distracted while you study will mean that you're not well prepared for the test. This may lead to cramming the night before, which will cause you to be physically and mentally exhausted for the test. Poor time management also contributes to feelings of stress, fear, and hopelessness as you realize you are not well prepared but don't know what to do about it.

Other times, test anxiety is not related to your preparation for the test but comes from unresolved fear. This may be a past failure on a test, or poor performance on tests in general. It may come from comparing yourself to others who seem to be performing better or from the stress of living up to expectations. Anxiety may be driven by fears of the future—how failure on this test would affect your educational and career goals. These fears are often completely irrational, but they can still negatively impact your test performance.

Review Video: 3 Reasons You Have Test Anxiety
Visit mometrix.com/academy and enter code: 428468

Elements of Test Anxiety

As mentioned earlier, test anxiety is considered to be an emotional state, but it has physical and mental components as well. Sometimes you may not even realize that you are suffering from test anxiety until you notice the physical symptoms. These can include trembling hands, rapid heartbeat, sweating, nausea, and tense muscles. Extreme anxiety may lead to fainting or vomiting. Obviously, any of these symptoms can have a negative impact on testing. It is important to recognize them as soon as they begin to occur so that you can address the problem before it damages your performance.

Review Video: 3 Ways to Tell You Have Test Anxiety
Visit mometrix.com/academy and enter code: 927847

The mental components of test anxiety include trouble focusing and inability to remember learned information. During a test, your mind is on high alert, which can help you recall information and stay focused for an extended period of time. However, anxiety interferes with your mind's natural processes, causing you to blank out, even on the questions you know well. The strain of testing during anxiety makes it difficult to stay focused, especially on a test that may take several hours. Extreme anxiety can take a huge mental toll, making it difficult not only to recall test information but even to understand the test questions or pull your thoughts together.

Review Video: How Test Anxiety Affects Memory
Visit mometrix.com/academy and enter code: 609003

Effects of Test Anxiety

Test anxiety is like a disease—if left untreated, it will get progressively worse. Anxiety leads to poor performance, and this reinforces the feelings of fear and failure, which in turn lead to poor performances on subsequent tests. It can grow from a mild nervousness to a crippling condition. If allowed to progress, test anxiety can have a big impact on your schooling, and consequently on your future.

Test anxiety can spread to other parts of your life. Anxiety on tests can become anxiety in any stressful situation, and blanking on a test can turn into panicking in a job situation. But fortunately, you don't have to let anxiety rule your testing and determine your grades. There are a number of relatively simple steps you can take to move past anxiety and function normally on a test and in the rest of life.

Review Video: How Test Anxiety Impacts Your Grades
Visit mometrix.com/academy and enter code: 939819

Physical Steps for Beating Test Anxiety

While test anxiety is a serious problem, the good news is that it can be overcome. It doesn't have to control your ability to think and remember information. While it may take time, you can begin taking steps today to beat anxiety.

Just as your first hint that you may be struggling with anxiety comes from the physical symptoms, the first step to treating it is also physical. Rest is crucial for having a clear, strong mind. If you are tired, it is much easier to give in to anxiety. But if you establish good sleep habits, your body and mind will be ready to perform optimally, without the strain of exhaustion. Additionally, sleeping well helps you to retain information better, so you're more likely to recall the answers when you see the test questions.

Getting good sleep means more than going to bed on time. It's important to allow your brain time to relax. Take study breaks from time to time so it doesn't get overworked, and don't study right before bed. Take time to rest your mind before trying to rest your body, or you may find it difficult to fall asleep.

Review Video: The Importance of Sleep for Your Brain
Visit mometrix.com/academy and enter code: 319338

Along with sleep, other aspects of physical health are important in preparing for a test. Good nutrition is vital for good brain function. Sugary foods and drinks may give a burst of energy but this burst is followed by a crash, both physically and emotionally. Instead, fuel your body with protein and vitamin-rich foods.

Also, drink plenty of water. Dehydration can lead to headaches and exhaustion, especially if your brain is already under stress from the rigors of the test. Particularly if your test is a long one, drink water during the breaks. And if possible, take an energy-boosting snack to eat between sections.

Review Video: How Diet Can Affect your Mood
Visit mometrix.com/academy and enter code: 624317

Along with sleep and diet, a third important part of physical health is exercise. Maintaining a steady workout schedule is helpful, but even taking 5-minute study breaks to walk can help get your blood pumping faster and clear your head. Exercise also releases endorphins, which contribute to a positive feeling and can help combat test anxiety.

When you nurture your physical health, you are also contributing to your mental health. If your body is healthy, your mind is much more likely to be healthy as well. So take time to rest, nourish your body with healthy food and water, and get moving as much as possible. Taking these physical steps will make you stronger and more able to take the mental steps necessary to overcome test anxiety.

Review Video: How to Stay Healthy and Prevent Test Anxiety
Visit mometrix.com/academy and enter code: 877894

Mental Steps for Beating Test Anxiety

Working on the mental side of test anxiety can be more challenging, but as with the physical side, there are clear steps you can take to overcome it. As mentioned earlier, test anxiety often stems from lack of preparation, so the obvious solution is to prepare for the test. Effective studying may be the most important weapon you have for beating test anxiety, but you can and should employ several other mental tools to combat fear.

First, boost your confidence by reminding yourself of past success—tests or projects that you aced. If you're putting as much effort into preparing for this test as you did for those, there's no reason you should expect to fail here. Work hard to prepare; then trust your preparation.

Second, surround yourself with encouraging people. It can be helpful to find a study group, but be sure that the people you're around will encourage a positive attitude. If you spend time with others who are anxious or cynical, this will only contribute to your own anxiety. Look for others who are motivated to study hard from a desire to succeed, not from a fear of failure.

Third, reward yourself. A test is physically and mentally tiring, even without anxiety, and it can be helpful to have something to look forward to. Plan an activity following the test, regardless of the outcome, such as going to a movie or getting ice cream.

When you are taking the test, if you find yourself beginning to feel anxious, remind yourself that you know the material. Visualize successfully completing the test. Then take a few deep, relaxing breaths and return to it. Work through the questions carefully but with confidence, knowing that you are capable of succeeding.

Developing a healthy mental approach to test taking will also aid in other areas of life. Test anxiety affects more than just the actual test—it can be damaging to your mental health and even contribute to depression. It's important to beat test anxiety before it becomes a problem for more than testing.

Review Video: Test Anxiety and Depression
Visit mometrix.com/academy and enter code: 904704

Study Strategy

Being prepared for the test is necessary to combat anxiety, but what does being prepared look like? You may study for hours on end and still not feel prepared. What you need is a strategy for test prep. The next few pages outline our recommended steps to help you plan out and conquer the challenge of preparation.

Step 1: Scope Out the Test

Learn everything you can about the format (multiple choice, essay, etc.) and what will be on the test. Gather any study materials, course outlines, or sample exams that may be available. Not only will this help you to prepare, but knowing what to expect can help to alleviate test anxiety.

Step 2: Map Out the Material

Look through the textbook or study guide and make note of how many chapters or sections it has. Then divide these over the time you have. For example, if a book has 15 chapters and you have five days to study, you need to cover three chapters each day. Even better, if you have the time, leave an extra day at the end for overall review after you have gone through the material in depth.

If time is limited, you may need to prioritize the material. Look through it and make note of which sections you think you already have a good grasp on, and which need review. While you are studying, skim quickly through the familiar sections and take more time on the challenging parts. Write out your plan so you don't get lost as you go. Having a written plan also helps you feel more in control of the study, so anxiety is less likely to arise from feeling overwhelmed at the amount to cover.

Step 3: Gather Your Tools

Decide what study method works best for you. Do you prefer to highlight in the book as you study and then go back over the highlighted portions? Or do you type out notes of the important information? Or is it helpful to make flashcards that you can carry with you? Assemble the pens, index cards, highlighters, post-it notes, and any other materials you may need so you won't be distracted by getting up to find things while you study.

If you're having a hard time retaining the information or organizing your notes, experiment with different methods. For example, try color-coding by subject with colored pens, highlighters, or post-it notes. If you learn better by hearing, try recording yourself reading your notes so you can listen while in the car, working out, or simply sitting at your desk. Ask a friend to quiz you from your flashcards, or try teaching someone the material to solidify it in your mind.

Step 4: Create Your Environment

It's important to avoid distractions while you study. This includes both the obvious distractions like visitors and the subtle distractions like an uncomfortable chair (or a too-comfortable couch that makes you want to fall asleep). Set up the best study environment possible: good lighting and a comfortable work area. If background music helps you focus, you may want to turn it on, but otherwise keep the room quiet. If you are using a computer to take notes, be sure you don't have any other windows open, especially applications like social media, games, or anything else that could distract you. Silence your phone and turn off notifications. Be sure to keep water close by so you stay hydrated while you study (but avoid unhealthy drinks and snacks).

Also, take into account the best time of day to study. Are you freshest first thing in the morning? Try to set aside some time then to work through the material. Is your mind clearer in the afternoon or evening? Schedule your study session then. Another method is to study at the same time of day that you will take the test, so that your brain gets used to working on the material at that time and will be ready to focus at test time.

Step 5: Study!

Once you have done all the study preparation, it's time to settle into the actual studying. Sit down, take a few moments to settle your mind so you can focus, and begin to follow your study plan. Don't give in to distractions or let yourself procrastinate. This is your time to prepare so you'll be ready to fearlessly approach the test. Make the most of the time and stay focused.

Of course, you don't want to burn out. If you study too long you may find that you're not retaining the information very well. Take regular study breaks. For example, taking five minutes out of every hour to walk briskly, breathing deeply and swinging your arms, can help your mind stay fresh.

As you get to the end of each chapter or section, it's a good idea to do a quick review. Remind yourself of what you learned and work on any difficult parts. When you feel that you've mastered the material, move on to the next part. At the end of your study session, briefly skim through your notes again.

But while review is helpful, cramming last minute is NOT. If at all possible, work ahead so that you won't need to fit all your study into the last day. Cramming overloads your brain with more information than it can process and retain, and your tired mind may struggle to recall even previously learned information when it is overwhelmed with last-minute study. Also, the urgent nature of cramming and the stress placed on your brain contribute to anxiety. You'll be more likely to go to the test feeling unprepared and having trouble thinking clearly.

So don't cram, and don't stay up late before the test, even just to review your notes at a leisurely pace. Your brain needs rest more than it needs to go over the information again. In fact, plan to finish your studies by noon or early afternoon the day before the test. Give your brain the rest of the day to relax or focus on other things, and get a good night's sleep. Then you will be fresh for the test and better able to recall what you've studied.

Step 6: Take a Practice Test

Many courses offer sample tests, either online or in the study materials. This is an excellent resource to check whether you have mastered the material, as well as to prepare for the test format and environment.

Check the test format ahead of time: the number of questions, the type (multiple choice, free response, etc.), and the time limit. Then create a plan for working through them. For example, if you have 30 minutes to take a 60-question test, your limit is 30 seconds per question. Spend less time on the questions you know well so that you can take more time on the difficult ones.

If you have time to take several practice tests, take the first one open book, with no time limit. Work through the questions at your own pace and make sure you fully understand them. Gradually work up to taking a test under test conditions: sit at a desk with all study materials put away and set a timer. Pace yourself to make sure you finish the test with time to spare and go back to check your answers if you have time.

After each test, check your answers. On the questions you missed, be sure you understand why you missed them. Did you misread the question (tests can use tricky wording)? Did you forget the information? Or was it something you hadn't learned? Go back and study any shaky areas that the practice tests reveal.

Taking these tests not only helps with your grade, but also aids in combating test anxiety. If you're already used to the test conditions, you're less likely to worry about it, and working through tests until you're scoring well gives you a confidence boost. Go through the practice tests until you feel comfortable, and then you can go into the test knowing that you're ready for it.

Test Tips

On test day, you should be confident, knowing that you've prepared well and are ready to answer the questions. But aside from preparation, there are several test day strategies you can employ to maximize your performance.

First, as stated before, get a good night's sleep the night before the test (and for several nights before that, if possible). Go into the test with a fresh, alert mind rather than staying up late to study.

Try not to change too much about your normal routine on the day of the test. It's important to eat a nutritious breakfast, but if you normally don't eat breakfast at all, consider eating just a protein bar. If you're a coffee drinker, go ahead and have your normal coffee. Just make sure you time it so that the caffeine doesn't wear off right in the middle of your test. Avoid sugary beverages, and drink enough water to stay hydrated but not so much that you need a restroom break 10 minutes into the test. If your test isn't first thing in the morning, consider going for a walk or doing a light workout before the test to get your blood flowing.

Allow yourself enough time to get ready, and leave for the test with plenty of time to spare so you won't have the anxiety of scrambling to arrive in time. Another reason to be early is to select a good seat. It's helpful to sit away from doors and windows, which can be distracting. Find a good seat, get out your supplies, and settle your mind before the test begins.

When the test begins, start by going over the instructions carefully, even if you already know what to expect. Make sure you avoid any careless mistakes by following the directions.

Then begin working through the questions, pacing yourself as you've practiced. If you're not sure on an answer, don't spend too much time on it, and don't let it shake your confidence. Either skip it and come back later, or eliminate as many wrong answers as possible and guess among the remaining ones. Don't dwell on these questions as you continue—put them out of your mind and focus on what lies ahead.

Be sure to read all of the answer choices, even if you're sure the first one is the right answer. Sometimes you'll find a better one if you keep reading. But don't second-guess yourself if you do immediately know the answer. Your gut instinct is usually right. Don't let test anxiety rob you of the information you know.

If you have time at the end of the test (and if the test format allows), go back and review your answers. Be cautious about changing any, since your first instinct tends to be correct, but make sure you didn't misread any of the questions or accidentally mark the wrong answer choice. Look over any you skipped and make an educated guess.

At the end, leave the test feeling confident. You've done your best, so don't waste time worrying about your performance or wishing you could change anything. Instead, celebrate the successful completion of this test. And finally, use this test to learn how to deal with anxiety even better next time.

Review Video: 5 Tips to Beat Test Anxiety
Visit mometrix.com/academy and enter code: 570656

Important Qualification

Not all anxiety is created equal. If your test anxiety is causing major issues in your life beyond the classroom or testing center, or if you are experiencing troubling physical symptoms related to your anxiety, it may be a sign of a serious physiological or psychological condition. If this sounds like your situation, we strongly encourage you to seek professional help.

Thank You

We at Mometrix would like to extend our heartfelt thanks to you, our friend and patron, for allowing us to play a part in your journey. It is a privilege to serve people from all walks of life who are unified in their commitment to building the best future they can for themselves.

The preparation you devote to these important testing milestones may be the most valuable educational opportunity you have for making a real difference in your life. We encourage you to put your heart into it—that feeling of succeeding, overcoming, and yes, conquering will be well worth the hours you've invested.

We want to hear your story, your struggles and your successes, and if you see any opportunities for us to improve our materials so we can help others even more effectively in the future, please share that with us as well. **The team at Mometrix would be absolutely thrilled to hear from you!** So please, send us an email (support@mometrix.com) and let's stay in touch.

If you'd like some additional help, check out these other resources we offer for your exam:
http://MometrixFlashcards.com/Addiction

Additional Bonus Material

Due to our efforts to try to keep this book to a manageable length, we've created a link that will give you access to all of your additional bonus material.

Please visit https://www.mometrix.com/bonus948/masteraddict to access the information.